Macroeconomic Issues Today

Macroeconomic Issues Today

Alternative Approaches

Eighth Edition

Robert B. Carson, Wade L. Thomas, Jason Hecht

M.E.Sharpe
Armonk, New York
London, England

We dedicate this edition of *Macroeconomic Issues Today* to
Robert L. Heilbroner
for making the dismal science of economics
readable and understandable.

Library of Congress Cataloging-in-Publication Data

Carson, Robert Barry, 1934–
  Macroeconomic issues today : alternative approaches / Robert B. Carson,
Wade L. Thomas, and Jason Hecht.—8th ed.
    p. cm.
  Includes index.
  ISBN 0-7656-1503-7 (pbk. : alk. paper)
    1. Macroeconomics. 2. United States—Economic conditions—2001–
I. Thomas, Wade L. II. Hecht, Jason, 1958– III. Title.

HB172.5.C37 2005
339'.0973—dc22   2004021685

Printed in the United States of America

The paper used in this publication meets the minimum requirements of
American National Standard for Information Sciences
Permanence of Paper for Printed Library Materials,
ANSI Z 39.48-1984.

∞

BM (p)   10   9   8   7   6   5

Contents

Figures and Tables   vii
Preface   ix
Acknowledgments   xvii

Part I. Introduction

Alternative Economic Philosophies: A Survey of
Conservative, Liberal, and Radical Critiques   3

Part II. Problems of Aggregate Economic Policy

Issue 1 Macroeconomic Instability: Are We
         Depression-Proof?   35

Issue 2 Economic Growth and Stability: Can We Maintain
         High and Steady Rates of Economic Growth?   60

Issue 3 Balancing the Federal Budget: Should We Be
         Worried About the Rising Federal Deficit?   87

Issue 4 Unemployment: Is Joblessness an Overrated
         Problem?   109

Issue 5 Inflation: Can Price Pressures Be Kept Under
         Control?   132

Issue 6 The New Population Problem: Can We Save Our
         Social Security System?   155

Issue 7 International Economics: Where Does America
         Fit into the New World Order?   179

Part III. Conclusion

Reprise. The Market Versus Planning and Controls:
          Which Strategy Works Better?   213

Final Thoughts and Suggested Readings   235

Index   239
About the Authors   245

Figures and Tables

Figures

3.1 Federal Budget Surplus or Deficit, 1969–2003   90

4.1 Employment and Joblessness in the United States, 1950–2003   111

4.2 Profile of the Nation's Unemployed, 1978–2003   122

5.1 Consumer Price Index, 1800–2003   136

5.2 Measures of Inflation   141

6.1 Projected Beneficiaries per 100 Workers and Cost of Social Security   170

7.1 Exports and Imports as a Percentage of Gross Domestic Product, 1929–2003   182

7.2 U.S. International Transaction Balances, 1970–2002   196

7.3 Major U.S. Tariff Laws, Trade Agreements, and Level of Effective Tariffs   199

Tables

2.1 Economic Growth, Unemployment, and Inflation Rates, 1959–2003   62

2.2 Trend in Real Gross Domestic Product per Capita and Productivity   65

2.3 Average Annual Changes in Gross Domestic Product per Capita   75

3.1 Measures of the Federal Debt   89

3.2 Government in the Economy   105

3.3 Outstanding Domestic American Debt, 1980–2000   108

7.1 Value of U.S. Foreign Investment, Selected Years, 1880–2001   205

Preface

More than a quarter century has passed since the publication of the first edition of *Economic Issues Today* (and its macroeconomic and microeconomic split versions). Needless to say, a lot of economic water has gone over the dam since 1978. Accordingly, the content of *Economic Issues Today* has undergone many changes through this, its eighth edition. Yet the underlying philosophy and pedagogical objectives of the book remain the same: to introduce those uninitiated in the ways of economists to the breadth and richness of economic reasoning.

Economic Issues Today maintains a distinctive approach with its first-person debate from Conservative, Liberal, and Radical views. The reader is advised not to approach these "ideological" positions as if they were etched in stone and not subject to change and adaptation. While each position has rather fixed philosophical foundations, the actual practice and the day-to-day politics of each has allowed appropriation of small ideological pieces from an opposing perspective on one issue or another. For example, the subject of automobile safety was a torrid debate between Left and Right twenty-five years ago. Now, it has mainstream acceptability and the debate over consumer protection has moved on to different products and problems. However, the comfortable conclusion of "issue solved" or the convenience of "score carding" which side came out ahead on a particular policy always has been fuel for this book's anticipation of the next turn of the wheel. Consider the wave of industry deregulation and other regulatory reversals that gave the impression that the bulk of regulatory institutions was on the path to oblivion. Now, corporate and accounting debacles of painful proportions have reinvigorated the public's interest in managing the ground rules for business conduct and prompted greater intrusion into lightly regulated areas such as financial reporting responsibilities and the broader accounting profession.

At the beginning of the twenty-first century and after more than twenty years of nearly uninterrupted economic prosperity, the contemporary scene is one where debates and argumentation over public policy generally have been muted. The tendency toward believing that old burning issues are solved or at least a high degree of consensus has been attained seems to have gained more traction over the past few years. Entire generations are weary of the continuing economic problems of farmers, the unemployed, environmental threats, the sustainability of the Social Security system, trade and budget deficits, poverty, and the like. These problems are supposed to be "fixed," not lingering sources of endless controversies! However, economic issues cannot be dismissed like overplayed songs and news stories or a bad season for the favorite sports team. The issues are troubling but it is more troubling when they are regarded as things too complex, too abstract, or too trivial with which to be bothered.

As it has since the first edition in 1978, *Economic Issues Today* (and the split versions) continues to plumb the depths of these debates. The book requires no background in the methods of economic analysis, and as much as possible it avoids the use of economic jargon in favor of everyday language. The eighth edition of *Economic Issues Today,* like previous ones, stresses the ideological choices that exist in economic thought and that often cause ordinary citizens to be confused about what economists *do* and what economists *believe.* As ever, it is meant to be a provocative book, more concerned with provoking discussion and thought than in presenting "right" solutions to problems. It remains committed to the belief that real economic solutions are possible in a democratic society only when all alternatives are known and considered.

Although longtime users are familiar with the text's philosophy and perspectives, new readers might benefit from an explanation of why the authors undertook this project in the first place and how the book is organized.

All too frequently, students begin their study of economics with the impression that economists are bland and monolithic when discussing important issues confronting the general society. We may as well admit that the profession sometimes exhibits a tendency to blandness in its public utterances, but surely any supposed unanimity toward social policy questions has vanished. With the rise of an influential Radical caucus within the discipline, beginning in the late 1960s, and the more recent resurgence of variations of laissez-faire ideology, any facade of consensus has clearly been broken down. The application of economic theory to issues of public policy more and more reflects a range of choice from Conservative to Liberal to Radical.

For the student struggling with basic theory and analytic tools, as well as for the ordinary citizen overwhelmed by economic data in the newspapers and on the TV evening news, it is hard to avoid confusion over what economists really think about the problems facing the nation. This book begins with the assumption that the answers economists give to policy questions can be usefully compared and analyzed according to the particular biases of their arguments and the probable outcomes of their proposals. In other words, differences in economic logic and interpretation of evidence are not so much a function of skill mastery as they are the expression of strongly held social and political opinions. The text also assumes that economics as a body of knowledge takes on greater meaning and is more readily comprehended when it is viewed in this way.

For each issue, a Conservative, Liberal, and Radical analysis and proposed solution are presented in turn as the valid approach to the problem. On one page, there may be a vigorous and unyielding defense of laissez-faire and the market economy; on another, a program for the elimination or modification of the free market. This is not the way economic analysis and theory are usually taught, but it is what the practice of economics is about. In the real world, the citizen and the economist make public policy choices that protect, attack, or modify the market mechanism. We may defend our positions in terms of economic logic, but behind our proofs lies our political and ideological view of the world. This book attempts to examine the relationship between ideological values and the economic theories and policies that are their outcome.

Since the text presents a wide range of perspectives on a number of currently sensitive issues, it should provoke disagreement, controversy, and discussion. In itself, the book does not urge a particular ideological position or a particular variety of economic analysis. The decision to select or reject this or that point of view is left—as it should be—to the reader.

Each chapter is self-contained and may be assigned in any order the instructor chooses. There are relatively few footnotes or direct references to specific economists, although the ideas of many contemporary economists and schools of economic thought will be apparent. The suggested readings at the end are offered for anyone wishing to dig a little more deeply into an issue or a particular economic perspective or approach.

What Is New in This Edition

The eighth edition represents a substantial revision over the seventh. Updating of critical changes in economic policy was undertaken for every issue. However, the introduction to the text keeps its time-tested development and explanation of the Conservative, Liberal, and Radical positions.

Macroeconomic Issues Today has noticeable changes. A new issue on social policy frames the debate about the Social Security system, becoming Issue 6. International economics is moved to Issue 7 where it takes up the intensifying controversies surrounding free trade agreements, recent episodes of protectionism, capital flight, and the outsourcing of American jobs. A revised Issue 1 launches the section with its familiar query regarding macroeconomic stability: "Are we depression-proof?" Issue 2 follows in a tightly designed sequence with a renewed focus on trends and prospects for economic growth and productivity growth in the U.S. economy. Issue 3 takes a sharp turn back to federal budget deficits from the previous edition's indulgence in budget surpluses with a fully revised discussion of causes and consequences. With unemployment once again ascending the ladder of the economic agenda, Issue 4 emerges as extensively redone to consider the various sources of unemployment, including the recent phenomenon of outsourcing, and examination of public policy options to deal with the problem. Issue 5 approaches the inflation debate more comprehensively than in the past edition by presenting alternative indices of price levels and a discussion of interest rate targeting in monetary policy.

"The Market Versus Planning and Controls," takes on a new identity as a "Reprise" to all the material that has gone before it. Placing it in a stand-alone position at the end of the book acknowledges the issue's summation of comparative economic systems.

Supplements

The instructors manual for *Economic Issues Today* is available on computer disk. Key terms, multiple-choice, true-false, and essay-discussion questions are provided for each issue. Some instructors like to use *Economic Issues Today* in conjunction with their preferred principles text. The instructor's manual provides a "correlation grid" that cross-references the issues from *Economic Issues Today* with related chapters in leading principles of economics textbooks. Potential adopters can request a copy of the grid from the publisher or view it online at www.mesharpe.com. The correlation grid is reproduced for your convenience at the end of the preface.

To assist with classroom presentations, instructors can download PowerPoint slides of all figures and tables in the text from the publisher's Web site at www.mesharpe.com. The authors also maintain a portal that is a quick and easy way to link to the PowerPoint slides and correlation grid at www.EconomicIssues.com.

Correlation Grid for Using *Economic Issues Today* with Leading Introductory Economics Textbooks

EIT issues	Baumol/Blinder	Case/Fair	Lipsey	McConnell/Brue	Mankiw	Mansfield/Bahraucsh	Miller	O'Sullivan/Sheffrin	Parkin	Ruffin/Gregory	Samuelson/Nordhaus	Schiller (one-semester text)	Stiglitz
Introduction: Alternative Economic Philosophies	1, 3, 4	1, 2	1, 2, 3	1, 2, 3, 4	1, 2	1	1	1, 2	1, 2	1, 2, 3	1, 2	1, 2	2
Issue 1: Responding to Market Outcomes: Competition or Protection for American Agriculture	5, 7, 8, 9	3, 4	4, 5, 6, 10	20, 23, 33	4, 5, 6	16, 17	3, 20	4, 5, 6	3, 4, 6	3, 4, 6	3, 4	3, 5	4, 5
Issue 2: Consumer Welfare: Is It Necessary to Protect the Consumer?	6, 7	5, 14	7	21	7, 21, 22	16, 18	19	7	19	7, 15	5	4	6, 14
Issue 3: Dealing with Externalities: How Can We Save the Environment?	8, 22	14	18, 19	30	10, 11	21	31	17	16, 19	5, 8, 20	18	5	21
Issue 4: Imperfect Competition: Is Big Business a Threat or a Boon?	10, 11, 12, 13, 20	11, 12, 13	11, 12	24, 25, 32	15, 16, 17	19	24, 25, 26, 27	10, 11, 12, 13, 14	11, 12, 13, 14	11, 12, 13, 14	9, 10	7	11, 12, 13, 14, 15
Issue 5: Economic Regulation. Which Path: Has Deregulation Worked?	14, 20		13, 18, 19	32	6, 7, 11	20	27	13, 14	14	14	2, 17	7, 9	13
Issue 6: Income Distribution: Does America Hve an Income Inequality Problem?	17, 18, 19	15	15, 16	28, 29, 34	19, 20	23, 24	6, 30	19	18	17, 19	12, 19	8	19

Relevant textbook chapters

Issue													
Issue 7: Financing Government: What Is a Fair System of Taxation?	21	16	20	31	8, 12	26	5, 6	16	31	21, 22	16	9	16, 26
Issue 8: Macroeconomic Instability: Are We Depression-Proof?	23, 24	17, 21, 23	21, 23, 24	8, 9, 10	26, 28	4, 5	7, 10, 11	22, 24, 25	21, 22, 24, 30, 31, 32	23, 25, 27, 34	20, 22, 23, 24	10, 11	24, 25
Issue 9: Economic Growth and Stability: Can We Maintain High and Steady Rates of Economic Growth?	15, 24, 29, 34	19, 25, 30	25, 26, 31	8, 11, 12, 17	25, 33, 34	6, 11, 14, 25	12, 13, 18	23, 25, 26	21, 23, 24, 25	26, 27, 31, 33	20, 22, 23, 24, 27, 34	10, 11	28, 29
Issue 10: Balancing the Federal Budget: Should We Be Worried About the Rising Federal Deficit?	33	16, 21	32, 33	18	33, 34, 35	12	13	25	31	31, 33	34	12	36
Issue 11: Unemployment: Is Joblessness an Overrated Problem?	26, 28	26	31	16, 19	28, 33, 35	4	7	21, 29, 30, 31	22	33	31	10	24, 31
Issue 12: Inflation: Can Price Pressures Be Kept Under Control?	25, 26, 28, 31	23, 25, 26	28, 29, 30	15, 16	30, 33, 35	7, 10, 12	7	21, 28, 29, 30	27, 28, 31, 32	32	26, 32	14	30, 31
Issue 13: The New Population Problem: Can We Save Our Social Security System?	21, 33	16		36		26	6	16, 19	34	19, 21, 22	16		
Issue 14: International Economics: Where Does America Fit into the New World Order?	35, 36, 37	32, 33, 34	35, 36, 37	37, 38	3, 9, 31, 32	27, 28	17, 18, 32, 33	32, 33	33, 34	35, 36, 37	29, 30	17	3, 18, 33, 34
Reprise. The Market Versus Planning and Controls: Which Strategy Works Better?	36	11, 31	38	16, 31, 39, 40	11, 36	26	5	22, 31	5, 16	21, 22, 38, 39	33	16	37

Acknowledgments

The senior author would like to thank Michael Weber, a longtime sponsoring editor of *Economic Issues Today* at St. Martin's Press (before St. Martin's dropped its college economics line), for signing the book with its new publisher, M.E. Sharpe, Inc. And, as with each new edition, the senior author feels duty bound to note the kind and thoughtful encouragement of Bertrand Lummus, then the college editor at St. Martin's, who made it possible for *Economic Issues Today* to see the light of day in the first place. Similarly, the senior author wishes to acknowledge the efforts of Paula Franklin and Emily Berleth, whose extraordinary editorial skills in the early editions of the work have survived, both directly and indirectly, right down to the current version.

The authors want to express appreciation to several teaching professors for their suggestions and comments that have led to improvements for this edition of the text: Michael McAvoy, William P. O'Dea, and David Ring (all from SUNY Oneonta), and Amy S. Cramer, Pima Community College. We are grateful to Campbell R. McConnell for his expert advice and encouragement over the past three editions of *Economic Issues Today*. The authors also thank Lynn Taylor, economics editor, for her editorial efforts on the eighth edition.

We sadly acknowledge the passing of our good friend and mentor of *Economic Issues Today*, Robert L. Heilbroner of the New School University. Bob Heilbroner was both a teacher and colleague of coauthor Jason Hecht, and we all drew much inspiration and intellectual strength from his numerous books and writings. In particular, the influence of his most famous book, *The Worldly Philosphers,* is evident within these pages. The eighth edition of *Economic Issues Today* is dedicated in memory of Robert L. Heilbroner.

Part I

Introduction

Alternative Economic Philosophies
A Survey of Conservative, Liberal, and Radical Critiques

The ideas of economists, both when they are right and when they are wrong, are more powerful than is commonly understood. Indeed, the world is ruled by little else. Practical men, who believe themselves to be quite exempt from any intellectual influences, are usually the slaves of some defunct economist. Madmen in authority, who hear voices in the air, are distilling their frenzy from some academic scribbler of a few years back.

—John Maynard Keynes, 1936

3

As of this writing (2005), the American economy had experienced only two brief recessions (in 1990–91 and 2001) during the past twenty-two years. Add to this the fact that the American economy remains the envy of the rest of the world. By such indicators, we should be—at least with respect to economic matters—a content and happy people. Right?

Alas, economic matters rarely seem to be a solid source of shared contentment. As the outcome of the 2000 and 2004 presidential elections indicates, the country remains equally divided on the question of whether or not the American economy was headed in the right direction. This down-the-middle division leads to an obvious conclusion (and one completely independent of who won and who lost the election): A great many Americans are uncertain about their nation's economic future. In fact, the uncertainty does not end there. Each thoughtful member of either side of the great divide in opinion has to wonder about what is going on in the minds of those who went the other way on the question of the "right direction."

As with all such periods of economic uncertainty and disagreement, the citizenry becomes increasingly interested in economic matters and the observations and advice that might be offered by the keepers of economic wisdom: *economists*. Mostly ignored in good times, economists can count on getting the public's attention when worries about bad times arise. And so, economists once again find a growing popular interest in their "dismal science."

Alas, when they are thrust into the spotlight, economists invariably reveal something about their discipline that ordinary citizens tend to forget during the good times. As those recently watching economists on TV or reading op-ed pieces by economists were soon to discover (or, if old enough, *rediscover*), economists are rarely of one mind with respect to matters of deep and immediate economic impact. Some Americans suffering unease about the economy in general may experience a heightening of this malady as a result of the evident lack of unanimity in the economics profession. However, this has been an abiding characteristic of the keepers of economic wisdom for a very long time.

It is well for the reader to remember that throughout the long history of human efforts to understand and explain economic matters, disagreement rather than consensus has been the rule. In a nation that puts great stock in consensus building as the ultimate tool of governance and the principal device for sustaining social order, this may be a disconcerting fact. In any event, it is one we should understand. Even in times of considerable national economic prosperity, real differences of political and economic opinion still circulate. And, as we should know from the historical record, economic prosperity itself has always been a transitory condition; when it fades, debate over alternative economic policies often becomes heated.

When that debate takes place, squabbling among economists over policy alternatives can scarcely be hidden from the public, and such disagreement can be downright unsettling. It often comes as a rude surprise to the person on the street, who, although paying due professional respect to economists, still sees the economist as a kind of mechanic. When one's car does not start, the car owner expects (at least hopes) that the diagnosis of mechanical trouble given at one garage is exactly the same as what will be heard at any other. If there is one mechanical problem, there should be one mechanical solution. The moral of this comparison is that the study of economics is more than studying a repair manual, and economists are not mechanics.

Economics and Ideology

How is such disagreement possible? Is not economics a science? Economists' answers to that question vary. A common and reasonable enough response is simply that scientists disagree too. While there is much truth to such an answer, it really begs the question. Plainly, economics is not a science like physics. Whereas economists may sometimes talk about the laws of supply and demand as if they were eternal verities like the law of gravity, there is abundant anthropological and historical evidence that many societies have behaved quite contrary to the laws of supply and demand.

To be sure, economists employ (or at least should employ) the rigor of scientific method and quantitative techniques in collecting data, testing hypotheses, and offering reasonable conclusions and predictions. However, economists deal with different "stuff" than their colleagues in the exact sciences. Their data involve human beings, and their laboratory is a world of behavior and perception that varies with time and place. On top of this, economists, like all social scientists, are called on to answer a question not asked of those in the pure sciences: "What *ought* to be?" Astronomers, for instance, are not asked what *ought* to be the gravitational relationships of our universe. That would be a nonsensical question. Economists, however, cannot evade making some determinations about optimal prices, optimal income distribution, and so forth. Their decisions, while perhaps based on a genuine effort at neutrality, detachment, and honest evaluation of the available evidence, finally must be a matter of interpretation, a value judgment based on their own particular world views. To put the point directly: *Economics, as a study of human behavior, cannot avoid value judgments. Struggle as it may, economics as a discipline is never free from ideology.*

The early economists of the eighteenth and nineteenth centuries—Adam Smith, David Ricardo, John Stuart Mill, and especially the heretic Karl Marx—perceived economics as merely part of a broader political economy context, but this view had been largely abandoned by the end of the nineteenth century. By the middle of the twentieth century, the economics profession generally approached ideology as if it were a dirty word, unprofessional, or, at the very best, too troublesome to deal with. The emphasis was on theoretical tools, considered both universal and neutral. All this changed in the 1960s and 1970s when well-known American economists thrust themselves into the powerful debates then sweeping American society. Their views on the war in Vietnam, poverty, civil rights, the extent of government power, the environmental crisis, the oil embargo, the causes of stagflation, high technology versus smokestack industries, and much more could be heard regularly on television talk shows and miniseries or read in the columns of weekly newsmagazines. Often there was the pretension that this "talking out of church" had little impact on the body of professional theory and judgment, but the pretension was unconvincing. For good or ill, the genie was out of the bottle, and the economics profession had again become involved in politics and in recommending political courses of action to pursue economic objectives.

Initially, through the 1960s and into the early 1970s, prevailing opinion among economic reasoners upheld a Liberal perspective on political economy, advocating an active interventionism by government to correct and improve the workings of the economy. However, during the late 1970s, this consensus began to break down as the national economy slipped into a long period of sagging growth, rising unemployment, and escalating inflation. In its place, a new consensus began to build on behalf of a Conservative, minimum-government approach to political and economic matters. As the Liberals' star fell and the Conservatives' rose, the intensity and bitterness of economic and political argument sharpened. Although the shrillness of the ideological debate calmed a bit during the Reagan years—no doubt a by-product of the long economic expansion that began in late 1982—the past four decades of shifting ideological perspectives have left their mark on the economics profession. To a considerable extent, the ordinary economics textbook illustrates this point. While economics texts continue to do what such books have always done, namely, to introduce the reader to a generally agreed-on body of theoretical and analytical techniques and tools that constitute the study of economics, most have also found it necessary to identify and discuss the alternatives of Liberals, Conservatives, and, sometimes, even Radicals in the practical extension of economic analysis to actual policy-making situations.

The significance of all this should not be lost on the beginning student of economics. Though many economists may stress the value-free nature of their studies, and of economics in general, common sense and observation suggest that this is at best a vastly exaggerated claim. The content and application of economic reasoning are determined ultimately by the force of what economists believe, not by an independent and neutral logic. But to say that economics is a matter of opinion is not to say that it is just a study of relatively different ideas: Here is this view and here is that one and each is of equal value. In fact, opinions are not of equal value. There are good opinions and there are bad ones. Different economic ideas have different consequences when adopted as policy. They have different effects—now and in the future. As we confront the various policy solutions proposed to deal with the many crises now gnawing deep into our economy and society, we must make choices: this one seems likely to produce desired outcomes, that one does not. No other situation is consistent with a free and reasoning society. Granted, it is a painful situation, since choice always raises doubts and uncertainty and runs the risk of wrong judgment, but it cannot be evaded.

This book is intended to focus on a limited number of the hard choices that we must make. Its basic premise is that economic judgment is fundamentally a matter of learning to choose the best policy solution among all possible solutions. The book further assumes that failure to make this choice is to underestimate the richness and importance of the economic ideas we learn and to be blind to the fact that ideas and analyses do indeed apply to the real world of our own lives.

On Sorting Out Ideologies

Assuming that we have been at least partially convincing in our argument that economic analysis is permeated by ideological judgment, we now turn to examine the varieties of ideology common to American economic thought.

In general, we may characterize the ideological position of contemporary economics and economists as Conservative, Liberal, or Radical. These, the same handy categories that evening newscasters use to describe political positions, presumably have some meaning to people. The trouble with labels, though, is that they can mean a great deal and, at the same time, nothing at all. At a distance the various political colors of Conservative, Liberal, and Radical banners are vividly different. Close up, however, the distinctiveness blurs, and what seemed obvious differences are not so clear. For instance, there is probably *not* a strictly Liberal position on every economic issue, nor are all the economists who might be generally termed Liberal consistently in agreement. The same is true in the case of many Radical or Conservative positions as well. Unless we maintain a certain open-endedness in our categorizing of positions, the discussion of ideological differences will be overly simple and much too rigid. Therefore, the following generalizations and applications of ideological typologies will attempt to isolate and identify only representative positions. By doing this we can at least focus on the differences at the center rather than on the fuzziness at the fringes of these schools of thought.

We are still left with a problem. How do you specify an ideological position? Can you define a Radical or a Liberal or a Conservative position? The answer here is simple. As the British economist Joan Robinson once observed, an ideology is like an elephant—you cannot define an elephant but you should know one when you see it. Moreover, you should know the difference between an elephant and a horse or a cow without having to resort to definitions.

There is a general framework of thought within each of the three ideological schools by which we can recognize them. Thus we will not "define" the schools but merely describe the salient characteristics of each. In all of the following, the reader is urged to remember that there are many varieties of elephants. Our specification of a particular ideological view on any issue is a representative model—a kind of average-looking elephant (or horse or cow). Therefore, the Conservative view offered on the problem of federal deficits, for instance, will probably not encompass all Conservative thought on this question. However, it should be sufficiently representative so that the basic Conservative paradigm, or worldview, can be distinguished from the Radical or Liberal argument. Where truly important divisions within an ideological paradigm exist, the divisions will be appropriately noted and discussed.

A Brief Footnote on the Paradigms

The reader should be aware that ideological labels and categories presently are used by Americans in an increasingly flippant fashion. For example, TV journalism's efforts to "dumb down" news reporting and editorial commentary on the news has produced the well-known talking-head format where analyses of events are sifted and sorted into "from the Right" and "from the Left" perspectives. Based upon the authors' experiences, this technique of dividing up Conservative, Liberal, and Radical political-economic ideas—handy as it may be for sound-bite making—creates some awful confusion.

Neat division into "Left" or "Right" is a dangerous oversimplification of the range and variety of ideological points of view. The Left presumably includes all Liberals and Radicals, and the Right catches all Conservatives. To dump Liberals and Radicals into a presumably shared-interest category is a monumental error of the first order. True Liberals and true Radicals have been at each other's throats for a century or more. Indeed, they have been at war with each other more than either one has been at war with Conservatives.

The Left-Right designation of ideologies rests on the false assumption that political-economic belief can be neatly segregated and compartmentalized along a continuum—with Adam Smith on one end and Karl Marx on the other. Accordingly, leaning Left or Right is apparently determined by where along this continuum one is located: nearer or further from Marx and Smith. Alas, ideas are not susceptible to arrangement along a continuum. To arrange political-economic ideas as if they were part of a unified spectrum is about as useful as arranging one's personal library according to book size or one's CD collection according to the color of the disks' cases.

However, the most troublesome and misleading aspect of the Left-Right categorization of American opinion is its habit of not sorting outlooks according to the types of issues that individuals might address.

Tasteless as some may find the following "for instances," where on the Left-Right spectrum should we locate a gay or lesbian couple who regularly vote Republican but are also seeking to obtain a marriage license or the aging Pentecostal Christian who is utterly dependent on Social Security monthly checks and Medicare to support himself and his wife?

The point is that sexual orientation or religious belief are questions of personal and social values (as is the matter of one's preferred major league baseball team) and not necessarily a reflection of one's political ideology at all. To be sure, political conservatives may court those who adhere to "conservative" personal values (sometimes called "family values") and liberal ideologues may cultivate those of a "liberal" bent with respect to their personal beliefs, but that is a separate matter from the examination of competing economic ideologies.

The purpose of this "footnote" is to underscore that the following Conservative, Liberal, and Radical paradigms are generalized representations of three long-recognized schools of ideological outlook. The reader is warned that they are not easily short-handed as Left or Right nor should any of our paradigms be presumed to advocate on behalf of specific "social values."

The Conservative Paradigm

What is usually labeled the Conservative position in economic thought and policy making was not always conservative. Conservative ideas may be traced to quite radical origins. The forebears of modern Conservative thought—among them England's Adam Smith (1723–1790)—were not interested in conserving the economic order they knew but in destroying it. In 1776, when Smith wrote his classic *Wealth of Nations*, England was organized under a more or less closed economic system of monopoly rights, trade restriction, and constant government interference with the marketplace and individuals' business and private affairs. This system, known as mercantilism, had been dominant in England and, with slight variations, elsewhere on the Continent for more than 250 years.

Adam Smith's Legacy

Smith's remedy was simple enough: Remove all restrictions on commercial and industrial activity and allow the market to work freely. The philosophical basis of Smith's argument rested on his beliefs that (1) all men had the natural right to obtain and protect their property; (2) all men were by nature materialistic; and (3) all men were rational and would seek, by their own reason, to maximize their material well-being. These individualistic tendencies in men would be tempered by competition in the marketplace. There, men would have to compromise with one another to gain any individual satisfaction whatsoever. The overall effect of these compromises would ultimately lead to national as well as individual satisfaction. Competition and self-interest would keep prices down and production high and rising, as well as stimulate product improvement, invention, and steady economic progress. For this to happen, of course, there would have to be a minimum of interference with the free market—no big government, no powerful unions, and no conspiring in trade. Smith's position and that of his contemporaries and followers was known as "classical liberalism." The Conservative label now applied to these views seems to have been affixed much later, when Smith's heirs found themselves acting in the defense of a status quo rather than opposing an older order.

Thus modern capitalist economic thought must trace its origins to Adam Smith. While this body of thought has been built on and modified over the past two hundred years, the hand of Adam Smith is evident in every conventional economics textbook. Common sense tells us, however, that a lot has changed since Smith's day. Today business is big. There are labor unions and big government to interfere with his balanced free market of equals. His optimistic view of a naturally growing and expanding system is now replaced by growth problems and by a frequent dose of pessimism in some glances toward the future. Nevertheless, modern Conservatives, among contemporary defenders of capitalism, still stand close to the ideals of Adam Smith.

Modern Conservative thought is anchored in two basic philosophic ideas that distinguish it from Liberal and Radical positions. First, the market system and the spirit of competition are central to proper social organization. Second, individual rights and freedoms must be unlimited and uninfringed.

Conservatives oppose any "unnatural" interference in the marketplace. In particular, the Conservative views the growth of big government in capitalist society as the greatest threat to economic progress. Milton Friedman, Nobel laureate and preeminent figure in the Conservative Chicago school, has argued that government has moved from being merely an instrumentality necessary to sustain the economic and social order to becoming an instrument of oppression. Friedman's prescription for what "ought to be" on the matter of government is clear:

> A government which maintained law and order, defined property rights, served as a means whereby we could modify property rights and other rules of the economic game, adjudicated disputes about the interpretation of the rules, enforced contracts, promoted competition, provided a monetary framework, engaged in activities to counter technical monopolies and to overcome neighborhood effects widely regarded as sufficiently important to justify government intervention, and which supplemented private charity and the private family in protecting the irresponsible, whether madman or child—such a government would clearly have important functions to perform. The consistent liberal is not an anarchist.*

The antigovernmental position of Conservatives in fact goes further than merely pointing out the dangers to individual freedom. To Conservatives the growth of big government itself causes or worsens economic problems. For instance, the growth of elaborate government policies to improve the conditions of labor, such as minimum-wage laws and Social Security protection, are seen as actually harming labor in general. A wage higher than that determined by the market will provide greater income for some workers, but, the Conservative argument runs, it will reduce the total demand for labor, and thus dump many workers into unemployment. As this example indicates, the Conservative assault on big government is seen not simply as a moral or ethical question but also in terms of alleged economic effects.

Another unifying feature of the representative Conservative argument is its emphasis on individualism and individual freedom. To be sure, there are those in the Conservative tradition who pay only lip service to this view, but for true Conservatives it is the centerpiece of their logic. As Friedman has expressed it:

> We take freedom of the individual . . . as the ultimate goal in judging social arrangements. . . . In a society freedom has nothing to say about what an individual does with his freedom; it is not an all-embracing ethic.

---

*Milton Friedman, *Capitalism and Freedom* (Chicago: University of Chicago Press, 1962), 34.

> Indeed, a major aim of the liberal [here meaning Conservative as we use the term] is to leave the ethical problem for the individual to wrestle with.*

Modern Conservatives as a group exhibit a wide range of special biases. Not all are as articulate or logically consistent as Friedman's Chicago school. Many are identified more readily by what they oppose than by what they seem to be for. Big government, in both its microeconomic interferences and its macroeconomic policy making, is the most obvious common enemy, but virtually any institutionalized interference with individual choice is at least ceremonially opposed.

Some critics of the Conservative position are quick to point out that most modern-day Conservatives are not quite consistent on the question of individual freedom when they focus on big business. In fact, until comparatively recently, Conservatives usually did demand the end of business concentration. Like all concentrations of power, it was viewed as an infringement on individual rights. The Conservative Austrian economist Joseph Schumpeter argued that "Big Business is a half-way house on the road to Socialism." The American Conservative Henry C. Simons observed in the depressed 1930s that "the great enemy to democracy is monopoly." Accounting for the change to a more accommodating position on big business is not easy. Conservatives offer two basic reasons. First, big business and the so-called monopoly problem have been watched for a long period of time, and the threat of their power subverting freedom is seen as vastly overstated. Second, by far the larger problem is the rise of big government, which is cited as the greatest cause of business inefficiency and monopoly abuse. Another factor that seems implied in Conservative writing is the fear of communism and socialism. To direct an assault on the American business system, even if existing business concentration were a slight impediment to freedom, would lay that system open to direct Radical attack. How serious this supposed contradiction in Conservative logic really is remains a matter of debate among its critics.

The Recent Resurgence of Conservative Economic Ideas

In the United States, until the drab years of the Great Depression, what we now call "Conservative economics" *was* economics, period. Except

---

*Milton Friedman, *Capitalism and Freedom* (Chicago: University of Chicago Press, 1962), 12.

for an occasional voice challenging the dominant wisdom, usually to little effect, few economists, political leaders, or members of the public at large disagreed greatly with Adam Smith's emphasis on individual freedom and on a free market economic condition.

The Depression years, however, brought a strong reaction to this kind of political and economic thinking. Many—perhaps most—of the millions of Americans who were out of work in the 1930s and the millions more who hung on to their jobs by their teeth came to believe that a "free" economy was simply one in free fall. While most staunch Conservatives complained bitterly about the abandonment of market economics and the "creeping socialism" of Franklin Roosevelt's New Deal, they had few listeners. For thirty-two of the next forty-eight years after Roosevelt's election in 1932, the White House, and usually the Congress, was in Liberal Democratic hands. For Conservatives, however, perhaps the greater losses were in the universities, where the old free market "ideas" of Adam Smith and his disciples quickly fell out of style. In their place, a generation of professors espoused the virtues of the "New Economics" of John Maynard Keynes and the view that a capitalist economy requires government intervention to keep it from destroying itself.

Driven to the margins of academic and political influence by the 1970s, the Conservatives seemed in danger of joining the dinosaur and the dodo bird as an extinct species. However, by the late 1970s, in the aftermath of the Vietnam War and the Watergate scandal and in a period when nothing government did seemed able to control domestic inflation and unemployment problems, there developed a growing popular reaction against government in general. As more and more Americans came to believe that government economic and social interventions were the cause of the nation's maladies, the Conservative ideology took off again under its own power.

In 1980, the Conservative economic and political paradigm succeeded in recapturing the White House. Ronald Reagan became the first president since Herbert Hoover to come to office after a private sector career. There was no doubting Reagan's philosophical commitment to the principles of a free enterprise economy.

As might be expected, Conservatives found themselves facing a difficult situation. Implementing a free market policy was, of course, much easier to accomplish in theory than in the real world—especially in a world vastly more complex than that envisioned by Adam Smith.

Reaganomics, the popular catchword for the new brand of Conservative economics, was quickly and sorely tested as the economy slipped into a deep recession in late 1981. To both friendly and hostile critics, Conservatives responded that quick solutions were not possible since the economic debris of a half century needed to be swept aside before the economy could be reconstructed. Despite the fact that Reaganomics proved to be somewhat less than an unqualified success (indeed, a good many Conservatives would now call it a failure), the Reagan years were a time of moderate but sustained economic boom—the second longest peacetime boom in American history. Despite some dark clouds—the near tripling of the federal debt, a worsening international trade situation, and a precipitous stock market collapse in 1987—the Reagan-Bush 1980s remained, in economic terms, a comparatively bright period in American economic history. Meanwhile, the collapse of communism in Eastern Europe and the Soviet Union and the Soviet bloc's shift toward a more open economic and political system in the last years of the decade could only be counted as frosting on Conservatives' ideological cake. As America approached the end of the century, Conservatives basked in the sunlight of success. Important for our study is the fact that a wide range of Conservative economic ideas and political perspectives that had been shunned in serious academic debates for over forty years have again made their way back into economics textbooks.

Indeed, the rise and refurbishing of market-based economic theory—and not simply in the United States—in the last decade or two of the twentieth century is one of the most important recent developments in economics. For today's young reader, who probably believes that market-based doctrine *is* economics, it may be difficult to believe that Conservative thinking in both economic theory and policy making was, not so many years ago, without much influence in the economics profession. That fact is a good one to keep in mind. It illustrates something that is often overlooked: The prevailing ideological mood, what we might call the conventional wisdom, is ever subject to change and reevaluation.

The Liberal Paradigm

According to a national poll, Americans tend to associate the term *Liberal* with big government, Franklin Roosevelt, labor unions, and welfare. Time was, not too long ago, when Liberal stood not just as a proud appellation but seemed to characterize the natural drift of the whole country. At the height of his popularity and before the Vietnam War toppled his administration, Lyndon Johnson, speaking of the new Liberal consensus, observed:

> After years of ideological controversy, we have grown used to the new relationship between government, households, business, labor and agriculture. The tired slogans that made constructive discourse difficult have lost their meaning for most Americans. It has become abundantly clear that our society wants neither to turn backward the clock of history nor to discuss the present problems in a doctrinaire or partisan spirit.*

Although what we will identify as the Liberal position in American economic thought probably still is alive and well in the teaching and practice of economic reasoning (as we shall see, even some Conservatives have adopted elements of the Liberal analysis), the Liberal argument is undergoing considerable changes. These changes, however, are more cosmetic than basic, and the central contours of Liberal belief are still visible.

The Interventionist Faith

Whereas Conservatives and Radicals are comparatively easily identified by a representative position, Liberals are more difficult to identify. In terms of public policy positions, the Liberal spectrum ranges all the way from those favoring a very moderate level of government intervention to those advocating broad government planning of the economy.

Despite the great distance between the defining poles of Liberal thought, several basic points can be stated as unique to the Liberal paradigm. Like their Conservative counterparts, Liberals are defenders of the principle of private property and the business system. These, however, are not categorical rights, as we observed in the Conservative case. Individual claims to property or the ability to act freely in the marketplace are subject to the second Liberal principle—that social welfare and the maintenance of the entire economy supersede individual interest. In a vicious condemnation of what we would presently call the Conservative position, John Maynard Keynes directly

---

The Economic Report of the President, 1965 (Washington, DC: U.S. Government Printing Office, 1965), 39.

assaulted the philosophy that set the individual over society. Keynes argued:

> It is not true that individuals possess a proscriptive "natural liberty" in their economic activities. There is no "compact" conferring perpetual rights on those who Have or on those who Acquire. The world is not so governed from above that private and social interest always coincide. It is not a correct deduction from the Principles of Economics that enlightened self-interest always operates in the public interest. Nor is it true that self-interest generally is enlightened; more often individuals acting separately to promote their own ends are too ignorant or too weak to attain even these. Experience does not show that individuals, when they make up a social unit, are always less clear-sighted than when they act separately.*

To the Liberal, then, government intervention in, and occasional direct regulation of, aspects of the national economy is neither a violation of principle nor an abridgement of "natural economic law." The benefits to the whole society from intervention simply outweigh any "natural right" claims. The forms of intervention may vary, but their pragmatic purpose is obvious—to tinker and manipulate in order to produce greater social benefits.

Government intervention in the economy dates from the very beginnings of the nation, but the Progressives of the early twentieth century were the first to successfully urge an extensive and systematic elaboration of governmental economic powers. In response to the excesses of giant enterprises in the era of the robber barons, the Progressives followed a number of paths in the period from 1900 to 1920. One was the regulation of monopoly power, to be accomplished either through antitrust prosecutions to restore competition or through the use of independent regulatory commissions in cases where a "break them up" policy was undesirable (for instance, railroads and other firms possessing *public utility* characteristics). A second was *indirect* business regulation, effected by such Progressive developments as legalization of unions, the passage of social legislation at both the federal and state levels, tax reforms, and controls over production (for example, laws against food

---

*John M. Keynes, "The End of Laissez Faire," in *Essays of Persuasion* (New York: Norton, 1963), 68.

adulteration)—all of which circumvented the power of business and subjected it to the public interest.

Although the legislation and leadership of the administrations of Theodore Roosevelt, William Howard Taft, and Woodrow Wilson went a long way in moderating the old laissez-faire ideology of the previous era, actual interference in business affairs remained slight until the Great Depression. By 1933 perhaps as many as one out of every three Americans was out of work (the official figures said 25 percent), business failures were common, and the specter of total financial and industrial collapse hung heavy over the whole country. In the bread lines and shanty towns known as "Hoovervilles" as well as on Main Street, there were serious mutterings that the American business system had failed. Business leaders, who had always enjoyed hero status in the history books and even among ordinary citizens, had become pariahs. Enter at this point Franklin Roosevelt, the New Deal, and the modern formulation of Liberal government-business policies. Despite violent attacks on him from the Conservative media, Roosevelt pragmatically abandoned his own conservative roots and, in a bewildering series of legislative enactments and presidential decrees, laid the foundation of public interest criteria for government regulation of the marketplace. *Whatever might work was tried.* The National Recovery Administration (NRA) encouraged industry cartels and price setting. The Tennessee Valley Authority (TVA) was an attempt at publicly owned enterprise. At the Justice Department, Attorney General Thurman Arnold initiated more antitrust actions than all of his predecessors combined. And a mass of "alphabet agencies" was created to deal with this or that aspect of the Depression.

Intervention to protect labor and extensions of social welfare provisions were not enough to end the Depression. It was the massive spending for World War II that finally restored prosperity. With this prosperity came the steady influence of Keynes, who had argued in the 1930s that only through government fiscal and monetary efforts to keep up the demand for goods and services could prosperity be reached and maintained. Keynes's arguments for government policies to maintain high levels of investment and hence employment and consumer demand became Liberal dogma. To be a Liberal was to be a Keynesian, and vice versa.

Alvin Hansen, Keynes's first and one of his foremost proponents in the United States, could scarcely hide his glee in 1957 as he described the wedding of Liberal Keynesian policies with the older government interventionist position this way:

> Within the last few decades the role of the economist has profoundly changed. And why? The reason is that economics has become operational. It has become operational because we have at long last developed a mixed public-private economy. This society is committed to the welfare state and full employment. This government is firmly in the driver's seat. In such a world, practical policy problems became grist for the mill of economic analysis. Keynes, more than any other economist of our time, has helped to rescue economics from the negative position to which it had fallen to become once again a science of the Wealth of Nations and the art of Political Economy.*

Despite the Liberal propensity for tinkering—either through selected market intervention or through macro policy action—most Liberals, like Conservatives, still rely on traditional supply-and-demand analysis to explain prices and market performance. Their differences with Conservatives on the functioning of the markets, determination of output, pricing, and so forth lie not so much in describing what is happening as in evaluating how to respond to what is happening. For instance, there is little theoretical difference between Conservatives and Liberals on how prices are determined under monopolistic conditions. However, to the Conservative, the market itself is the best regulator and preventive of monopoly abuse. To the Liberal, monopoly demands government intervention.

Varieties of Liberal Belief

As noted before, the Liberal dogma covers a wide spectrum of opinion. Moreover, the Liberal position has shifted somewhat in response to the economic disappointments of the 1970s and certain successes of the Reagan years.

On the extreme left wing of the Liberal spectrum, economists such as Robert Heilbroner and John Kenneth Galbraith have long argued that capitalism as the self-regulating system analyzed in conventional economic theory simply does not exist. Heilbroner contends: "The persis-

---

*Alvin H. Hansen, *The American Economy* (New York: McGraw-Hill, 1957), 175.

tent breakdowns of the capitalist economy, whatever their immediate precipitating factors, can all be traced to a single underlying cause. This is the anarchic or planless character of capitalist production."* For a time, this critical defect led Heilbroner to flirt with central planning as the only possible cure. However, he eventually backed away from this position, holding instead that capitalism plus government regulation to provide periodic corrections has proved to be more durable than central planning efforts.

To the left-leaning and always iconoclastic John Kenneth Galbraith, who sees problems of technology rather than profit dominating the giant corporation, a more rational atmosphere for decision making must be created. In brief, the modern firm demands a high order of internal and external planning of output, prices, and capital. The interests of the firm and state become fused in this planning process, and the expanded role of Liberal government in the whole economy and society becomes obvious. While Galbraith has in the past maintained that he was a socialist, the Liberal outcome of his program is obvious in that he (1) never explicitly takes up the expropriation of private property, and (2) still accepts a precarious social balance between public and private interest.

Although Galbraith's Liberalism leads to an economy heavily reliant on planning, most Liberals stop well before this point. Having rejected the logic of self-regulating markets and accepted the realities of giant business enterprise, Liberals unashamedly admit to being pragmatic tinkerers—ever adjusting and interfering with business decision making in an effort to assert the changing public interest. Yet all this must be done while still respecting basic property rights and due process. Under these arrangements, business regulation amounts to a protection of business itself as well as the equal protection of other interest groups in pluralist American society.

In the not-too-distant past, business itself adapted to and embraced this position. Whereas certain government actions might be opposed, the philosophy of government intervention in the economy was not necessarily seen as antibusiness. The frequent Conservative depiction of most Liberals as being opposed to the business system does not withstand the empirical test. For instance, in 1964 Henry Ford II organized a

---

*Robert Heilbroner, *The Limits of American Capitalism* (New York: Harper and Row, 1966), 88.

highly successful committee of business leaders for the Liberal Lyndon Johnson, while Conservative Barry Goldwater, with Friedman as his adviser, gained little or no support from big business. However, the extent of government regulation soon reached a level that was wholly unacceptable to the private sector. In the late 1960s and early 1970s, a blizzard of environmental, job safety, consumer protection, and energy regulations blew out of Washington. Added to what was already on the ground, the new legislative snowfall seemed to many observers at the end of the 1970s about to bring American business to a standstill. Many who a decade before frankly feared the economic freedom of the Conservative vision now embraced that position.

The distress of economic *stagflation* in the 1970s (lower growth, rising unemployment, *and* price inflation), for which the Liberals seemed to have no programmatic cures, along with a growing popular sentiment against big government in general, drove Liberals from positions of political influence. Even within universities, the Liberal consensus began to collapse, with some former Liberal theorists deserting to the Conservative camp and most others adopting a lower profile in their teaching, writing, and research. Yet by the end of the 1980s, most of the analytical and policy positions associated with Liberal economic reasoning still survived—a bit subdued from the high-flying days of Kennedy's New Frontier and Johnson's Great Society but distinguishable nonetheless. Among the more reform-minded Liberal reasoners, the old economic agenda items—income distribution, discrimination, the environment, consumer protection, monopoly abuse, labor unions, structural shifts in the economy and their resulting dislocations—remained vital concerns in any policy-making effort. However, Liberal hopes for a fairly swift and sweeping resolution of these problems had diminished greatly from the expectations of the 1960s and early 1970s. The new realities of a slow-growth economy, massive federal deficits, reduced American competitiveness in world markets, and costly entitlement programs put serious constraints on even a visionary reformer's dedication to interventionism. But this commitment had not been extinguished. When the Eastern European communist states toppled like dominoes and the long-time cold war confrontation with the Soviet Union seemed to move steadily toward a peaceful end, there was brave talk among Liberals of the prospects for a "peace dividend." The ending of the cold war was envisioned as freeing up vast sums for favored social agenda items that had long been shelved.

Meanwhile, in the business community, the old propensity to enlist government on the side of improving the stability of domestic markets was given new life in the face of rising foreign competition, the decline of certain basic industries, and the double frights provided by Black Monday (the sudden collapse of the stock market on October 19, 1987) and the savings-and-loan industry crisis. In particular, the last two events seemed to show that too much market freedom might not be as desirable as it sounded.

The present-day ambivalence of Liberals on the degree and type of intervention will be evident in our survey of economic issues in this book; nevertheless, this tendency should not be misunderstood. Specific Liberal approaches to problem solving may be debatable, but the essence of Liberal economics remains unchanged: *The capitalist economy simply requires pragmatic adjustment from time to time to maintain overall balance and to protect particular elements in the society.*

The Radical Paradigm

For most readers, specification of a Radical paradigm will seem to be a difficult and unfamiliar exercise. The identifications of Right and Left, or Conservative and Liberal, are used nightly on the television news and talk shows, and presumably these labels have self-evident political meaning to most viewers. The Radical label is not so well known, nor is it used very much by the media. For the most part, Americans are generally uninformed about the content and objectives of a Radical social outlook. Yet in a variation on the old adage about familiarity breeding contempt, we find also that ignorance breeds contempt, at least with regard to ideological matters. Quite simply, most Americans—even if they know little about a Radical ideological outlook—believe it to be essentially wrongheaded and, at bottom, un-American. Nevertheless, there is a Radical tradition in American economic thought, and it needs to be understood.

The principal litmus test for accepting the Radical position requires the rejection of production-for-profit capitalism as an economic system —both the free market capitalism of Conservatives and the regulated capitalism of Liberals. Such a minimum membership standard, needless to say, leads to the lumping of a large number of very different anticapitalist critiques into the Radical category. Nonetheless, there is an important shared outlook among true Radicals. The essence of this perspective is nicely illustrated by a comment made some years ago by Tony Benn, a political and ideological leader of the British Labour Party. Queried by an interviewer in 1992 as to what was going to happen to socialists around the world now that the Marxist-socialist regime in the Soviet Union had collapsed, Benn offered a pregnant response. "The real struggle," Benn observed, "was never between capitalism and socialism. It was and is between capitalism and democracy."

In Benn's remark lies the common core of contemporary Radical thought: Radicals espouse a social and economic order in which institutions are expected to respond to people's needs and people are to be empowered politically and economically so as to ensure democratic outcomes.

At such a general level of articulation, Radical ideology may appear deceptively benign. Who, after all, can be opposed to "empowering people?" However, the economic and political empowerment of people quickly takes on a more serious and, to some, more threatening meaning when the Radical analysis is examined in greater detail. As the Radical tradition understands the economic and social dynamic of societies, power is intricately connected to the ownership of property: Whoever owns or controls the use of a society's things invariably possesses political and economic power commensurate with such ownership or control. In capitalism, ownership of things, particularly the things (capital) that produce other things, is disproportionately held in the hands of a comparative few. These owners of the means of production are seen by Radicals as exercising excessive influence for their own personal (or class) gain in the society's decisions about what will be produced, how that output will be produced, and who will share in this output. In our Radical paradigm, empowerment necessarily leads to limiting private and individual economic power and to increasing the social ownership and control of the things within a society. For most readers, a word should spring to mind: *socialism.*

Socialism as a political, social, even religious outlook probably predates the rise of capitalism. And the term *socialism* is an umbrella that can cover a multitude of ideological tendencies. Utopian communitarians, Christian socialists, anarchists, Marxists, syndicalists, communists, guild socialists, and many other ideological variants can crowd under the socialist umbrella. The common thread to membership in any socialist tradition is acceptance of the advocacy for the social or community ownership of all, or most, of the means of production and for a societally determined standard for the distribution of the output of the society.

While it is pretty clear that all socialists would qualify as Radicals, it is by no means true that all Radicals see themselves as socialists. Partly, this is the case because socialism has long been and certainly remains a dirty word among most Americans—an ideological outlook that directly challenges the nation's historical proclivity to explain social and economic life in largely individualist terms. Partly, it reflects the fact that the term socialism is simply too big an umbrella and therefore includes a lot of ideological outlooks that, once you get past a few basic theoretical similarities, do not agree on important issues of specific programs and goals.

Moreover, many American Radicals are not political activists at all. For them, commitment to a Radical perspective is mostly an intellectual and analytical exercise aimed at attacking and revealing the deficiencies of conventional Conservative and Liberal thought. Their purpose is not to build an alternative political party, such as socialism has tended to become, but to supply an alternative critical analysis that Americans might act upon within the constraints of the existing political order. In any case, in specifying a Radical paradigm, it is wise to remember that membership includes many different marchers not necessarily listening to the same drummer, or at least not hearing the same beat even if there is a single drummer. But then again, the same can be said for Conservative and Liberal paradigms.

However, as a practical matter, an extended explanation of the Radical paradigm must be assigned an ideological starting point. And most, but surely not all, American Radicals would admit their intellectual debt to Karl Marx and his nineteenth-century critique of capitalism.

The Marxist Heritage

Since the Marxist critique is likely to be less familiar to many readers than the basic arguments of Conservatives or Liberals, it is necessary to be somewhat more detailed in specifying the Radical position. As will be quickly apparent, the Radical worldview rests on greatly different assumptions about the economic and social order than those of the Conservatives and Liberals.

According to Marx's view, the value of a commodity reflects the real labor time necessary to produce it. However, under capitalism workers lack control of their labor, selling it as they must to capitalists. The workers receive only a fraction of the value they create—according to Marx, only an amount sufficient in the long run to permit subsistence. The rest of the value—what Marx calls *surplus value*—is retained by capitalists as the source of their profits and for the accumulation of capital that will increase both future production and future profit. As the appropriation of surplus value proceeds, with the steady transference of living labor into capital (what Marx called *dead labor*), capitalists face an emerging crisis. With more and more of their production costs reflecting their growing dependence on capital (machines) and with surplus labor value their only source of profit, capitalists are confronted with the reality of not being able to expand surplus appropriation. Unless they are able to increase their exploitation of labor—getting more output for the same, or less, wages paid—they face a falling rate of profit on their growing capital investment. Worse still, with workers' relatively falling wages and capitalists' relatively increasing capacity to produce, there is a growing tendency for the entire capitalist system to produce more goods than it can in fact sell.

These trends set certain systemic tendencies in motion. Out of the chaos of capitalist competitive struggles for profits in a limited market there develops a drive toward *concentration and centralization.* In other words, the size of businesses grows and the number of enterprises shrinks. However, the problems of the falling rate of profit and chronic overproduction create violent fluctuations in the business cycle. Each depression points ever more clearly toward capitalist economic collapse. Meanwhile, among the increasingly impoverished workers, there is a steady growth of a *reserve army of the unemployed*—workers who are now unemployable as production decreases. Simultaneously, increasing misery generates class consciousness and revolutionary activity among the working class. As the economic disintegration of capitalist institutions worsens, the subjective consciousness of workers grows to the point where they successfully overthrow the capitalist system. In the new society, the workers themselves take control of the production process, and accumulation for the interest of a narrow capitalist class ceases.

The Modern Restatement of Marx

Of necessity, the modern Radical's view of the world must lack the finality of Marx's predictions. Quite simply, the capitalist system has

not self-destructed and, in fact, in a good many respects is stronger
and more aggressive than it was in Marx's day. Although the present-
day Radical may still agree with Marx's long-run predictions about
the ultimate self-destructiveness of the capitalist order, the fact is that
Radicals must deal with the world as it is. While the broad categories
of Marx's analysis are retained generally, Radical thought must focus
on real-world, current conditions of capitalist society and present an
analysis that goes beyond merely asserting the Marxist scenario for
capitalist collapse. Useful economic analysis must be offered in ex-
amining contemporary problems.

The beginning point for modern Radical critiques, as it was also for
Marx over a hundred years ago, is the unquenchable capitalist thirst
for profits. This central organizing objective of all capitalist systems
determines everything else within those systems. The Radical analysis
begins with a simple proposition about how capitalists understand
market activity:

> Total sales = total cost of materials and machinery used up in production
> + total wages and salaries paid + (– in the case of losses) total profits

Such a general view of sales, costs, and profits is, thus far, perfectly
consistent with traditional accounting concepts acceptable to any Conservative or Liberal. However, the Radical's analytic mission becomes
clearer when the proposition is reformulated:

> Total profits = total sales – total cost of materials and machinery used up
> in production – total wages and salaries paid

It now becomes evident that increasing profits depends on three general conditions: (1) that sales rise, *ceteris paribus* (all things being equal);
(2) that production costs (composed of wage costs and material and
machinery costs) decline, *ceteris paribus;* or (3) that sales increases at
least exceed production cost increases. The capitalist, according to the
Radical argument, is not simply interested in total profits but also in the
rate of profit, or the ratio of profits to the amount of capital the capitalist
has invested.

With capitalist eyes focused on raising profits or raising profit rates,
it becomes clear to Radicals which individual economic policies and
strategies will be advanced by capitalists: *Every effort will be made to*

keep costs low, such as reducing wage rates, speeding up the production line, introducing so-called labor-saving machines, seeking cheaper (often foreign) sources of labor and materials, and minimizing outlays for waste treatment and environmental maintenance. At the same time, *efforts will be made to keep prices high,* especially through the development of monopolistic price-making power on both a national and an international scale. In all of these activities, capitalists will make every effort to use government economic intervention to their own advantage—both in domestic markets and in expanding capitalist hegemony into the world.

However, taking the system as a whole, the effort of individual capitalists—either on their own or aided by government—to expand profit produces a crisis in obtaining profits. For instance, the capitalist goals of keeping wages low and prices high must lead to situations where workers as consumers simply cannot clear the market of available goods. Accordingly, the aggregate economy deteriorates into periodic recession or depression, with rising unemployment among workers and falling profits for capitalists. With capitalist support, a variety of government monetary and fiscal efforts may be employed to offset these ups and downs in the capitalist business cycle—in particular to improve the profit and profit rate of capitalist enterprises. However, so-called mixed capitalism (a mixture of private sector and government planning of the economy) cannot overcome the fundamental contradictions of a dominantly private, production-for-profit economy. And, of course, with the expansion of capitalism throughout most of the world, the capitalist crisis takes on international proportions. Quite as Marx predicted, the general economic crises deepen and occur more frequently. The search for profit becomes more frantic and more destructive to the lives of ever greater numbers of people living under capitalist hegemony throughout the world.

From the Radical point of view, periodic crisis in capitalism is not the result of excessive tinkering with the market system, as Conservatives claim; nor will the tendency toward crisis be contained by Liberal interventionism. *Periodic and deepening crisis* is *capitalism.*

Radical analysis is, of course, more penetrating than this short résumé can indicate. One further point that should be examined briefly is Marx's view of the relationship between a society's organization for production and its social relations. To Marx, capitalism was more than an economic system. Private values, religion, the family, the educational system, and political structures were all shaped by capitalist class domination and by the goal of production for private profit. It is important to recognize this tenet in any discussion of how Marxists—or Radicals with a Marxist orientation—approach contemporary social and economic problems. Marxists do not separate economics from politics or private belief. For instance, racism cannot be abstracted to the level of an ethical question. Its roots are seen in the capitalist production process. Nor is the state ever viewed as a neutrality able to act without class bias. Bourgeois democracy as we know it is seen simply as a mask for class domination.

Marx, in his early writings before his great work, *Capital,* had emphasized the "qualitative" exploitation of capitalism. Modern Radicals have revitalized this early Marx in their "quality of life" assaults on the present order. In these they emphasize the problems of worker alienation, commodity fetishism, and the wasteful and useless production of modern capitalism. The human or social problems of modern life are seen as rooted in the way the whole society is geared to produce more and more profits.

In addition to their Marxist heritage, modern Radicals derive much of their impulse from what they see as the apparent failure of Liberalism. Liberal promises to pursue policies of general social improvement are perceived as actions to protect only *some* interest groups. In general, those benefiting under Liberal arrangements are those who have always gained. The corporation is not controlled. It is more powerful than ever. Rule by elites has not ended, nor have the elites changed. Moreover, the national goals of the Liberal ethic—to improve our overall national well-being—stimulated the exploitation of poor nations, continued the cold war, and increased the militarization of the economy.

The Question of Relevance

Quite obviously, the Marxist prediction of capitalism's final collapse has not yet come to pass. In fact, Radicals—particularly those very closely associated with the Marxist tradition—are increasingly obliged to account for what many non-Radicals see as a historical turning away from all collectivist political economic alternatives with the rise of market economies in previously socialist states. These trends, along with certain internal analytical problems of Marxist analysis, are quite sufficient for most non-Radicals to consign the whole Radical paradigm to the garbage heap of worthless, worn-out ideas.

A thoughtful observer may question whether this is an entirely enlightened conclusion to reach. First, the tendency to lump Marxism and real-world communist systems together as one and the same, while long a habit in the noncommunist as well as the communist world, rests on a grossly inaccurate understanding of Marx's philosophy. Second, Marxism—at least as American Radical scholars have developed and used it—is more a way of looking at how our economy works than a prophecy of things to come. It is the technique of analysis rather than the truth of Marx's specific analysis that counts.

A third point might also be worth considering. Freed of the Soviet millstone, Radical critiques, which were easily evaded during the cold war epoch, might take on more meaning and appeal. Radicals no longer have to explain away the Soviet errors of authoritarian politics, decrepit bureaucracies, and failed planning before putting forth their own critique of contemporary capitalism and their own democratic-socialist programs. Moreover, and of increasing importance to the relevance of Radical arguments, the post-Soviet world economy has yet to show the robustness that the victors of the cold war might have expected. Standing unchallenged in the world, capitalism and variants of capitalism may loom as larger targets for Radical attack than is generally appreciated. Consequently, it may be just a bit early to count out the Radical paradigm, as non-Radicals are presently inclined to do.

As noted before, not all Radicals subscribe to all Marxist doctrine, but Marxism in one form or another remains the central element of the Radical challenge. Marx's fundamental contention that the system of private production must be changed remains the badge of membership in the Radical ranks. This sets Radicals apart from mainstream Conservative and Liberal economists.

Critics of the Radical position usually point out that Radical analyses are hopelessly negativistic. Radicals, they say, describe the problems of capitalism without offering a solution other than the end of the whole system. While there is much truth to this charge, we shall see in the following sections that indeed some solutions are offered. But even if their program is vague, Radicals would argue that their greatest contribution is in revealing the truth of the capitalist system.

Despite lessened political influence, modern Radical economic thought still looms as a logically important alternative to the more broadly supported Conservative and Liberal paradigms. The force of an idea is not dependent on the number of true believers. Were that the case, Conservative economic doctrine would have disappeared thirty years ago.

Applying the Analysis to the Issues

We have identified the three representative paradigms; now we will put them to use. The following selected issues by no means exhaust the economic and political crises troubling the nation; nevertheless, they provide a good-sized sampling of the social agenda confronting us. The issues presented here were selected because of their immediacy and representativeness in illustrating the diverse ideological approaches of Conservative, Liberal, and Radical economic analyses.

In each of the following issues, the representative paradigms are presented in a *first-person advocacy approach*. The reader might do well to regard the arguments like those in a debate. As in a debate, one should be careful to distinguish between substantive differences and mere logical or debating strategies. Thus some points may be quite convincing, whereas others seem shallow. However, the reader should remember that, shallow or profound, these are representative political economic arguments advanced by various economic schools.

The sequence in presenting the paradigms is consistent throughout the text: first Conservative, then Liberal, then Radical. In terms of the logical and historical development of contemporary economic ideologies, this sequence is most sensible; however, it certainly is not necessary to read the arguments in this order. Each one stands by itself. Nor is any ideological position intentionally set out as a straw man in any debate.

Readers should look at each position critically. They should test their own familiarity with economic concepts and their common sense against what they read in any representative case. Finally, of course, as students of economics and as citizens, they must make their own decisions. They determine who, if anyone, is the winner of the debate.

Because of space limitations, the representative arguments are brief, and some important ideas have been boiled down to a very few sentences. Also, within each of the three major positions there is a wide range of arguments, which may sometimes be at variance with one another. Conservatives, Liberals, and Radicals disagree among themselves on specific analyses and programs. For the sake of simplicity, we have chosen not to emphasize these differences but arbitrarily (although after much thought) to select the most representative arguments. Each paradigm's discussion of an issue presents a critique of present public policy and, usually, a specific program proposal.

In all of the arguments, the factual and empirical evidence offered has been checked for accuracy. It is instructive in itself that, given the nature of economic facts, they can be marshaled to prove a great variety of different ideological positions. Different or even similar evidence supports different truths, depending on the truth we wish to *prove*.

Problems of Aggregate Economic Policy

Part II focuses on issues that are primarily *macroeconomic* in origin. In other words, our attention will be directed to issues affecting the economy as a whole and to variables affecting its aggregate economic performance. Specifically, we shall examine such problem areas as business cycle behavior, stabilization policy, the federal deficit, unemployment, inflation, international trade and monetary policy, and the changing demographics of the nation's population.

Macroeconomic Instability

Are We Depression-Proof?

We have nothing to fear but fear itself.
—President Franklin D. Roosevelt, 1933

This is a unique moment in U.S. history, a time of unrivaled prosperity and progress, with few internal crises or external threats. We have the responsibility to use our good fortune wisely. If we maintain our current economic strategy, we can sustain our prosperity, expand the circle of opportunity, meet the long-term challenges of this new century, and provide our children the chance to live their dreams.
—President Bill Clinton, 2001

The economy of the United States has been through a lot. If you really think about it, it's pretty remarkable to be able to stand up and say to you that our economy is strong and getting stronger, that we're witnessing steady, consistent growth. After all, we've been through a recession, a national emergency, a war, corporate scandals.
—President George W. Bush, 2004

In world market crisis, the contradictions and antagonisms of bourgeois production break through to the surface. But instead of investigating the nature of the . . . catastrophe, the apologists content themselves with denying the catastrophe itself.
—Karl Marx, 1867

The Problem

Fluctuations in the general level of economic activity have long been one of the more prominent features of the macroeconomy. Throughout the nineteenth century and the first third of the twentieth, the cyclical pattern of national economic performance was more or less accepted as the normal state of affairs: first a period of boom and expansion, then a stage of general contraction (until the 1930s usually called a "panic"), followed by a recovery that culminated in yet another boom, and, sooner or later, another contraction. Always a matter of some interest to economists, public interest in the business cycle varied inversely with the ebb and flow of business conditions. Not until the long contraction of the 1930s did the business cycle become a matter of serious and enduring discussion among ordinary citizens. The dreary decade after the stock market crash in 1929 directed almost everyone's attention to efforts to understand the causes of economic fluctuations. This was especially true because the Great Depression was, by most past standards of cyclical behavior, exceptionally deep and protracted. Although the Great Depression is no longer a part of recent American history, and is remembered only dimly by a comparative handful of living Americans, its impact on our economic thinking and reflexes remains extraordinarily strong.

That Americans might have a special concern about severe business downturns is not surprising when the severity of the "Great Rupture" in American history is recalled. Between 1929 and 1933, the gross domestic product (the nation's annual output of goods and services) was sliced almost in half. Unemployment, which had averaged about 3.2 percent in 1929, soared to 24.9 percent by 1933. Unemployment for 1933 totaled 13 million men and women, but this figure was deceiving because several times that amount, perhaps 65 percent of the labor force, suffered some unemployment or could obtain only part-time work. On the business side, before-tax corporate profits fell from a record $11 billion in 1929 to an operating loss of $1.2 billion four years later, and industrial production declined by more than 45 percent.

Historians have documented the wrenching effect of the Depression on institutions and values. However great the changes in modes of American thought and behavior, none were more profound than those in economic thinking and practice. Before Black Tuesday's stock market collapse on October 29, 1929, and the crisis that followed, conventional economic wisdom unashamedly espoused the virtues of laissez-faire. The economy was to operate freely. Although this meant the periodic toleration of bad times as business activity occasionally slowed, these downturns were offset by succeeding periods of expansion and prosperity. Left alone, economic analysis held, the economy would right itself and, over time, move upward to new, higher levels of output, employment, and real income.

But recovery was not spontaneous, and for good or ill, the orthodox belief in the self-regulating business cycle fell from favor. Ruminating in England on the worldwide depression, John Maynard Keynes concluded it was time to clear the intellectual stage of all the old furniture of economic orthodoxy. In 1936, his *General Theory of Employment, Interest, and Money* proclaimed that capitalist economic institutions were not self-balancing mechanisms but instead tended toward chronic stagnation. This situation required action by governments through fiscal and monetary policy to forestall collapse. The solution: Raise aggregate demand for goods through massive government spending, thereby putting to work unemployed people and idle factories. Not given to modesty, Keynes correctly warned his readers that his ideas would change the way people thought about modern capitalist economies. And they did, as Keynes's "New Economics" became the dominant wisdom in economic matters.

For most of the first three decades after World War II, Keynesian orthodoxy reigned. The Keynesian view that periodic slumps in the economy could and should be offset by government efforts to stimulate the demand for goods went virtually unquestioned, and many economists began to think and act as though fluctuations in business activity were only a feature of the past, pre-Keynesian era. With the new economic logic maintaining that depressions were unnecessary and could always be headed off by appropriate use of public policy, a good many Americans came to believe in the 1960s that we were now "depression-proof." However, events in the mid-1970s prompted a reexamination of the New Economics. Although no depression developed, the economy did suffer through stagflation as economic growth slowed, unemployment rates rose, and price inflation gnawed deep into the economy.

Meanwhile, the general economic uncertainty that prevailed during and after the 1970s had reopened old debates among contending economic philosophies about what were the appropriate and most effective strategies for dealing with business fluctuations or any impending depression. Liberals had to reexamine their earlier claims that the business cycle had indeed been brought under control through demand-management policies. While not abandoning their view on the inherent instability of production-for-profit economies, modern Keynesian Liberals have accepted more modest countercyclical targets, no longer arguing so vigorously that the economy can be sustained on a permanent expansionary course by simply fine-tuning levels of aggregate demand. For Conservatives, the stagflationary epoch provided first visibility (which had all but disappeared during the era of "High Keynesianism") and then a high degree of respectability. In the new economic setting, it was appropriate to challenge the Keynesian explanation of the Great Depression as well as Keynesian policy making in general. For Radicals, the stagflationary crises of the 1970s and early 1980s were seen, at least in the short run, as a vindication. They had always viewed the 1930s as proof that unregulated capitalist economies were inherently self-destructive, and the economic problems of the 1970s had shown that regulated capitalism did not work either.

Then, along came the economic boom of the 1990s. Its durability was such that a great many ordinary citizens became inclined to believe that the Great Depression and its consequences should be consigned to the trash bin of "forgettable historical events." Of course, not many thoughtful economists believed that the good times of the nineties were *proof* that the business cycle had been repealed. Most, if pressed on the question of whether or not another Great Depression was *possible*, would have responded with a cautious affirmative answer: *Possible but really unnecessary as long as we responded to a downturn "intelligently."*

By early September 2001, the evidence indicated that the boom was over and the nation had descended into recession—but a recession of ordinary and tolerable dimensions. However, the terrorist attacks on the World Trade Center and the Pentagon on September 11, 2001, and the resulting commitment of the United States to a "war on terrorism" caused considerable professional reconsideration about the prospect of a "normal recession." The New York Stock Exchange's biggest one-day loss of value in its history (although the loss was overcome in the following three weeks), the particularly heavy blow to transportation and entertainment industries, the American consumer's decision to reduce current spending, and the resulting cut back on employment and investment outlays by business dealt the sagging economy a heavy blow.

Although the 2001 recession officially lasted only nine months, as of June 2004, employment still remained below its prior peak level. Though the economy is not likely to slide down a precipice resembling the Great Depression, the last recession was notable for the breadth and duration of unemployment—especially among college-educated workers. Perhaps this will be a new feature of the American business cycle where employment prospects in recessions are not that much different from expansions. The prospects of another Great Depression may be greatly muted, but they have not been silenced.

Synopsis

The Conservative position maintains that depression and protracted economic stagnation are not central to capitalist economic systems and that the business cycle downturn after 1929 was worsened, not moderated, by government intervention in the economy. Liberals argue that only through vigorous, active countercyclical policies by government can the economy's natural propensity toward recession and depression be controlled. To Radicals, crisis and depression are quite natural to production-for-profit systems, and although crises may be delayed by governmental actions, they cannot be eliminated in the long run.

Anticipating the Arguments

- On what grounds do Conservatives argue that Liberals and Radicals have failed to prove their case that capitalism naturally tends toward protracted periods of economic stagnation? How do they account for economic downturns?
- In what ways did the Keynesian critique depart from the conventional wisdom of the 1930s?
- How does the Radical scenario of capitalism's chronic tendency toward crisis differ from the Liberal Keynesian view?

THE CONSERVATIVE ARGUMENT

The classical economic tradition from which most Conservatives draw their analytical perspectives and their strength of purpose holds to a simple proposition: *When free human beings operate freely in free markets, this necessarily will lead to optimal economic and social outcomes.* This view is not limited to microeconomic (individual market) operations, but extends to an aggregate or macroeconomic analysis of economic activities. Left to operate freely, the aggregate economy, like an individual market, will be self-correcting over time, setting optimal output, price, and employment conditions to avoid excessive long-term swings in business activity.* Business fluctuations over the short term are, of course, not surprising since an economy must from time to time adjust to changing conditions. But long-run or violent contractions are essentially the result of unwarranted interventions by government or others seeking to *improve on* market outcomes.

For a long time this point of view did not enjoy extensive currency among economic reasoners nor much practice by Western political leaders. The long Depression of the 1930s signaled a decline in classical economic modes of thought that was not reversed until the late 1970s. Given the long economic boom of the 1980s and the record-breaking expansion of the 1990s, however, it is easy to forget the economic past. Yet two important points need to be recalled lest we repeat, in our forgetfulness, our past errors. First, we need to understand the real causes and effects of economic events in the era that came to be known as the Great Depression. Second, we must comprehend how our errors in understanding these events led to the development of economic doctrines and policies that produced the near catastrophic economic crises of the 1970s. Much mythology surrounds these questions, but also much danger if we are not historically and factually accurate in our understanding of the past seven decades of economic history.

To put matters directly, most of what is believed about the causes of the Great Depression is wrong. More important, the body of economic policy developed to make us depression-proof was dangerously irrelevant, constructed to deal with a problem that never existed. Alas, the cumbersome structure of government intervention in the economy through countercyclical fiscal and monetary policy has been unnecessary. Indeed, government intervention has been more of a threat to stability than a bulwark.

On Misreading the Significance of Causes of the Great Depression

Contrary to popular economic beliefs, the initial business downturn between 1929 and 1930 was not in itself a unique event. As most econo-

---

*This principle, sometimes called Say's law after the French economist Jean-Baptiste Say, who formulated it in 1803, is, of course, directly challenged by Liberals and Radicals.

mists know but sometimes overlook, the general economic performance of the United States, both before the Great Depression and after (even with the tools of the New Economists), has followed a cyclical course. Indeed, the expansion/contraction rhythm of economic affairs had fascinated many students of business cycles long before the 1930s. Business contractions had appeared at intervals of about eight to twelve years, each eventually succeeded by a counteracting stage of growth and prosperity. Economists offered a variety of explanations for such cyclical behavior, including new inventions, changes in investment or consumer behavior, and even sunspot activity. But before the 1930s, few, except perhaps Marxists committed to the destruction of the system, held that business contraction could become a permanent state of affairs. Just as surely as the business cycle turned downward, it would sooner or later turn upward.

This pattern, however, did not occur in 1929–30. To obtain a clearer understanding of modern-day economic tendencies, we must ask why. According to the zealots who quickly snatched up John Maynard Keynes's ideas and perverted them for their own uses, the depression of the 1930s was not merely a periodic movement within the business cycle. Instead, it was a problem of chronic *stagnation,* a situation in which the economy could no longer maintain high levels of employment and output because of the inadequacy of business investment. In short, depression had become a permanent state of affairs.

Such a situation, according to Keynes's followers, demanded firm action. First, the economy would have to be managed by government since the Treasury and monetary authorities could no longer count on the natural bottoming out of the depression. Second, government would have to act to *stimulate demand*—by undertaking efforts to increase consumer spending and business investment. Third, this demand stimulation would probably have to come from enlarged state expenditures, purposely unbalanced budgets and deficit spending for public goods, and transfer payments to business and individuals.

Thus began the modern period of economic thought. The epoch of laissez-faire was to be closed, with government replacing private accumulation and private instincts as the driving force of the economic system. Never mind the past spectacular performance of the private and open economy in building the nation. Never mind the implied assaults on individual economic freedom and choice that were the underpinnings of political freedom in the United States. Lord Keynes and his followers had determined that these now were outmoded beliefs and that only through massive government intervention in the economy could survival be assured.

A Better Interpretation

Ordinarily, the best test for a hypothesis that interprets a set of events is to ask whether the hypothesis adequately explains the situation and is the best explanation possible. Applying this rule to the Keynesian critique, we find it wanting.

There is no evidence to support the idea that the Great Depression was, at its beginning in 1929, exceptional or that it differed markedly from past business downturns. Therefore, there is nothing to support the Keynesian belief that depression had become a permanent, congenital economic condition by the 1930s. What we do know, however, is that the depressed business conditions were worsened by the money policy actions of the Federal Reserve Board (the Fed), the government authority charged with maintenance of the nation's money and banking system. The Fed succeeded in transforming the difficulties of an excessively careless epoch of stock market speculation, coupled with an ordinary downturn in the business cycle, into an economic catastrophe of the first magnitude.

Lowering interest rates had always served to bring forth new investment and stimulate recovery in past downturns. However, reacting to the speculative bull market, the Fed had pursued a tight money policy even when it was apparent in early 1929 that a business downturn was forming. With high interest rates discouraging new business borrowing and reducing the stock of money (the money supply), business investment and consumer buying sagged even before the stock market collapsed. This was the Fed's first mistake. Its second came in December 1930 when the Bank of the United States in New York City closed its doors. Although it was an ordinary commercial bank, many people believed it to be an official government bank, and panic set in. Depositors in New York City and elsewhere rushed to withdraw their savings. Bank after bank faced liquidity crises. Unable to meet depositors' demands, banks began to fall like a line of dominoes. Meanwhile, the Fed, created in 1914 for just such an emergency, failed to take any action to improve bank liquidity. In fact, its next action was simply disastrous. In September 1931, as economic and financial problems spread worldwide and more and more gold was drained from the United States, the Fed raised interest rates in an attempt to stop the flow of gold overseas. Banks, now unable to borrow from the Fed (because of the high interest rates), had insufficient funds to meet their customers' demands and had to fold. Fourteen hundred closed their doors in three months, and the nation's money supply (consisting largely of *demand deposits* held in the form of checking accounts) fell by 12 percent. Meanwhile, on the business side, high interest rates discouraged new investment, and consumer spending fell as the money supply contracted. An ordinary depression had been transformed into an unprecedented financial crisis and, in turn, a near-complete prostration of business.

One other misguided economic action deserves special note: passage in 1930 of the protectionist Smoot-Hawley Tariff Act. Under pressure from businesses seeking to protect domestic markets from foreign competition, the Hoover administration, caught up in the anxiety following the market crash, encouraged Congress to pass a tariff that established the highest duties on imported goods in American history. Predictably, our protectionism was quickly matched by similar actions by our trading partners, and while we were protected from imports, we soon found it impossible to sell our products overseas.

The foregoing analysis differs sharply from the Keynesian stagnationist approach. While the Keynesians are partially correct that the Depression did finally become a matter of insufficient aggregate demand that happened only after and as a result of the failure of the Federal Reserve System and the passage of Smoot-Hawley. Rather than the economy manifesting some sinister and fatal stagnationist flaw, the evidence suggests that the Great Depression was largely accidental. That being the case, there is no proven analytical foundation for the Keynesian prescription that only through massive government intervention can free enterprise economies be kept afloat. Ironically, when we focus on the critical failures of monetary and tariff policies between 1929 and 1933, we find the reverse of the Keynesian analysis to be true: that government actions (through the Fed and the Smoot-Hawley Tariff) in fact caused the Great Depression.

The worsening and deepening of the Depression after 1933 was also the result of government activity. Liberal defenders of Franklin Roosevelt like to depict the New Deal as an experimental, pragmatic program to *prime* the economy. Not yet convinced by the Keynesian arguments, Roosevelt is usually presented as doing too little with countercyclical policy to get things going (until the government spending boom of World War II). This interpretation of the New Deal period of the Great Depression is guilty of a serious error of omission.

Roosevelt's antidepression strategy, Keynesian or not, was antibusiness and antibanker. The president's public addresses identified these two groups as both the cause of the Depression and the reason why his own policies had not turned the economic tide. Roosevelt's attempts to increase regulatory agency power, to insert government in the pricing mechanism, to reform the banking community, and especially to reform the Supreme Court when it threw out key pieces of his interventionist legislation created considerable business uncertainty. Within such a charged political atmosphere, business expectations, key to the undertaking of new investment and critical to recovery, remained essentially negative. Thus the interventionist policies of the New Deal tended to deepen and broaden the already crucial business depression.

The Painful Legacy of the Depression

The passing of the Depression did not signal the passing of Keynesian ideas; indeed, it only marked the beginning of a long era of wrongheaded economic thought and policy. The victory of the Keynesian analysis led to the building of ever more elaborate theories to justify the enlargement of the government sector. The size of federal spending grew, and the extent of fiscal and monetary manipulation of business activity was expanded. For decades, beginning students of economics were taught, as if it were received religious truth, that deficits do not matter, that the growth of the public sector is healthy, and that the macro performance of the economy can be insulated from depression and *fine-tuned* to produce desired levels of output, employment, and price stability instantaneously as well as in the long run.

By the 1970s, however, the basic flaws of such an analysis were becoming uncomfortably evident as the nation slipped into a decade of inflation, unemployment, and disappointing growth. The Keynesian emphasis on *maintaining demand* meant neglecting and even restricting the production or supply side of the economy. As we shall see in subsequent issues, it led by the 1970s to an explosion of the federal debt, which in turn triggered an inflationary spiral that discouraged savings and slowed business investment. Incorrectly deciding that business had caused the Great Depression led, naturally enough, to forgetting that business was the very foundation of the economy. The situation was a bit like concluding that the health of the goose that laid the golden eggs would be improved by increasing the demand for eggs.

Looking back over the years of Keynesian dominance, with its patchwork of countercyclical and income-redistribution programs, George Gilder has observed:

> When government gives welfare, unemployment payments, and public service jobs in quantities that deter productive work, and when it raises taxes on profitable enterprise to pay for them, demand declines. In fact, nearly all programs that are advocated [by Keynesian economists] . . . in actuality reduce demand by undermining the production from which all real demand derives. . . . This is the essential insight of supply side economics. Government cannot significantly affect real aggregate demand through policies of taxing and spending.*

At best, the demand-side management efforts of the Keynesians amounted to a zero-sum game, merely shifting the earnings of some to others. At worst, as we shall see in the next issue, Liberal Keynesian fiscal and monetary policies drove the economy downward. The growing political, professional, and even popular reaction against Liberal economic and political policies, which commenced in the late 1970s and has continued to grow, is heartening.

Are We Really Depression-Proof?

Turning to the original question of whether or not another Great Depression is possible, the Conservative position, although similar to the Liberal Keynesian position in giving a negative response, should be seen in light of its own assumptions. First, a massive depression is not the natural outcome of a free enterprise economy. Second, the elaborate policy tools developed in an effort to insulate the economy from depression are both unjustified and inherently dangerous. Third, the fact that we have not experienced a serious depression since the 1930s should not be accepted as proof that Keynesian macro policy ever worked. Rather, it might just as easily prove that the private economy is basically durable and adaptable—even with Keynesian roadblocks thrown in its way.

Thus we can conclude that another Great Depression is not inevitable unless, of course, we continue to rely on mistaken interpretations and cures in the formation of public policy. The "cures" we learned from the

---

*George Gilder, *Wealth and Poverty* (New York: Bantam Books, 1981), 62–63.

last depression are a far greater menace to future stability than anything else on the horizon.

THE LIBERAL ARGUMENT

Riding the crest of a relatively less volatile business cycle since the mid-1980s, Conservatives have found it expedient to rewrite American economic history. Accordingly, they dismiss the significance of the Great Depression and the elaboration by John Maynard Keynes and his followers of modern macroeconomic theory and policy making. It is necessary, therefore, to go back and set the record straight. The exercise will be helpful in putting our subsequent examination of contemporary macroeconomic issues in a proper perspective as well as addressing the immediate question of whether or not we are *depression-proof.*

At the outset, however, it must be conceded that the *stagflation* of the 1970s with its high rates of inflation, slow economic growth, and high levels of unemployment—events that helped propel Conservative economic reasoning back onto center stage—did demonstrate that a too narrow Keynesianism has limitations in dealing with *all* the problems of the modern economy. However, the events of the 1970s should not be misread and used as dismissal of all that we have learned over the past sixty years or so. The stagflationary problems of high unemployment *plus* inflation did not prove the essential Keynesian critique to be in error. The absence of self-adjusting and self-regulating mechanisms in a laissez-faire capitalist economy is just as true today as in the 1930s. Similarly, the tendency of mature capitalist systems toward stagnation remains as much a characteristic as ever (as the current anemic employment growth confirms). Whatever the benefits of emphasizing the production side of the economy—and most Liberals would admit that some benefits have been obtained from the *supply-side* debate of the past several decades—this does not amount to a proof that Keynes's basic analysis should be abandoned in favor of a return to the discredited laissez-faire assumptions of a bygone era.

The Collapse of Orthodox Ideas in the 1930s

The prevailing economic view in 1929 was that the economy was a natural, self-adjusting mechanism. Wages, interest, and rents were paid to individuals according to the value of their contributions to national output. Such payments were, over time, equitable and just rewards for work and risk. The general mode of economic activity was assumed to be pure competition. Interference in the economy, whether by government, labor unions, or collusive business practice, was condemned. The economy was thus described and analyzed theoretically in terms of an open laissez-faire system. To be sure, periodic downturns in the national economy were possible, just as periodic stickiness in wages, savings, and business investment was possible. However, the focus was on the long haul, and over time, such deviations were thought to be self-correcting.

Within this general economic structure, traditional economists based their analysis of the national economy on a four-cornered foundation. First, there would be no long-run overproduction of goods (or, to look at it from the other side, no long-run underconsumption). This was true because payments to producers, labor, business, and so forth were always equal to the value of the goods produced. As the nineteenth-century French economist Jean-Baptiste Say put it in what has since come to be known as Say's Law, "Supply creates its own demand."

Second, and following from the first point, there could be, again in the long run, no such thing as involuntary unemployment. With flexible wages and prices, there would always be sufficient work at any given wage level to employ all those willing to work at that wage. Individuals who chose not to work at a particular wage (supposedly because they valued leisure more) were not "unemployed" at all.

Third, through free and flexible interest rates, private savings would be just enough to meet the investment (or borrowing) needs of businesses. If business sought greater investment, interest rates would rise, people would choose to save more, and funds would become available for business expansion. This, in turn, would create jobs, raise wages, and stimulate balanced economic growth.

Fourth, the level of prices in the society was determined by the rate of growth of the money supply. An increase in money would stimulate spending and demand for goods, which would raise market prices. A decrease in money would lower prices.

To the orthodox, these theories offered policy solutions to the periodic downturns in the economy. If business output exceeded consumer demand, just wait! Prices would fall to clear the market of goods. Wages would fall, and the number of workers seeking employment would be reduced until an equilibrium wage was reached. Interest rates would fall, and individuals would shift savings to consumption. With lower interest rates and increasing consumption, business would again invest. Public policy within such a self-balancing economic order could be described quite easily: *Do nothing.*

As the international economy continued to inch downward after 1929, John Maynard Keynes began to rethink the orthodox analysis and reach his own conclusion on the evidence at hand. First of all, he observed that the automaticity of Say's Law was unfounded. Indeed, it was possible for overproduction or underconsumption to develop if individuals held money rather than saved it (lent it to borrowers). Second, wages were not, in the real world, freely flexible. Business could and did keep prices up and laid off workers while awaiting the sale of inventories. The alternatives available to workers were not lower wages or leisure but simply increased involuntary unemployment. Third, lowered interest rates did not induce business investment at a time of overproduction. With goods on hand, business would be unlikely to produce more goods even if the cost of borrowing was near zero. Finally, businesses will neither invest nor hire additional workers without the *expectation* of future sales.

Thus in Keynesian analysis, the allegedly *short-run* business fluctuations of the economy could become very long indeed. The self-correcting nature of the economy was an incorrect premise. And squaring with the real evidence that continued to build after the early 1930s, it was possible to have a continuing low level of output that left large numbers of workers and factories idle. Indeed, it was not only possible, it was quite natural in an unregulated economic system.

The Keynesian Solution

Keynes's objective in his *General Theory* was to lay out the path to a high-employment economy. His approach emphasized aggregate economic performance rather than the microeconomic aspects of orthodox analysts. First, he explained, aggregate levels of employment depended on the total demand for goods, including consumer purchase of goods and services and business investment as well as government spending. Second, the primary culprit in the cyclical downturn of an economy was the activity of businesses because changes in investment outlays most directly affect changes in total demand for goods and services. Consumer spending, he maintained, was a fairly constant function of total income, with consumer outlays rising and falling directly as national income fluctuated. Government spending was small, and in depression conditions it tended to get smaller as governments tried to live within the orthodox doctrine of annually balanced budgets.

Keynes's position was that only through artificially induced higher levels of aggregate demand would it be possible to attain full employment and full utilization of plants and equipment. The course was clear: Business investment had to be stimulated, government spending had to be inflated, or, more likely, some combination of both had to be tried. The combined effects of expansionary fiscal policy (greater government spending and/or tax cuts usually accompanied by a budget deficit) and expansionary monetary policy (lower interest rates and easier money) were to produce enlarged aggregate demand and diminished unemployment.

The Victory of the New Economics

Although Keynes quickly gained academic adherents for his ideas, he made little headway in Washington during the Depression. For all his alleged fiscal profligacy, Franklin Roosevelt, with his pump priming and "ABC" government agencies, never grasped the Keynesian analysis and never embraced massive federal spending until he was forced—during World War II.

There was enormous federal spending during the war (with government spending in 1944 nearly twice the GDP of 1933), which produced a rapid growth of demand that was restrained only by rationing and price controls. Simultaneously, there was an equally rapid growth in the federal debt. When the war ended, many economists still feared the economy would drop back into depression. Instead, the stored-up wartime demand became the engine for a long postwar boom. Even before the inadvertent Keynesianism of World War II proved to be effective, however, the United States had rung down the curtain on the laissez-faire era. On February 20, 1946, President Truman signed Public Law 340, better known as the Employment Act of 1946. This act committed the federal government to the three objectives of (1) providing high levels of employment, (2) maintaining stable prices, and (3) encouraging economic growth. The groundwork had been laid for countercyclical fiscal and monetary policy.

The lessons of World War II fiscal expansion and the license for government fiscal and monetary intervention in the economy granted by the act of 1946 opened American economic thinking to the New Economics. Although Presidents Truman and Eisenhower showed only passing interest in the new doctrines and the new possibilities for public policy, university economists were quickly won over.

With the election of John Kennedy in 1960, Keynesian theory became policy. Coming to office during the third Eisenhower recession (1960–61), Kennedy introduced a fiscally experimental program. With an investment tax credit worth $2.5 billion to businesses in 1962 and a proposal for an $11 billion general tax cut in 1963, the Kennedy agenda offered sound Keynesian medicine. Lyndon Johnson continued and elaborated on the Kennedy theme. For almost eight years the economy moved forward, and Americans learned (although they were soon to forget) that economic crisis, whether periodic or inherent, need not be the nature of the economy.

Is the Keynesian Analysis Still Relevant?

There is little denying that the simultaneous appearance in the 1970s of high unemployment, slow growth, and raging inflation was very unkind to Keynesians. Displaying a propensity to throw the baby out with the bathwater, many economists (including some previously ardent Keynesians), politicians, and ordinary citizens incorrectly identified Keynesian thinking and policy making as the cause of the stagflationary crisis. True, the Keynesian focus had not prepared the nation for all economic crises—it had not anticipated the severe *supply shocks* of the 1970s. Moreover, Keynes's original critique had emphasized an economy caught up in severe and pervading depression. It saw this chronic contraction as the result of insufficient private spending and argued that correction required massive offsetting government spending. While, as we have seen, the events of the Depression and war seemed to prove Keynes correct, it was discovered by the late 1960s that Keynesian demand-management efforts did not work well when the focus of policy attention was on a nearly or fully employed economy.

Although some of Keynes's followers argued for *fine-tuning*—simply turning on or off the demand spigot as conditions dictated—events soon showed that closing the spigot, when such anti-inflationary actions were called for, was painful and unpopular. The short-run benefits of expansionary economic policies were quickly perceived by politicians, as were the politically suicidal effects of contractionary policies that required raising taxes and reducing government spending. Indeed, as much as anything else, it was this politicization of Keynesianism that transformed what was mostly a technical shortcoming into a near catastrophic deficiency.

Keynesian ideas, however, did not disappear even though the limitations of fine-tuning and anti-inflationary policy were exposed. Based simply on a survey of the content of the average college introductory economics text, as well as the op-ed pages of the *Wall Street Journal,* it becomes obvious that most economists still use the Keynesian identities and causalities in setting up the framework of macroeconomic analysis. Most texts retain the Keynesian view that production-for-profit economies still tend naturally toward periodic stagnations. They still outline the potential uses of government policy to remedy such situations, although these exercises are decidedly more theoretical than policy-oriented, reflecting the constraints imposed by the experiences of the 1970s. However, those accepting the Keynesian framework (whether they actually use the label or not) pay a great deal more attention now than in the past to the role played by private investment in the long-run maintenance of high levels of employment.

While Conservative economists like to claim credit for ending inflation, their cures were little more than an application of Keynesian principles. How was inflation finally halted in the 1980s? The Federal Reserve closed off investment and consumer spending by raising interest rates and bringing on the worst recession since the 1930s. How was the long period of peacetime growth after 1982 achieved? The tax cut of 1981 and enormous defense outlays produced a tripling of the national debt—to $3 trillion by 1990—that provided sufficient demand stimulation to keep the boom going (although the boom was quite moderate by past standards).

In a perverse and economically dangerous way, Conservatives were applying Keynes's aggregate demand analysis without giving appropriate credit or understanding the long-term consequences. The administration of President George W. Bush has rerun the tired fiscal policies of the Reagan-Bush period of the 1980s. The large tax cuts of 2001–3 and significant increase in defense expenditures are a mixed message, with demand-side and supply-side stimuli reasoning tossed together with a plea for "tax fairness" that principally benefits only the wealthy.

As a result (as we shall see in the following issues), the economy remains plagued by serious fundamental problems. During the 1990s there was a significant increase in the share of national income going to the top 20 percent of households, while the vast majority of nonsupervisory production workers experienced growing indebtedness and inflation-adjusted wages remained below their early 1970s all-time peak. The destruction of the World Trade Center, the attack on the Pentagon, and mail distribution of potentially deadly anthrax delivered a shock to an economy already caught in the tightening grip of a slowdown. Policy makers responded with a visibly Keynesian slant, relying upon expansionary fiscal and monetary policies. To be certain, Keynesian economics is as relevant as ever to the task of macroeconomic stabilization. Indeed, Liberals may not possess *all* the answers, but at least they understand the question when asked: Are we depression-proof?

THE RADICAL ARGUMENT

For both Conservatives and Liberals, albeit for different reasons, the imminent or future collapse of the American economy is not an inevitable event. Their views, of course, are not very startling. That defenders of varieties of capitalism believe the system has a future should be expected; however, the evidence, if looked at closely, points to a different conclusion. Contrary to the cheery Conservative view that free enterprise economies suffer only periodic and inconsequential business downturns, it is apparent from both historical and recent perspectives that crisis is part of the nature of production-for-profit economies. The Liberal contention that the countercyclical use of fiscal and monetary policy can insulate us from depression enormously understates the systemic roots of economic crisis and fails to comprehend the costs and effects of the tools of countercyclical policy.

The Chronic Tendency Toward Crisis

Economic crisis and instability are not peculiar to capitalist societies alone. However, with the dawn and maturity of capitalism, crisis (or what we presently might call depression) took on a new dimension. In precapitalist societies, economic contraction resulted largely from wars, plagues, crop failures, or other natural disasters. The granaries were empty, people starved, and there were shortages of goods of all kinds. Crisis was associated with underproduction. Paradoxically, in the capitalist era of crisis, this situation has been reversed. Capitalist contraction usually appears after an era of growth in the productive forces of a society. With excess goods on hand and no market, producers reduce current output, unemployment rises, and wages and prices fall. In short, capitalist crises usually begin when the granaries are full.

To be sure, the periodic panics and depressions that strike capitalism have usually been followed by recoveries. For many years before the appearance of Keynes's work, the periodicity of boom and bust (especially boom) allowed Conservatives to describe economic contractions as "mere disturbances" that would go away and therefore did not merit very serious analytical study. No effort was made to see stagnation as fundamental to the capitalist order. Nor has this view changed much among modern Conservative economists. Keynesian Liberals, meanwhile, have accepted the fact that underconsumption generally leads to depressions in modern capitalism, but they hold that the tendency is easily manageable through the tools of modern public policy.

From the Radical perspective, however, economic crises are both fundamental to capitalism and beyond capitalists' capacity to resolve in the long run. As Karl Marx pointed out long ago, the crises are inherent in the capitalist system of production. In their perpetual search for expanded profits, capitalists must create *surplus value*—that is, they forever attempt to maximize the difference between the higher price for which goods sell and the lower price of the labor involved in production. To acquire greater profits, the capitalist must enlarge surplus value through the introduction of greater amounts of capital equipment, through the direct exploitation of labor, or through some combination of the two. The object is to produce greater output per unit of wage labor paid. As capitalists endeavor to produce more and more at greater profit, the capacity of the workers (consumers) to purchase this output declines. Although the people may *need* the goods, they do not have the *effective demand* to obtain them. Overproduction and underconsumption create periodic gluts of goods, which in turn cause crises wherein production ceases, capital is destroyed or left idle, and human beings starve.

As capitalism progresses, Marx argued, its productive capacity constantly enlarges. The possible depths and duration of production-consumption crises are heightened, and the ultimate end of the system is brought that much closer. Nineteenth-century Marxists observed the growing incidence of capitalist crises and predicted, a bit prematurely, early collapse.

While the capitalist system has not collapsed, this does not mean that

Marx's analysis is wrong or outdated. In fact, Marx foresaw several sources of macroeconomic instability that are easily observable today, including the accelerating pace of labor-displacing technological change, increasing financial fragility, growing income and wealth inequality, continued corporate concentration and centralization (through ever-larger mergers and acquisitions), and the ongoing conflict over global trade. Looking a little closer at two of these current trends will underscore the continuing relevance of Marx's arguments to the Radical position.

As was noted, profitability is crucially dependent on the ability of capitalists to extract as much surplus value per unit of output as possible from employees by working them harder or longer and/or by equipping them with better machines. Unfortunately for capitalists, there are legal constraints in most advanced industrialized countries that limit the length of the working day. While firms can try to evade or change these laws, there can be penalties as well as intangible costs such as loss of goodwill. Moreover, a worker's physical capacity to labor at a given task is limited by the need for rest and sleep. Thus, the only substantive way to increase the rate of profit is to mechanize and automate production such that fewer workers are required for a given level of output. The present *new economy* strategy of wringing labor costs out of any product or service is central for understanding the surge in profitability over the past several years. While mainstream macroeconomists rejoice at the recent growth in labor productivity, it is clear that these gains have been obtained by the continual displacement, deskilling, and degradation of occupations as diverse as mining, engineering, farming, teaching, and medicine. The macroeconomic consequences of persistent job destruction and diminishment are clear: lowered living standards, greater income and wealth inequality, more indebtedness, and economic insecurity for the vast majority of workers.

A second source of current macroeconomic instability identified by Marx, is the ever-increasing income gap between rich and poor. Despite the smug and self-congratulatory tone of Conservatives and Liberals over *productivity-led* growth and prosperity during the 1990s, real wages and working conditions for most Americans have not shown much improvement. For example, the inflation-adjusted income of the bottom 40 percent of households grew much more slowly during the last decade compared to the 1970s and 1980s. Thus, the vaunted acceleration in productivity of the New Economy did *not* translate into higher wages or reduced work hours for most Americans. In fact, the number of hours it would take a worker who is paid the average wage to earn the average family income is about 3,700 hours per year (a seventy-one-hour workweek). It is painfully obvious to working American families—despite admonitions to acquire more education and improve their work ethic—that capitalists and their high-paid functionaries have appropriated most of the productivity dividend. Thus, it is no surprise that both the share of national income going to capital and the aggregate profit rate (20.2 percent and 8.0 percent, respectively, in 2002) have returned to levels last seen in the 1960s.

Finally, it should be noted that capitalist societies have adopted policies —such as a progressive income tax structure, free public education, and an end to child labor—that Marx recommended in the *Communist Manifesto*. While Marx never developed his ideas about the role of the state in the economy, he understood, like Keynes, that government could be a stabilizing (albeit only temporary) force. In particular, the state could foster or sanction monopoly behavior, mitigate the effects of labor exploitation and unemployment, and act directly to absorb the surplus production through government purchases (especially during war) and transfer payments. Yet, such efforts to "rationalize" capitalism by temporarily disguising or hiding its self-destructive propensities cannot eliminate capitalism's chronic tendency toward crisis.

The Collapse of 1929

The expansion of overseas markets and sources of cheap labor and resources, the increasingly monopolistic behavior of business enterprises, and the enlargement of government protective actions held back the breaking of the dike before 1929. It did not, however, stop serious leaks.

In the case of the United States, seven major business cycles can be identified between the panic of 1893 and the beginning of World War I. Each downturn lasted longer and became more pronounced. As the United States entered World War I and a wartime business boom, unemployment stood at about 10 percent. The Roaring Twenties were not much better. Probably the worst depression in U.S. history to that point occurred in 1921–22, and throughout most of the decade unemployment was higher than 4 percent. Meanwhile, real wages moved upward only slightly. Only the phenomenal expansion of consumer debt buoyed the economy. For those who wished to see the evidence or could at least understand it, it was apparent that the dike would soon collapse.

The crisis after 1929 was a near-classic example of Marx's overproduction-underconsumption scenario. Moreover, it precipitated a general international collapse. The mature capitalist economies had exhausted their markets for goods. Overseas, the underdeveloped economies had little capacity to absorb output. At home, warehouses bulged because consumers lacked effective demand. As the first signs of crisis appeared, the banking and financial system, which itself rested on the capitalists' ability to realize their surplus, tottered and collapsed: first the Wall Street crash, then New York bank failures, then European bank failures. Full-scale industrial contraction followed.

The Old Economics in a New Package

The Keynesian response to the deepening depression was to accept the essential outline of the older Marxist critique of capitalism: Overproduction and crisis were endemic to the system. However, the Keynesians neatly evaded the Marxian conclusion. According to their analysis, insufficient business and consumer demand could be either manipulated by fiscal and monetary policy or supplemented by government spending that would raise the level of aggregate demand. In Marxian terms, government now became the vehicle to realize surplus value.

Much has been made of this new thinking on the problem of the capitalist system. The "Keynesian Revolution" came to describe dominant economic opinion; however, it was no revolution at all. Keynes and his followers have sought not to end capitalism but to save it. The central features of capitalism—private property, production for profit, wage labor, the business system, and all the rest—were retained. Indeed, as business leaders came to appreciate the profit (surplus value) possibilities of increased government spending during World War II and the trial-and-error Keynesian years after the war, corporate America enthusiastically accepted the New Economics. The frequent Liberal posturing against big business should be recognized as pure political rhetoric. In the 1964 Johnson-Goldwater presidential election, big business showed its colors by rejecting the Conservative, laissez-faire Republican in favor of the big-spending Democrat from Texas. Giant corporations poured millions of dollars into Johnson's campaign.

The Keynesian Mirage and Back to Reality

Through the 1960s and most of the 1970s (remember that even Richard Nixon had proclaimed himself a Keynesian), the New Economics seemed to be just what capitalism needed. The old capitalist business cycle of roller-coaster ups and downs simply disappeared as the economy underwent continuous expansion. In silly self-congratulation, economists wrote and talked of "no more depressions" while they enjoyed a place never before reserved for them in the public's esteem.

With the Vietnam War and other government spending growing and an easy monetary policy usually operating to encourage private borrowing, high levels of demand kept factories operating at near-peak utilization rates and kept unemployment rates low. Yet these signs of success through the 1960s were actually danger signals, for in capitalism success invariably sows the seeds of doom. The basic problem, as with all expansionary phases of the capitalist business cycle, was that expanding demand put serious pressures on business by causing rising costs, which in turn squeezed profits. With unemployment at very low levels, workers—unionized and nonunionized alike—enjoyed a seller's market for their labor. Real wages rose as businesses bid against each other for needed employees. Between 1960 and 1973, real (adjusted for inflation) after-tax weekly earnings rose by 35 percent. Since this exceeded productivity (output per worker-hour) growth, it translated into rising per-unit costs for producers. To make matters worse, resource costs worldwide began rising, the principal source being rising energy costs resulting from the Arabs' opting to challenge their former colonial and neocolonial masters.

At any rate, after-tax corporate profits peaked in 1965 (at about 10.4 percent on investment) and fell thereafter (to about 5.9 percent in 1974). With profits falling, businesses continued to reduce their investment outlays through the late 1960s and into the 1970s. At first the decline was scarcely felt as demand remained high for a time, but in the late 1960s, unemployment began to edge upward. By the early 1970s, regardless of expansionary fiscal policy efforts to offset the trend, unemployment grew as profits fell. Prices, meanwhile, began to rise, producing the new phenomenon of *stagflation* (rising unemployment *and* rising prices). Inflation took hold simply because demand, fueled by government and private borrowing, remained high. Without an expansion of business production facilities and with productive efficiency falling as the investment base got older and more outmoded, the high levels of demand caused price increases rather than output expansion. Meanwhile, the high levels of demand had few salutary effects on employment since profits remained low and business actually reduced its rate of investment. The outer limits of runaway Keynesianism had been reached.

There remained only one solution, the old solution: recession. Through the mid- and late 1970s, under enormous pressure from rising prices, government fiscal policy turned less expansionary. Predictably, unemployment crept upward. Inflation, however, was not significantly slowed until Conservative Ronald Reagan supported a bone-chilling tight money policy that shut off private borrowing. The immediate result was the recession of 1981–82, which produced Great Depression levels of unemployment.

Although Conservatives crowed about their victory over inflation and enjoyed pointing out that Keynesianism had proved itself a failure, they, as we shall see in the next issue, understood little about what had happened. They offered no new solution to the capitalist system. However, as we shall see in subsequent issues, the Conservatives have enjoyed a considerable measure of popular support during their recent return to policy-making power.

The dislodgement of the Republicans from the White House in 1992, after the brief recession under George H. Bush, did not bring a return of traditional Liberal political economy. Although President Clinton leaned toward a Liberal position during his first two years in office, the election of Republican majorities in both houses of Congress in 1994 was a fair measure of the popular ascendancy of Conservative political and economic outlooks. Clinton quickly adapted to the new realities, winning reelection in 1996 after allowing that the era of big government was over and more or less conceding to the Conservative insistence that fiscal policy should be subordinated to the necessity of balancing the federal budget. In all this, both Clinton and Conservatism benefited from a long economic expansion through the mid- and late 1990s. Everyone seemed caught up in the boom.

Conservative burbling about a "new world economic order" in the aftermath of the demise of the USSR in 1992 and their growing praise for a technology-based New Economy were muted upon the predictable arrival of yet another recession in early 2001. Ironically, the crisis materialized just as the administration of George W. Bush unleashed an explosion of deficit-financed tax cuts for the rich.

To Radicals, the recent resurgence of Conservative antigovernment and probusiness ideology and practice, after a generation of Liberal ascendancy, is a matter of considerable irony. Marx, commenting on the ironies of history, once remarked that when history repeats itself, it first appears as tragedy and then as farce. However, to the more thoughtful, the idea of America returning to the "good old days" of Calvin Coolidge and Herbert Hoover is both farcical *and* tragic.

Yet, in a sense, that is precisely where we are. Indeed, production-for-profit capitalism, in any substantial sense, has never really passed much beyond the era immediately preceding the Great Depression. Is another great depression possible? *Very definitely.*

Economic Growth and Stability

Can We Maintain High and Steady Rates of Economic Growth?

We must recognize that only experience can show how far
the common will, embodied in the policy of the state, ought
to be directed to increasing and supplementing the
inducement to invest.

—John Maynard Keynes, 1935

Is fiscal policy being oversold? Is monetary policy being
oversold? . . . My answer is yes to both of those
questions. . . . What I believe is that fine tuning has
been oversold.

—Milton Friedman, 1968

Originating in a liberal effort to respond to the popular will
and relieve the pressures of poverty, demand-oriented
politics ends in promoting unemployment and dependency.

—George Gilder, 1981

Although the evidence is widespread that there really is
something new about the economy, it is not clear just how
much the basic parameters of macroeconomic performance
have changed.

—Economic Report of the President, 2001

The Problem

Conservative, Liberal, and Radical paradigms are strikingly divided on the matters of long-term growth and stability and the economic role to be played by government to best ensure rising living standards. The problems of short-term economic performance tend to attract the attention of the public, policy makers, and economists. In other words, more day-to-day concern is placed on the trim of the economic ship than on what might be done if it actually capsized. Looming in the background are larger and more spectacular questions about whether living standards can rise at an appreciable pace and if the economy is actually depression-proof. The issue can be conveniently divided between the maintenance of short-term macroeconomic stability and the subject of long-term growth. The two are intertwined, but in this issue we set our sights principally on the long-run outlook for sustained economic growth and rising living standards.

Since the passage of the Employment Act of 1946, the federal government has had the responsibility

> to use all practicable means consistent with its needs and obligations and other essential considerations of national policy, with assistance and cooperation of industry, agriculture, labor and State and local governments, to coordinate and utilize all its plans, functions and resources for the purpose of creating and maintaining, in a manner calculated to foster and promote free competitive enterprise and general welfare, conditions under which there will be afforded useful employment opportunities, including self-employment, production and purchasing power.

This rambling and wide-ranging statement has been interpreted over the years to mean that government is charged with three basic public policy objectives:

- Providing high levels of employment
- Maintaining stable prices
- Encouraging economic growth

For better or worse (the reader may already be anticipating in the arguments to come who might think it better and who might think it worse), the government had assumed some level of responsibility, albeit indistinct, over the great trinity of employment, prices, and growth.

Table 2.1 (see p. 64) shows how well the economy performed in the last half of the twentieth century with respect to the three objectives. The economy had enjoyed 120 months of economic expansion before the 2001 recession. The very length of the boom was impressive, but the period had also been impressive when compared to the previous boom of the 1980s and the dismal stagflationary years of the 1970s because of its uncharacteristically high rates of economic growth and correspondingly low inflation. Not surprisingly, Conservatives used the boom of the 1980s as proof of the errors of the earlier Keynesian heresy and evidence that a policy relying predominantly on market-directed forces is capable of maintaining both economic stability and growth. Liberals could counter that the 1960s and 1990s, under political leadership of closer affinity to their views, produced economic success that surpassed the Conservative heydays. Radicals would, of course, be unconvinced by either.

Thus, even during good economic conditions, the paradigms differ on why these events occurred, the principal forces that drive the operation of the macroeconomy, and how very similar policies affect economic performance. Conservatives tend to emphasize supply-side economics while Liberals place greater faith in the demand-management theories of Keynesian heritage;* Radicals assert that capitalist economies are fundamentally unstable and prone to long-term crises of underconsumption, overproduction, and accumulation. While achieving full employment and building upon the productive base of the economy are common objectives, the different sides possess very divergent opinions about how this is to be accomplished.

---

*The supply-siders' analytical critique of Keynesian theory can be fairly easily demonstrated. For supply-siders the inflationary episode of the 1970s was directly traceable to the Keynesian error of believing that increases in demand had only a salutary effect on output and employment and no impact upon prices. The supply-side argument is illustrated in Panel 1 on page 63. With aggregate demand (AD) and aggregate supply (AS), respectively, illustrating the total demand and total supply of goods at all possible combinations of gross domestic product (GDP) and price level, the economy is in equilibrium in Panel 1 where AD = AS. It can be noted at a low level of equilibrium output (Q), an increase in the total demand from AD_1 to AD_2 has a far greater impact in increasing GDP than in raising the price level. However, the shift from AD_2 to AD_3 has a far greater impact upon prices. This is because as the economy approaches full employment, the aggregate supply curve slopes upward more steeply reflecting higher resource prices that are caused by increased competition for scarcer resources. The solution to the problem is demonstrated in Panel 2. Actions should be taken to increase aggregate supply. This appears as the shift from AS to AS_1, resulting in higher GDP and a decrease in prices.

A second, but closely related, dimension of the problem is labor productivity growth. A slowdown in productivity growth started in the middle
of the 1970s. Table 2.2 illustrates that the rate of growth in output per
worker had assumed a slower long-term pace, dropping from an average
annual rate of 3.1 percent between 1960 and 1973 to 1.6 percent between 1973 and 1995. Productivity growth accelerated to 2.7 percent
between 1995 and 2003, largely due to widespread use of information
technologies, more capital goods, and improved labor force skills, among
other things.

Although an increase in labor productivity does not guarantee that
society's economic well-being will be improved, there is general agreement
that productivity is closely related to living standards. A rough-and-ready
gauge of a country's standard of living is to look at output per capita, and
this measure is closely connected to productivity, that is, the output per
worker that in turn determines available output per person. Table 2.2 illustrates the connection between the rate of growth in gross domestic product (GDP) per capita and productivity growth. Recognize that even during
periods of comparatively rapid GDP growth such as exhibited by the majority of years in the 1990s, rates of growth in productivity and living standards can be comparatively slow.

The data in Table 2.2 reveal that growth rates in productivity are more
than a full percentage point higher in the period 2001–2003 than 1973–
95. How important is a percentage point or so? The answer is found by
turning to a rule of thumb known as the *rule of 72,* which permits a quick
approximation of how long it will take something (such as living stan-

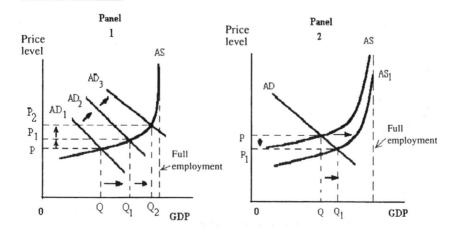

Table 2.1

Economic Growth, Unemployment, and Inflation Rates, 1959–2003

Year	Annual percentage change in real GDP	Annual unemployment rate (percentage)	Annual percentage change in consumer price index
1959	7.1	5.5	0.7
1960	2.5	5.5	1.7
1961	2.3	6.7	1.0
1962	6.1	5.5	1.0
1963	4.4	5.7	1.3
1964	5.8	5.2	1.3
1965	6.4	4.5	1.6
1966	6.5	3.8	2.9
1967	2.5	3.8	3.1
1968	4.8	3.6	4.2
1969	3.1	3.5	5.5
1970	0.2	4.9	5.7
1971	3.4	5.9	4.4
1972	5.3	5.6	3.2
1973	5.8	4.9	6.2
1974	−0.5	5.6	11.0
1975	−0.2	8.5	9.1
1976	5.3	7.7	5.8
1977	4.6	7.1	6.5
1978	5.6	6.1	7.6
1979	3.2	5.8	11.3
1980	−0.2	7.1	13.5
1981	2.5	7.6	10.3
1982	−1.9	9.7	6.2
1983	4.5	9.6	3.2
1984	7.2	7.5	4.3
1985	4.1	7.2	3.6
1986	3.5	7.0	1.9
1987	3.4	6.2	3.6
1988	4.1	5.5	4.1
1989	3.5	5.3	4.8
1990	1.9	5.6	5.4
1991	−0.2	6.8	4.2
1992	3.3	7.5	3.0
1993	2.7	6.9	3.0
1994	4.0	6.1	2.6
1995	2.5	5.6	2.8
1996	3.7	5.4	3.0
1997	4.5	4.9	2.3
1998	4.2	4.5	1.6
1999	4.5	4.2	2.2
2000	3.7	4.0	3.4
2001	0.8	4.7	2.8
2002	1.9	5.8	1.6
2003	3.0	6.0	2.3

Source: Bureau of Economic Analysis, *Economic Report of the President* (Washington, DC: Government Printing Office, 2004) and authors' calculations.

Table 2.2

Trend in Real Gross Domestic Product per Capita and Productivity
(annual rates)

Year	Growth in real GDP per capita (percentage)	Growth in output per worker hour (percentage)
1960–1973	2.9	3.1
1973–1995	1.9	1.6
1995–2000	2.6	2.2
2001–2003	0.9	3.9

Source: Bureau of Economic Analysis and U.S. Bureau of the Census. Calculations by the author.
Note: GDP = gross domestic product.

dards, price levels, population, or output) to double if it grows at a specific percentage rate. For the example at hand, the percentage rate of increase in real GDP per capita is divided into seventy-two to yield the number of years it will take for living standards to double. The growth rate for the period 1960–73 would permit living standards to double in less than twenty-five years (= 72/2.9) By comparison, the rate of growth in GDP per capita had slowed to just under a 1 percent average annual rate for the period 2001–3. Were that rate to be sustained, it would take seventy-two years (= 72/1) for living standards to double.

The difference a percentage point can make is indeed profound. At the 1960–73 rate of growth in real GDP per capita, living standards could easily quadruple in one lifetime, whereas at the slower rate of the 2001–3 period, it takes most of a lifetime to experience a doubling of living standards.

Although output per worker hour is the usual basis for measuring productivity, it is obvious that the American productivity dilemma goes much deeper than the question of how hard the individual American works. After all, workers can be more or less productive if they have more or fewer capital goods (machinery) with which to work. An hour of work by a person equipped with a shovel will be trifling by comparison to an hour of work performed by a backhoe operator. This leads to another dimension of the issue: Is capital, even if it is of great quantity, being dedicated to its best purpose? Furthermore, we might ask: Is the available technology the best we are capable of producing? Overarching all of these components of productivity is the question of the management skill of American industry: Does it possess the qualities necessary to make the best decisions about what is to be produced, how much is to be produced, and under what production arrangements?

When evidence suggested that something was wrong somewhere within the labyrinth of economic forces that determine productivity, a long list of culprits was submitted. Depending on ideological viewpoint, government intervention, excessively powerful labor unions, poor business decision making, the "quick profit" motive, too much dependence by business upon government, a decline in entrepreneurship, deterioration in the work ethic, too many lawyers and not enough engineers, insufficient investment spending, decline in the quality of primary and secondary education, and so on were identified as causes of the productivity slowdown. The acceleration in productivity exhibited from 1995 to 2003 poses the challenge to explain whether something was *going right* at that time within the economic forces that determine productivity. The differing assessments of the productivity puzzle go to the very roots of the ideological differences among economic paradigms.

The robust expansion of the 1990s rebuilt American confidence but did not allay all trepidation about the future. Macroeconomic stability and growth had produced a minor miracle in employment opportunities and reduced rates of unemployment. Yet Americans realize that not all jobs are created equal. Full-time opportunities seem less plentiful, employment security is seemingly more tenuous, benefit packages are skimpy, and employees' urine is something that demands testing. The 2001 recession had a particularly harsh and lingering impact on college-educated workers who experienced lengthy periods of unemployment. The attention-grabbing, but falsely robust, recorded music industry actually experienced a collapse as the industry's value of shipments shrank by 19 percent between 1999 and 2003, eliminating thousands of jobs.* Collectively, these developments temper the typical exuberance or euphoria incited by economic booms. At the same time, America's confidence is probably not uplifted by past experience and recurring controversies with macroeconomic policy that reveal no clear consensus on the proper course.

Lackluster economic prospects are hard for Americans to accept, especially those generations conditioned by the unusually rapid gains of the long postwar boom. A longing for the "good old days" is not lost on policy

---

*Based on manufacturers' shipments data reported by the Recording Industry Association of America.

makers who understand that the citizenry wants a quick but long-lasting fix for productivity and living standards.

The twenty-five years of economic growth and dominance that America enjoyed following World War II were the consequences of unusual circumstances. While the New Economy was thought to be impervious to business cycles, the recession of 2001 refuted such hubris. Rather, it appears that the New Economy—despite its vaunted technological prowess and dynamism—is more akin to the nineteenth-century economy where economic opportunity went hand-in-hand with economic insecurity.

Synopsis

Conservatives argue that efforts to stabilize the economy and foster economic growth have been ill fated in the past. They argue that such policy initiatives are actually the cause of poorer macroeconomic performance. They generally favor tax reductions, budget balancing, and smaller government as the means for returning the economy to the growth track. Liberals cite random shocks, over which economic policy makers had no control, and society's negligence of crucial areas in need of government investment and guidance as largely responsible for the economic difficulties that have beset the economy since the 1970s. They argue in favor of activism and contend that careful examination of the historical record of intervention indicates that the results have been quite favorable. If anything, the problem has been a lack of adequate and properly timed intervention. Radicals argue that Liberals are impelled to intervene in the economy's performance less out of social conscience than on behalf of business and ruling-class interests. The protracted trend of sluggish growth in GDP per capita and productivity reflects the deepening crisis of modern capitalism and presages worsening economic and social decay.

Anticipating the Arguments

- What policies do Conservatives advocate to maintain macroeconomic stability and maintain rising living standards?
- If the economy is not delivering desirable results in terms of stability or growth in living standards, how would Liberals respond?
- Why do Radicals reject the idea that the economy can be managed by either the Conservative or Liberal prescriptions for stabilization and maintenance of economic growth?

THE CONSERVATIVE ARGUMENT

Understanding the Conservative program for stabilization and growth requires recognition of the fact that consumption is at the center of economic life. Accommodating consumption necessitates production and the means for production. On the macroeconomic level, it is the production or supply side of the economy that is the source of income that permits consumption. It does not happen the other way around. The Conservative prescription is composed of two basic elements:

- Redirect fiscal and monetary policy from attention to the demand or consumption side of economic activity to the supply or production side. Ultimately, fiscal and monetary policy must be neutral. The government should perform only its most necessary functions and under the regimen of a balanced budget. Monetary authorities would set a rate of growth in the money supply that approximates the potential growth in the economy and spurn trying to manipulate interest rates in the interest of stabilization. Markets will be the workhorse and coordinator of economic activity, not the government or the central bank.
- Deregulate and eliminate various impositions and controls upon industry and labor markets. The government's imposition of regulatory costs and outright obstruction, which has hindered production, work incentives, innovation, and productivity growth, needs to end.

The Errors of Demand-Management Economics

Until recently, conventional macroeconomics had acquired a one-dimensional perspective that had its origins in the Keynesian critique of an economy mired in the depths of the Great Depression. With large numbers of people unemployed and much of the nation's plants and equipment sitting idle, Keynes's logic in retrospect was nearly artless: Find the means to increase demand for goods and services, which would generate the demand for men, women, and machines to go back to work. The supply side could be taken for granted because of the sheer volume of idle resources. Demand would dictate the level of output with a near-instantaneous response from the supply side. The only constraint upon output is when full employment is reached. With an economy far from full employment, the Depression-built economics of Keynes was hardly concerned with the consequences of forcing the economy toward full employment.

The Keynesian remedy for the prostrate economies of the 1930s was seductively simple and painless: *Spend your way out of the Depression.* Moreover, it had even seemed to work during the late 1930s and during World War II, when massive government outlays did rejuvenate the economy. As an antidepression strategy, Conservatives will admit, Keynesian policies were—in the short term at least—a politically attractive alternative to simply allowing the business cycle to undergo a natural correction. However, their political appeal in no way made it sound economic policy. Worse still, their superficial success led to the eventual institutionalization of demand-management fiscal and monetary policies, reserved not for exclusive use to counter an economic depression but for persistently fine-tuning the economy.

The preoccupation with unemployment that had hung over from the Great Depression and the fact that the Keynesian contingent of the economics profession had expressed a theoretical and practical justification for government spending was simply too alluring for government policy makers. Now they had experts to support the implausible: Taxes could be cut, government spending increased, the money supply expanded, and perennial deficits incurred, all in the interest of improving macroeconomic performance. Yet, the agenda expanded beyond lowering unemployment. Grand expenditure and social engineering programs were introduced to advance President Johnson's vision of the Great Society. Simultaneously, America's growing involvement in the Vietnam War led to increased military spending.

It looked as if a holiday from economic reason had been declared. The old principle of a guns-versus-butter trade-off was placed in abeyance. More of both military and civilian goods could be attained. The cake could be eaten and had too!

Likewise, the ramifications of excessive government spending were blissfully ignored until the nation moved into the final years of the 1960s and made the transition into the awful decade of the 1970s. Demand-pull inflation appeared in the late 1960s. Then came the incongruous situation of *stagflation*—both high rates of unemployment and high rates of inflation. Growth rates faltered, the trend in rates of personal and gross saving flattened, and the climate for investment spending suffered as government deficits gobbled up loanable funds and inflation elevated interest rates and lowered after-tax capital income.

Regulatory Burdens and Other Disincentives

While fiscal and monetary meddling proved a major force in fostering the long descent to slower progress in living standards and productivity, ample assistance in battering the nation's productive base came from other steps taken by the Liberal-leaning policy makers of the times.

- The economic inefficiencies of industry regulation were now to be hugely amplified through the social engineering measures of the 1970s that were aimed at consumer, environmental, and worker protection. This added to business costs at a time when general economic conditions were depressing profits. Investment and innovation were further stifled by the strictures of regulation. By some estimates, billions of dollars are transferred annually from productive purposes to the bureaucracy that was given life through regulation, and hundreds of billions are squandered on compliance costs.
- A "soak the rich and business" taxation mentality pervaded the thinking of the time. Of course, such policies appropriate resources from those who do the most saving, investing, and producing. Although Liberals ostensibly favor growth, their zeal about income equity seems to dominate.

The combination of inflationary fiscal and monetary policies, overzealous regulation, and punitive taxes was the formula that sank the economy in the 1970s and established a foundation for enduring hardship that has proven difficult to reverse. Economic policy from the period of high Keynesianism unwittingly worked to slow the growth of the nation's productive base—to kill the goose that laid the golden eggs.

Reversing the Trend

Perhaps growth and productivity, more than any issue, have given historical legitimacy to the Conservative position. The 1980s ushered in the political administration of President Ronald Reagan and with it at least a partial reversal of demand management and social engineering. Although the Reagan policies were but rough and incomplete proxies for the Conservative agenda, their rapid success was striking. More progress was made in particular areas in the years to follow right up to the present. A brief summary is instructive.

- Conservatives focus on the supply side of the economy as the source of increases in output, employment, productivity, and living standards. Supply-side growth policy calls for greater incentives to work, save, invest, and engage in entrepreneurial risk taking. Punitively high tax rate brackets drove a *tax wedge* between before- and after-tax labor income, interest income from savings, investment income, and profit. Because a large share of the rewards associated with work, savings, investing, and entrepreneurship was forfeited to taxes, people were discouraged from these productive activities. The drag on production caused by high tax rates actually retards the growth in government revenue as well. The Economic Recovery Tax Act of 1981 and the Tax Reform Act of 1986 provided much needed relief from the tax wedge by greatly reducing income tax brackets. Thankfully, the three consecutive tax cuts proposed by the Bush administration and passed by Congress from 2001 to 2003 have all helped to reverse the higher tax rates enacted during the Clinton administration, restoring the focus on supply-side growth policy.
- Conservatives also call for less government regulation and restrictions upon business investment and risk taking. Progress in this area advanced in the 1980s with an acceleration in industry deregulation that saw completion of the deregulation of airlines, elimination of price controls on most oil and natural gas, and inroads into the deregulation of trucking and railroads. The result has been measurable cost savings and innovations in those industries as well as lower overall inflation. By the 1990s, it seemed as if the government was getting over its penchant for regulating business and fearing markets. This is exemplified by government auctioning off the electromagnetic spectrum for communications, the development of a market for pollution permits, and reluctance (or perhaps its real inability) to regulate or tax the Internet.
- Economic growth and growth in living standards are best served by a global environment of free trade (discussed in detail in Issue 7). Fortunately, a strengthening trend of trade liberalization has come into vogue and the economy is reaping the benefits of that course.
- The nation's public education system is dysfunctional. American high school students are now routinely performing well below their counterparts in other industrially advanced countries and also, to our chagrin, some not-so-advanced countries. Privatizing the system or introducing competition through a voucher system that would

allow individuals the choice of what school to attend would instill the incentive to deliver high-quality education. This would strengthen the base of *human capital* that is essential to restoring productivity growth.

Greater Acceptance of the Conservative Paradigm and Its Success

The Conservative paradigm has enjoyed greater acceptance in the last two decades because it successfully reversed the misguided policies of the past, placing America back on the track of economic growth and rising per capita GDP. Liberals' criticism of supply-side policies in the 1980s for not delivering immediate results has been increasingly muted as the course of lower taxes, deregulation, and reliance upon market forces set the stage for the significant economic boom that has since transpired. It took long-term adherence to the Conservative program to nullify the long downward slide caused by the policies of the past. A glance back at Table 2.1 confirms the impressive long-term response of GDP growth to Conservative policies that stimulated work, savings, investment, and enterprise; promoted freer trade; and trimmed government. The economy will continue to thrive if it is freed from the social engineering of affirmative action, government favoritism toward labor unions, and the propping up of ailing businesses.

The greater stability of GDP growth since the mid-1980s and unprecedented acceleration in labor productivity since 2001 conclusively demonstrate the superiority of Conservative policies to promote long-term growth and prosperity. This was accomplished in large part because fiscal policy manipulation of the macroeconomy was shelved. Unfortunately, just as the American economy is currently poised for continued growth the Federal Reserve System is resuming its monetary activism in response to a perceived threat of inflation. Their overreaction with a tight money policy was plainly responsible for the unnecessary recession in 2001. Frightened first by the slowdown they helped to create and then by the economic ramifications of the September 11 terrorist raid on the United States, the Fed radically reversed the policy with thirteen interest rate cuts in rapid succession. Now, the Fed is currently reversing that policy in favor of rate increases that can only foster instability. Conservatives can only hope for a return to a less activist monetary policy and continued shrinking of government involvement in the economy.

THE LIBERAL ARGUMENT

It is wise to remember that the experience of the Great Depression and the shortcomings of classical economic thought gave rise to the Keynesian critique. Classical economists had no answers and no solutions. Their recommendation was to wait around until the economy corrected itself through the *automatic stabilization mechanism of markets.* After a decade of waiting for self-correction, the Keynesian prescription was by happenstance put to the test by the coming of World War II and the massive military spending it required. National defense budgetary outlays rose from $1 billion in 1939 to $81 billion by 1945, accounting for 82 percent of federal spending and absorbing nearly 40 percent of the nation's output. Although the principal purpose behind this effort was to defeat the Axis powers of Nazi Germany, Italy, and Japan, the economic results of rising output and employment served as confirmation for Keynes's proposition that we could indeed spend our way out of the Depression. Since then, we have come to understand and refine the analytic and policy tools necessary to manage the general level of economic activity. At the same time, our understanding of the productivity and growth problems has advanced, ensuring improvement in the management of those problems as well.

Conservatives, who do not believe in the efficacy of macroeconomic stabilization policy, are in fact long on theory and short on evidence. Their pessimism about government's role in regulating economic growth and in addressing the related problem of the slowdowns in productivity and GDP per capita growth illustrates not only a lack of faith but also a disregard for specific troubles that can be countered only by government intervention.

Having made this point, Liberals do acknowledge that possessing the tools of correction and using them properly are different matters. There was outright misuse of countercyclical policy during most of the 1970s, and indeed there were examples of overzealous regulation and some poorly conceived efforts at social experimentation. However, it was not so much these errors as it was unpredictable random shocks and structural changes in the economy that were mainly to blame for the economic crisis of the 1970s and its lingering effects. On the other hand, the assertion that Conservative-leaning policies in the 1980s and the continuing drift toward the practice of Conservative economic policy making have produced a great turnaround for America is simply unfounded.

A Different View of the Economic Record

The general framework for policy making to counter the business cycle was in place by the beginning of the post–World War II period. Steps to end the Depression, wartime spending, and the legal commitment of the Employment Act of 1946 helped end the traditional government commitment to balance the budget. Nevertheless, between 1946 and the early 1960s, the political leadership of the nation showed little mastery of the new policy possibilities. Fiscal policy, as it was practiced, was unplanned and ill timed. Deficits or surpluses appeared at the wrong time or quite accidentally at the right time. Manipulative monetary policy was not practiced at all.

After inheriting a stagnant macroeconomy, President Kennedy sought recommendations from economic advisers who were schooled in Keynesian economics. A reluctant Kennedy was convinced to propose a discretionary tax reduction. In 1964, three months after Kennedy's assassination, Congress passed a bill to reduce personal taxes by $11 billion and corporate taxes by $2.6 billion. The results were quite good: By 1965, unemployment fell, the growth rate in output per capita nearly doubled from 1963 levels, and prices were stable. However, the Vietnam War, coupled with Lyndon Johnson's adamant stance that the economy could produce guns *and* butter, gave rise to excessive demand for goods and chronic inflationary pressures.

Elementary Keynesian economics would have called for a tax increase and a reduction in government spending. Neither of these, especially a tax increase, looked politically appealing to Johnson. His successor, Richard Nixon (a Republican), sidestepped that dilemma by invoking the extraordinary measure of wage and price controls.

Consequently, there is a relatively short period within which to evaluate countercyclical policy. However, the data in Table 2.3 show that the 1960s, the decade most affected by the judicious exercise of macroeconomic policy, stands out in terms of gains in living standards. Referring back to Table 2.2, generally impressive rates of economic growth prevailed.

Thereafter, the economy faltered, but not precisely for the reasons expressed by Conservatives. Economic policy making's expansionary bias was certainly not designed to counter the economic challenges besetting the economy in the 1970s. Inflation and the growth slowdown were exacerbated.

Table 2.3

Average Annual Changes in Gross Domestic Product per Capita

Year	Change in real GDP per capita (percentage)
1950–1959	2.3
1960–1969	3.1
1970–1979	2.2
1980–1989	2.1
1990–1999	1.9
Entire period 1950–1999	2.3

Source: Bureau of Economic Analysis and U.S. Bureau of the Census. Calculations by the author.

Random Shocks and Structural Change

The 1970s presented a confluence of problems found in no other period. Contrary to the Conservative view, Keynesian stabilization policy does not bear primary responsibility for the stagflationary malaise of the times. The real culprit was a series of random events and structural changes in the economy.

- By 1971, the American economy was faced with worsening balance-of-payments problems (which were caused mostly by Vietnam War spending). Simultaneously, the world began to doubt the sturdiness of the gold-backed dollar, and the collapse of confidence was confirmed when America suspended the conversion of dollars into gold on the international level. The dollar lost stature as an international reserve asset and had to be devalued by the Nixon administration in an attempt to correct the balance-of-payments deficits. While this made American goods less expensive to foreign buyers, prices of imported goods rose, contributing to inflationary pressure.
- In October 1973, the United States exported 19 million metric tons of wheat to the Soviet Union, reducing American wheat supplies to practically nothing. This resulted in higher food prices.
- In late 1973, the Organization of Petroleum Exporting Countries (OPEC) imposed a temporary embargo on oil exports to the United

States and began a long series of increases in the price of crude oil, which rose from less than $2 per barrel in 1970 to nearly $40 per barrel in 1981 (or about $50 per barrel in 2004). The rapid escalation in oil prices affected the costs of heating, transportation, chemical processing, plastic production, and virtually everything else. Price levels soared. Given that the price of oil is stated in dollars on the international market, each announcement of a price increase delivered an almost instant shock to consumer prices in America.

- Structural changes of various sorts that had quietly evolved were now exerting a downward pressure on productivity and economic growth. Inexperienced teenagers and women had entered the labor force in large numbers. The economy was prominently exhibiting a shift from manufacturing and agriculture (where productivity is rather readily observable) to services (where productivity gains are less obvious). Research and development spending (the engine of technological advancement) as a share of national output had been declining since the mid-1960s. The amount of capital per worker was in a state of decline as war had seized and wasted the best technology and capital, and evidence of poorer management and a diminished work ethic mounted.

The situation's complexity is but incompletely summarized above. The 1970s proved to be a tar baby for policy makers of any ideological stripe. Each use of the blunt tools of fiscal and monetary policy mired the economy more deeply than before. Nixon's mandatory wage and price controls (1971–74), Ford's WIN (Whip Inflation Now) buttons, and Carter's feeble efforts to maintain wage-price guideposts were a testimonial to bafflement.

Supply-Side Paradox

It is difficult to understand why supply-side economists, with their attachment to tax cutting, see their policy efforts as uniquely different from the maligned Keynesian economics of the past. While income tax reductions may vary in magnitude, timing, and targeting, there is no solidly logical way to predict whether it is the demand side or supply side of the economy that is most affected by such actions. Economists have clearly determined that the Economic Recovery Tax Act of 1981 had little supply-side effect. Advocates asserted that it worked, but just as Keynesian stabilization efforts were not responsible for the lousy economic performance of the 1970s, the same could be said about supply-side economic policy's impact upon the improved performance in the 1980s.

Fortuitous circumstances gave the illusion of success: A tight money policy that had begun in August of 1979 wrung the inflation out of the economy by inducing a severe recession. The OPEC oil cartel lost unity and oil prices fell. Labor union membership as a percentage of the labor force went into major decline, perhaps relieving upward pressure upon wages.

Unemployment rates dropped, as they usually do, once the economy emerged from the recession of 1981–82. Ironically, the 1980s became the *go-go* years of stimulative fiscal policy, with seemingly unrestrained increases in annual federal deficits piling up federal debt and tripling the federal debt per capita. In the end, inflation-adjusted GDP per capita had not improved and labor productivity turned in a worse performance than in the 1970s (Table 2.2). The 1990s continued this trend with real per capita output slightly lower than the prior decade while labor productivity was almost half a percent faster. In retrospect, despite a sustained focus on supply-side considerations, the last two decades of the twentieth century were periods of below-average growth in real per capita output and productivity.

What Is Wrong?

If the macroeconomy is performing well, what else needs to be in place to alter the course of productivity and GDP per capita? The fact is economic science has no exact answer. Differing perceptions of the main causal factors and what policies might work are at issue. Liberals maintain that neglect of pressing social and economic problems has helped to worsen the structural changes that resulted in the productivity slowdown and weakened growth in living standards.

For one thing, the rate of technological change may have slowed beginning in the mid-1960s. This was suggested by the lower percentage of GDP going to research and development spending. The market system tends to devote insufficient resources to research and development because the payoffs of such investments may be risky or uncertain, or hard to claim if competitors are swift and unobstructed imitators. Government can play a critical role in stimulating technological progress by offsetting the risks and uncertainty of research and development (R&D) spending through such measures as tax credits and subsidies. Government also establishes and lays the groundwork for enforcement of intellectual property rights through the patent system and copyrights—invention and innovation will be stifled if not protected from theft. Given that most of the productivity slowdown can be blamed on slower technological change, it is instructive to look at the late 1940s and the 1950s when productivity was speeding up. In this era, private sector business productivity was the beneficiary of a government-inspired surge in innovation. Government has to engage in planned peacetime encouragement of R&D spending to reverse or prevent productivity slowdowns. Indeed, government directly and indirectly subsidized research and development into computing and information systems technologies, which fed the productivity acceleration experienced from 1995 to 2000.

Although deficient investment in human capital cannot be identified as a major contributor to the slowdown, quite plainly a better-educated, more highly skilled, and healthier labor force is essential to maintaining and advancing productivity growth. Conservatives' obsession with shrinking the public sector and nonintervention is part of a deeper social and political agenda aimed at privatizing public schools and dismantling affirmative action. Again, the knee-jerk Conservative response is to prescribe a competitive market as the solution for nearly every complex problem. This ignores the fact that the real source of failure for public education is a starvation diet on which schools are supposed to thrive. The constraints imposed on public school budgets have decimated specialties such as foreign language and music education, and now threaten the basic fields of mathematics and science. Meanwhile, poverty rates among children have been allowed to climb, worsening preparation for learning and acquisition of human capital. The scaling back of affirmative action simply promises a return to the inefficiencies caused by labor market discrimination. Productivity growth could be improved through *more* spending and intervention in these areas, not less.

There is some evidence that the quantity and quality of the nation's basic infrastructure, namely, transportation systems, sewer and water systems, and so forth, also have an impact upon a nation's productivity. There is also evidence that the slowing of public investment in infrastructure correlates with America's productivity slowdown. Deteriorating highways and difficulties with air traffic control systems may not figure prominently in explaining the slowdown, but the public sector must be vigilant in maintaining and improving transportation infrastructure to prevent drags on productivity growth.

While Conservatives argue vehemently on behalf of free trade, they seem to ignore that many of America's trading partners use industrial policies to obtain the best advantages from international commerce. This crosses over from the earlier point that government can use tax incentives or subsidies to target technological progress in promising industries to help bolster productivity growth. In other areas, America can make judicious use of selective trade barriers to give ailing industries time to reindustrialize.

In the face of sustained economic and employment growth in the 1990s, the American economy did not display above average gains in living standards until the last half of the decade. Conservatives initially said that productivity measures were not detecting the gains. When the same measures began recording a big acceleration, they proceeded to celebrate victory for a fairly predictable collection of Conservative favorites. Free markets, globalization, technological supremacy of American business enterprises, and reductions in affirmative action programs were credited. However, there was little Conservatives could say about their main obsession: onerous taxes wreaking havoc on incentives, productivity, and living standards. Clearly, supply-side tax policies have minimal influence on economic growth and stability, and Conservatives are having a hard time accepting it.

Summary

Conservatives do not make a believable case against discretionary stabilization policy. No more convincing are their pronouncements of a shift in national sentiment toward the Conservative position and their claims that Conservative policies have led to rising productivity growth and living standards. Most thoughtful Americans would expect their living standards to be visibly improving if the United States were undergoing the productivity growth that Conservatives celebrate. However, it is mainly the elite few who have seen tangible gains in their own real income and wealth. Productivity growth is the engine for the development of future wealth. Sustaining it requires government to wage a strong and concerted effort to promote innovation, investment in human capital, and public investment, and adopt sensible industrial policies.

THE RADICAL ARGUMENT

The debate between Liberal demand managers and Conservative supply-siders has produced considerable confusion among thoughtful Americans. The arguments have usually been framed in either/or terms: Either you intervene to manage the aggregate economy or you do not. Either an unregulated economy works better than a managed one or it does not. Given the record of the past seventy years of American economic history, there is little evidence to make either side's claims very convincing. Thus it is not surprising that modern macroeconomic policy debates produce more heat than light. In both actual policy making and the classroom teaching of economics, the result has been "a little of this and a little of that." From a Radical perspective, however, there is no confusion about the issues: both Liberals and Conservatives, albeit for different reasons, are *wrong*.

Why Neither Demand-Side nor Supply-Side Efforts Work

The fundamental flaw of both Liberal and Conservative approaches begins from the same error: Neither truly understands what powers a capitalist economy. Although both agree that investment is the driving force, each sees investment as depending on different determinants.

Conservatives understand investment as being determined by the level of savings in the society. As savings grow, interest rates (the cost of borrowing) decline, and investors step forward in greater numbers to obtain funds. In turn, their investment actions propel the economy, providing growth and jobs. Accordingly, Conservative policy focuses on actions that will enhance savings. The Reagan tax cut of 1981 was called a supply-side tax cut (although it differed little from earlier demand-side cuts) because it was aimed at giving very large tax reductions to the very rich, who were expected to save their windfall, and to corporations, who were expected to translate after-tax profits directly into investment.

Similarly, Conservatives oppose government deficits that are financed in capital markets in competition with private seekers of funds. Government borrowing is supposed to *crowd out* private investment by raising interest rates. In monetary policy matters, although low interest rates are attractive to investors, too-low rates are opposed because they might discourage saving and encourage consumer borrowing. Therefore, an expansionary money policy is discounted as having no useful effects on investment. In focusing on savings and the interest rate, along with their views on the excessive power of labor unions to raise wage rates, it is apparent that Conservatives take a cost-based approach to explaining how investment occurs and capitalism supposedly flourishes.

Liberals, meanwhile, see the chief determinant of investment as the actual level of aggregate demand. Abundant savings and low interest rates, they argue, will not induce a firm to invest if, as a result of an economic slump, it has a great deal of unused plants and equipment. As demand rises, utilization rates grow, and new investment becomes attractive as the firm actually seeks to expand output. Faced with an underemployed economy, Liberals are accordingly biased toward tax cuts that raise consumption, toward increases in government spending, and, under some circumstances, toward very low interest rates (which in their view encourage borrowing). Their built-in bias focuses on demand conditions. Increase demand to stimulate the economy; decrease it to slow down economic activity.

To be sure, Liberals and Conservatives view the "natural state" of the economy in two different ways. Conservatives assume that, left to itself and without government tinkering, an economy naturally runs at full employment and capacity utilization. Liberals view the natural state as being less than full employment but believe that full employment may be reached by means of adroit policy actions. In many other respects, Conservatives and Liberals are quite alike. Both zero in on business investment as the key that unlocks the economy; they differ, however, on their *cost* versus *demand* explanations of why investment takes place. *The difference is a very crucial one.*

To see this issue more clearly and to understand why Liberals and Conservatives are both wrong, we must first see that each is a little bit right in understanding how capitalism works. *Profit, not savings or aggregate demand, is the real determinant of investment.* Although few Liberals or Conservatives would disagree with the assertion that profit drives capitalism, they fail to recognize that profit has both a cost side and a demand side. Remember: Profit equals sales minus expenditures. Thus lower costs increase profits and increased sales raise profits, *ceteris paribus.* The trouble, of course, is with *ceteris paribus.*

The very actions aimed at lowering costs (the supply-side menu of cutting the taxes of only the rich, keeping government spending in check, balancing the budget, and so on) lowers demand and thus business sales.

Meanwhile, actions intended to increase demand (increased government spending, tax cuts to stimulate consumption, budget imbalance, and the like) raise costs as resource prices are bid upward in an expanding economy. This was precisely the dilemma of the 1970s, as we saw in the last issue.

Ironically, both demand-based and supply-based stabilization policy scenarios are doomed to fail in the long run. The problem lies deep in a production-for-profit system. The normal search for profits produces overproduction and underconsumption crises and falling profits. Marx identified both outcomes as inherent features of growth under capitalism. Why? Because capitalist competition compels businesses to squeeze every penny of profit from their payroll while simultaneously seeking new ways to automate and mechanize as many jobs as possible. In this way, technological change—rather than being some passive or neutral factor in the production process—has a very specific role and objective: to reduce the labor content in the production of any good or service. Thus, the capitalist system is always under threat because of its inherent labor-displacing tendency and continual need to exploit workers to increase profitability. Efforts to remedy overproduction and underconsumption through macroeconomic stabilization policies lead to rising costs and falling profits. In either case, profits, the driving force of the system, are perpetually threatened.

Over the past half century, stabilization policy has been simply a matter of trying first one and then the other of these bankrupt approaches. Although many economists have tried to reconcile the Liberal and Conservative extremes and build an eclectic system, that is bound to fail too. Invariably, cost-based and demand-based approaches come into conflict. The result is that they either negate each other or one comes to dominate the other.

The Class Bias and Irrationality of Conventional Stabilization Policy Efforts

Regardless of its failure, stabilization policy efforts in our time have had one permanent effect: They have erected government as a central feature of the modern capitalist economy. In turn, the modern capitalist state has become a vehicle for class domination and increasing productive irrationality.

Liberals and Conservatives both hold that government policy is capable of being neutral; that is, tax cuts or money policy actions, regardless of the particular kind of action, are viewed as having only economic effects. The social and political biases of any of these policies are never put up front for examination. This misses an important aspect of public policy making, namely, its role as a class instrument, a tool for perpetuating ruling-class domination. Ordinary Americans better appreciate the social inequalities of stabilization policy than most economists admit, but they might usefully be laid out in detail.

There is an upper-income bias in taxation policy. A brief survey of important tax-cutting efforts to stimulate expansion—either the cuts of 1964 or those of 1981 or the most recent tax cuts of the Bush administration throughout 2001–3, for example—indicates that upper-middle-class and upper-income taxpayers received the largest percentage reduction and the bulk of the total cut. These same groups, of course, benefit the most from the legal loopholes of the tax system, such as the ability to deduct interest payments on home mortgages and home equity loans and business expenses from their tax bills. The poor and the lower middle class, without the benefits of tax loopholes (or even much opportunity to cheat), have lost economic ground in the tax-cutting measures of demand-side Keynesians and supply-side Conservatives. In the case of tax increases, the poor again are hit hardest. The recent increase in Social Security withholding taxes is a good example. Over the past few years, both the taxable base and the rate of the taxes have risen at the lower end of the income scale. (In 2005 the rate paid by employees was 6.2 percent on earnings up to $90,000.) Such taxes are regressive, since they fall most heavily on lower incomes. Moreover, nearly three out of four workers pay more in Social Security taxes than they do in federal income taxes. Obviously, the solution is to reduce significantly the payroll tax rate at the lower end of the income scale while imposing a progressive rate structure on *all* income.

Low-income Americans have also lost out on the spending side. While Conservatives and Liberals (for different reasons) point to the magnitude of federal transfers to the poor and indigent, this is a massive deception. The federal government's spending in this area amounts to about the same percentage of the GDP today as it did in the pre-Keynesian 1930s.* At the same time, transfers to large farmers, businesses, and professional work-

---

*This fact may seem startling to Americans, who are constantly bombarded with propaganda about the alleged extravagance of social spending on the poor. In reality, ers have grown. Government spending for goods, meanwhile, directly benefits the ruling class and higher-income workers. A good illustration of the capitalized bias of such expenditures is military and space spending. The recipient firms are among the largest in the nation and also the most capital- and skill-intensive. Spending funneled into these firms strengthens capital's power and has little or no impact on creating jobs for less skilled and lower-paid workers (see Issue 4).

Looked at in this way, government spending, even for stabilization purposes, is not neutral at all. It actually heightens class divisions in the society. Spending on low-income housing, medical care, and other social goods that would improve the poor's quality of life has always ranked very low among fiscal priorities. This is because the poor, regardless of their numbers, are not yet a powerful constituency and also because spending for certain social goods would actually create competition with the private sector. Subsidized public housing would destroy the lucrative low-income housing market in the private sector, free clinics would bankrupt private hospitals, and so on. Moreover, when the stabilization experts call for a contraction in government spending (to balance the budget or reduce aggregate demand), services and transfers to the poor are the first items sacrificed.

Although Liberals in the heyday of Keynesian policy were less inclined to cut so deeply or so obviously, the Conservative budget cutters of the Reagan years brutalized the poor. In the name of "trickle-down" economics, poor children were told that catsup now qualified as a vegetable in the school lunch program, and the unskilled were told that there were plenty of jobs in most newspapers' classified sections. And all social service budgets were chopped.

Monetary policy is equally selective and unfair in its class effects. For instance, the 1982 pursuit of high interest rates (a tight money policy) as an anti-inflation tool especially burdened the working class. For consumers, high interest rates mean that greater portions of their income must go toward such necessities as home mortgages and for the "luxuries" provided by credit buying. Upper-income groups, of course, face the same interest rates, but their burdens are a much smaller proportion of their income and more easily borne without sacrifice of their living

---

we currently spend only a little over 2 percent of our output on programs directed specifically to low-income groups. In 1938, for example, the $1.5 billion spent on various poor relief programs by federal, state, and local governments amounted to a little less than 2 percent of the output.

standards. Meanwhile, for workers, tight money translates into reduced business output and fewer jobs or lower pay.

Thus stabilization policy perpetuates and accentuates the normal class inequalities of capitalism. Expansionary policy never benefits the poor as much as the rich. And contraction always demands that the least affluent American citizens tighten their belts the most. The normal exploitative tendencies of traditional capitalism are merely reinforced under both Liberal and Conservative approaches.

Apart from the upper-class biases of stabilization policies, there is also the problem of the irrational production and consumption that it encourages. Foremost among these irrational activities are the huge amounts of government spending on the military. Presently, we are spending about $450 billion on national defense for goods and services that only waste the social surplus and have been a significant source of inflation during the postwar period. This is because once warplanes, tanks, guns, ordnance, and the like are produced, they can only be stockpiled and not recirculated throughout the economy. Although wages have been paid, there is no concomitant increase in socially useful output.

Second, while defense expenditures give the appearance of increasing GDP, in actuality they add little to the material well-being of the vast majority of workers. Furthermore, military expenditure programs are also extremely costly and untenable in an era of austerity and shrinking federal budgets. Thus, it should be obvious that rather than being a source of macroeconomic stability, defense expenditures are a persistent net drain on society's resources and need to be drastically curtailed. Significantly cutting the defense budget would have other salutary effects, such as lowering the national debt and deficit, freeing up money for needed social programs, and discouraging politicians from getting involved in unnecessary military adventures (such as the invasion of Iraq).

Rather than reconstructing a stable economy, uncritical and unplanned government spending policy has reinforced the irrational production and consumption patterns of a capitalist system.

With government nondefense spending now poised to be restrained by yet another round of supply-side tax and expenditure cutting, it would be erroneous to conclude that government has ceased contributing to productive irrationality. By cutting corporate taxes and reducing other burdens on the private sector, encouragement of irrational production and investment decisions has shifted from the spending side of the government budget to the revenue side. The technique differs, but the outcome is the same: more socially useless goods and a more meaningless life for consumers and workers.

The Emerging Contradiction

Overall, the past forty years of public policy have heightened internal capitalist contradictions. The unequal distribution of benefits and losses has produced growing conflicts—big business versus little business, capital versus labor, worker versus worker, worker versus nonworker, and, always, rich versus poor. Overarching everything is the mounting evidence that Liberal economics cannot deliver on any of its promises of full employment, growth, and price stability. After peaking during the 1960s, the growth rate of real per capita income has been steadily falling (see Table 2.3). In fact, neither the Reagan nor Clinton administrations were able to reverse this long-term trend even as labor productivity accelerated right through the 2001 recession. In essence, American capitalism becomes more and more productive at the expense of worker's livelihoods and jobs.

The temporary rise of worn-out laissez-faire economics, however, may have one positive effect: revealing the class-biased nature of capitalism much more quickly. Consequently Americans may finally be willing to go beyond the narrow and oppressive economics of their past. When the Conservative ideology fails, as it must, and the Keynesian alternative remains discredited, we will be forced to consider an economic and social agenda we have evaded thus far. Under these circumstances, we will go beyond merely stabilizing the economy to reorganizing it and planning it so that oppression and irrationality no longer exist.

Balancing the Federal Budget

Should We Be Worried About the Rising Federal Deficit?

When national debts have once been accumulated to a
certain degree, there is scarce, I believe, a single instance
of their having been fairly and completely paid. The
liberation of the public revenue, if it has ever been brought
about at all, has always been brought about by a bankruptcy; sometimes by an avowed one, but always by a real
one, though frequently by a pretended payment.

—*Adam Smith*, The Wealth of Nations, *1776*

A decline in income due to a decline in the level of employment, if it goes far, may even cause consumption to exceed
income not only by individuals and institutions using up the
financial reserves which they have accumulated in better
times, but also by Government, which will be liable, will-
ingly or unwillingly, to run a budgetary deficit.

—*John Maynard Keynes*, The General Theory of
Employment, Interest, and Money, *1935*

We recognize loud and clear the surplus is not the
government's money. The surplus is the people's money
and we ought to trust them with their own money.

—*President George W. Bush, 2001*

A balanced budget amendment is a rigid, simple-minded
approach to a very complex problem. Sometimes you need a
deficit to kick-start a stalled economy. But that doesn't mean I
think it's ok to run deficits year after year. Borrowing money
from rich people is a cowardly substitute for taxing them.

—*Doug Henwood*, Left Business Observer, *2004*

The Problem

Over the past seven decades, majority economic and political thinking on the question of government deficits has undergone a 360-degree swing. The prevailing view in the early 1930s, which had been held as long as economists had been speaking out on the subject, was that government budgets should be balanced annually. Experience had shown that when governments financed spending by printing new money or by borrowing, general economic misfortunes such as inflation, currency devaluation, and general financial instability tended to follow. Ironically, Franklin D. Roosevelt campaigned hard against Herbert Hoover in 1932, lambasting his "spendthrift" opponent for running deficits in the previous two years of depression.

The growing popularity of John Maynard Keynes's ideas in the 1930s and 1940s, along with the actual experience of watching budget deficits grow precisely as the economic gloom of depression receded, caused a shift in opinion. Few economists by the 1960s seriously advocated an annually balanced federal budget. A number talked about cyclically balanced budgets, in which expenditures and revenues should reach parity over a complete business cycle. The focus on the budget in such an approach was to use deficits to finance needed economic expansion while surpluses naturally accumulated during periods of prosperity. Clearly related to this view was "functional finance," which showed no real concern in any accounting sense for balance or imbalance at all but focused exclusively on using deficits or surpluses as policy tools. To the functional finance theorists, there was no fundamental limitation on government's capacity to create and finance deficits, regardless of the size of the debt.

It is important to recognize that the federal government deficit is different from the federal debt. The federal government experiences a *budget deficit* when its revenues are less than its expenditures during a given time period, typically a fiscal year or a calendar year. If deficits are not paid off and become a recurring phenomenon, then the government accumulates *debt*. Economists distinguish between a budget deficit and debt when speaking of government finance by referring to the revenue shortfall of a given year as a budget deficit and the year-to-year accumulation of budget deficits as the federal debt.

By the 1980s, the sudden explosion of the federal debt forced a change in majority economic thinking again. As Table 3.1 shows, both debt as a share of gross domestic product (GDP) and interest payments as a percent of GDP moved sharply upward. With debt and interest outlays on

Table 3.1

Measures of the Federal Debt

Year	Public debt (billions of current dollars)	Real debt (billions of 2000 dollars)	Debt as percentage of GDP	Interest as percentage of GDP
1929	16.9	98.8	16.0	0.7
1940	50.7	582.7	52.4	1.3
1945	260.1	2498.8	117.5	1.5
1950	256.9	1995.7	94.0	1.6
1955	274.4	1885.7	69.3	1.3
1960	290.5	1660.1	56.0	2.0
1965	322.3	1671.8	46.9	1.9
1970	380.9	1612.0	37.6	2.2
1975	541.9	1601.4	34.7	2.4
1980	909.0	1807.6	33.4	3.2
1985	1817.4	2680.2	43.8	4.9
1990	3206.3	4067.9	55.9	5.1
1995	4920.6	5395.4	67.2	4.8
2000	5628.7	5628.7	58.0	3.7
2003	6760.0	6396.0	62.4	1.4

Source: Economic Report of the President (Washington, DC: Government Printing Office, 2001) and data from Bureau of Economic Analysis.
Note: Entries for 1929 relied on gross national product figures. GDP = gross domestic product.

the debt growing faster than national output and also seeming to accompany an inflationary period of high unemployment and slow growth, many economists (mostly Conservatives at first but soon many Liberals as well) began to believe that deficits did have an adverse effect on the general economy. Needless to say, Conservatives have been increasingly vulnerable to Liberal criticism on the debt and deficit issues. The administrations of Ronald Reagan and George H. Bush, irrespective of their official condemnation of deficits and their posturing on behalf of spending restraint on budget balance, ran up in the 1980s the greatest deficits in American history to that point—nearly tripling the national debt (see Figure 3.1). Their defenders will correctly point out that Congress collaborated with the debt explosion too, but the irony of supposedly Conservative administrations being the most profligate is not lost on many observers.

Annual deficits mounted in the mid-1980s creating pressure for legal restraints on government's capacity to create debt. Proposals for a constitutional amendment that would require annually balanced federal budgets represented the strongest opposition to deficit spending. Whether or not

90

Figure 3.1   **Federal Budget Surplus or Deficit, 1969–2003**

Source: Economic Report of the President (Washington, DC: Government Printing Office, 2004).

such an amendment will ever be passed remains to be seen. However, alarmed by their inability to slow the flow of red ink, Congress and President Reagan produced rather mechanical budget-balancing legislation in the form of the Gramm-Rudman-Hollings Act (GRH) in 1985. A schedule was laid out for obtaining annual budget balance by 1991, but this was later revised to 1993. Absolute deficit limits were imposed. If budgets came in at higher-than-allowed deficits, the act called for across-the-board cuts by the percentage of the excess deficit to all spending categories except Social Security and some defense outlays.

Few economists expressed much satisfaction with GRH's automatic, across-the-board budget-cutting machine as a substitute for human judgment and decision making about spending. Conservatives worried about defense spending cuts and insufficient cuts in social spending. Conservatives were also concerned about the distinct possibility that tax increases and not spending cuts would ultimately be used to meet deficit targets. Liberals and Radicals, on the other hand, saw the imposed cuts in social spending as "balancing the budget on the backs of the poor."

GRH's historical significance is that it *briefly* cooled debate about debt and deficits. The Black Monday meltdown of the stock market on October 19, 1987, reopened the debate. Postmortems of the securities market crash held that loss of investors' faith was traceable to America's "double deficits": the persistent federal deficit and the equally persistent deficit in international trade balances. Then the deficit reduction targets set by GRH were missed in 1988 and 1989 by more than the $10 billion margin for error allowed by the statute. The 1990 deficit was off target by more than $120 billion. In 1990, the Congress and the president eliminated the GRH mechanism and resorted to increasing taxes.

Agreeing to raise taxes in 1990 to reduce the deficit was the undoing of George H. Bush's presidency. Ironically, successor William Clinton promised and delivered higher tax rates at the upper end of the income scale. Top rates rose from 31 percent to 39.6 percent. Both the Clinton administration and the Congressional Budget Office had predicted rather modest deficit reduction using what turned out to be quite conservative forecasts of economic growth.

The expansion of the 1990s upstaged all tools of discretionary policy by outperforming even the most optimistic expectations of economic growth and deficit reduction. A deficit of $290 billion in 1992 shrank dramatically to a mere $22 billion in 1997. The year 2000 saw a $236 billion surplus in the federal budget. The best of all possible worlds had occurred: Economic growth had painlessly eliminated federal budget deficits. Federal debt as a percentage of GDP leveled off. Paying down the debt became a real option.

President George W. Bush's tax cutting policies, combined with the 2001 recession and initiation of war first against Afghanistan and then with Iraq, combined to move the federal budget from a position of record surplus to record deficit in just three years. In fact, with the exception of the Korean War, every major American armed conflict has been financed with debt. Historically, the financial capacity for the American economy to assume and manage very significant increases in wartime debt is rather remarkable. For example, during World War II the total stock of federal debt increased fivefold from 1940 to 1945 (see Table 3.1). The call for balanced budgets will likely become more vocal as the issue and its immediate effects will not disappear. As of this writing, financial markets remain nervous about prospective financing needs, and this has caused a notable increase in the yields on long-term federal government bonds. In sum, while there is fair agreement among all ideological shades that deficits do matter, it should also be clear that mainstream ideological differences could become quite blurry—especially during periods of national crises such as wars. Although the heyday of functional finance is over, there is wide disagreement on the precise consequences of deficits, on their real significance, and on how they might be eliminated.

Synopsis

Conservatives oppose government budget imbalance because it is inherently destabilizing, producing inflation, rising interest rates, and reduced private investment. Furthermore, the discretionary nature of demand-management fiscal policy, which they see as the source of the rising debt, is singled out as particularly unwise. Liberals, although concerned with recent trends in debt growth (which they see as the result of Conservative management), generally view debt as a tool of fiscal management. Radicals see the debt issue as a reflection of the economy's general inability to realize surplus value. They point not only to the growth of public debt to support this view but also to the even faster growth of private debt.

Anticipating the Arguments

- What is the logic of the Conservative argument that links budgetary deficits with inflationary pressures?

- Explain the Liberal argument that it is not the size of the deficit that is important but the way in which the deficit is acquired.
- Why do Radicals maintain that permanent elimination of the deficit is impossible?

THE CONSERVATIVE ARGUMENT

If there is a particular gauge of the failure of demand-management policies, it must be the federal debt. The growth of the debt and a general indifference to this growth were, until comparatively recently, aspects of Liberal doctrine that were scarcely ever criticized. Introductory economics textbooks devoted a few pages to discussion of federal debt but quickly moved on to other topics, leaving the distinct impression that "debt doesn't matter." In fact, the debt does matter. Not only is it the undesirable outcome of wrong policy choices, but annual operating deficits by the federal government and mounting aggregate debt also throttle an economy, encouraging inflation and general economic stagnation.

Although Liberals have little understanding of the real problems posed by growing deficits, they are quick to point out that much of the current federal debt was acquired during a Conservative presidency. The implication is that what Conservatives say on the debt question is really just hot air. The charge is inaccurate and begs the evidence. Although the federal debt more than doubled during Reagan's years in office, this debt explosion was actually the result of pre-Reagan fiscal excesses and the reluctance of a Liberal Congress to cut federal spending. As much as ever, budget balance remains the central objective of Conservative fiscal thinking, and the debt expansion during the Reagan presidency—whatever its sources—does not change this.

Deficits as a Source for Inflation and Unemployment

One of the more objectionable features of government's running high and persistent annual deficits is its inherent inflationary effect. When government spends more for goods and transfers than it collects in taxes, it increases the total demand for all goods produced in the economy. If an increase in the supply of goods equal to the increase in government-generated demand were instantaneously forthcoming, there would be no problem: more demand, more goods, prices unchanged. However, this is not how an economy works. Even in an underemployed economy capable of producing a greater output by simply adding productive resources, there is bound to be some *demand-pull* inflation as the existing output is bid upward in price. When the economy is operating near full employment levels, as it was through most of the 1960s and the early 1970s, and when government is at the same time piling up large annual deficits, the demand-pull pressure on prices is very much greater. Approaching the outer limits of the society's actual productive ability, demand increases by themselves cannot raise production.

Apart from their demand effect, deficits also have an inflationary effect through the money supply. Deficits must, after all, be financed. Two options are open: Bonds may be sold to financial institutions and the general public (which creates its own special problems, as we shall presently see), or the Federal Reserve System (the Fed) may purchase the new securities and in turn increase the Treasury's account, providing the government with funds to pay its mounting bills. When the latter takes place, as it will when the Fed attempts to complement an expansionary fiscal policy with an accommodative (and expansionary) monetary policy, new money is created.

To comprehend the effect of monetizing the debt, we need simply to understand the traditional explanation of inflation: too many dollars chasing too few goods.

The long-term growth of output and employment in any economy depends on the society's utilization of resources. Prices are nothing more than the measure by which money is exchanged for commodities. Accordingly, the general tendency of prices in any society will be determined by changes in the stock of money available for transactions. The stock of money, of course, must increase or decrease as the general level of economic output expands or contracts. A relative decrease in money stock compared to output must produce general price reductions. A money expansion rate above the rate of increase in output will lead to price expansion. Quite simply, more money does not, and by itself cannot, create more goods. Instead, it will be spent on the available goods at higher prices.

This analysis of the fundamental cause of inflation is amply supported by evidence. Every significant inflationary episode in U.S. history has followed excessive growth in the supply of money. However, neither logic nor the evidence has succeeded in deflecting modern state policy from pursuing an inflationary course. As we indicated in our discussions of stabilization policy and unemployment, public policy has been committed too long to the Keynesian belief that high levels of output can be created and maintained by manipulating aggregate demand. Through the 1960s and 1970s, deficits were the intended outcome of fiscal policy. Their excess demand effects were enlarged as the Fed, often pursuing an easy money policy, monetized the deficits.

Eventually, the economy was seized by an inflationary episode it could not control. The sequence of events producing the stagflation of the mid- and late 1970s should be carefully understood. The Conservative analysis of how underlying economic forces are affected runs as follows: The immediate impact of expansionary monetary and fiscal policy will probably be to induce new business investment and additional consumer spending. Thus an increase in output and employment may occur. However, the expansion is only temporary at best. Tricked by a sudden increase in earnings, businesses and consumers have overspent and overborrowed. While money income has risen, their real situation has not improved; indeed, it has probably worsened if they have overspent. Over time, however, people learn. Anticipated discretionary actions by monetary and fiscal authorities merely induce businesses and consumers—who, after all, are not stupid—to take any action they see fit to protect themselves. Their *rational expectations* negate the impact of the authorities' policies. Expansion of the money supply over time no longer stimulates economic expansion (even temporarily); it merely fuels demand inflation without any employment benefits. In fact, unemployment gets worse. The situation is a bit like a kitten chasing its tail. Excess demand inflation (aided by other Liberal tinkering with the market) lowers real income and demand for goods, which in turn lowers employment. Further economic intervention is therefore required to offset these employment losses. This in turn generates more inflationary pressures, which consequently lead to more unemployment. The more the kitten tries to catch its tail, the faster it must run.

Crowding Out: The Impact of Deficits on Investment and Business

As noted earlier, the monetary authorities do have an option other than monetizing the debt. They can sell new government bonds, financing government's deficit spending out of private savings. While this is certainly less inflationary, it has equally undesirable effects. When government goes into financial markets as a borrower, it competes with private borrowers. With increased competition among all borrowers—government as well as private seekers of investment funds—interest rates (the price of borrowing) are pushed upward. For business borrowers, the cost of obtaining funds rises. The result is to *crowd out* some private business investment that would otherwise have taken place at a lower interest rate.

The magnitude of the crowding-out effect is a matter of some debate. A few economists hold that a dollar of government borrowing squeezes out a dollar of private investment. But even if the outcome is much smaller, government borrowing adversely affects the productive base of the economy, which is, after all, the real determinant of output and employment.

Deficits and Trade Balances

By the early 1980s, it was apparent that the high and rising federal deficits had yet another undesirable consequence: They were adversely affecting our international trade position. This is examined in detail in Issue 7, so a brief outline here will suffice.

Through the 1970s and early 1980s, accompanying both the deficits and the deficit-generated inflationary pressures, there was a steady upward push in interest rates. From the perspective of lenders around the world, the comparatively high American interest rates made investment in all kinds of U.S. securities highly desirable. Large portions of the new government bond issues, floated to finance the swelling debt, were purchased abroad. To buy American securities, it was essential to obtain American dollars. The resulting demand for dollars pushed the price of dollars upward relative to other world currencies. With a strong and strengthening dollar (some would call it an overvalued dollar), American goods sold at relatively higher prices in foreign markets, while foreign goods sold relatively inexpensively in our own domestic markets. With imports rising and exports falling, the balance of trade turned decidedly against the United States.

While it is not accurate to lay all U.S. trade problems at the door of the deficit, it is obvious that insofar as deficit spending and deficit financing place upward pressure on interest rates, they helped create an artificially strong dollar, which translated directly into a worsening international trade position.

Deficits Do Matter

The foregoing arguments make it clear that deficits have an extraordinary impact on the contemporary economy. Paradoxically, they bring about the opposite of their intended effects. Rather than leading to a demand-powered expansion of output and employment, as Liberals have long claimed, deficits lead in the other direction, toward inflation, rising interest rates, dwindling investment, and ultimately lower levels of output and employment.

The legislative process of budgeting is influenced by far too many powerful voting interests with personal stakes in keeping spending high and thus keeping deficits high. Too many candidates for high political office have learned that the briefly stimulating effects of a political fiscal policy that pumps up demand just before election time can ensure victory at the polls. A balanced budget amendment would solve this problem, but the political balance in the House and Senate has obstructed its enactment. The Cato Institute has proposed the alternative of a "balanced budget veto" amendment that would allow the president to exercise line-item veto power to reduce government spending only in years following a deficit. Congress would have the incentive to restrain spending to avoid losing control of the budgeting process. Thus, a check and balance would be restored in that the president's veto authority would be checked by the ability of Congress to balance its spending prerogatives against available revenues.

Conservatives maintain that mandatory budget balancing is the long-term solution to the problem of deficits and debt. The need for fiscal discipline is grounded in recognizing that the role of the central government must be curtailed. More aggressive efforts to privatize and contract out governmental operations to the private sector support that end. The savings and efficiencies from pursuit of these policies provide society with the rewards of a reduced tax burden and less government intrusion into economic affairs.

THE LIBERAL ARGUMENT

During the Reagan presidency, when Conservative policy influence was at its greatest, the nation saw a near tripling of the federal debt. History seems to be repeating itself. The administration of George W. Bush has been relatively quiet about the exploding federal deficits it has induced on the heels of the comfortable surplus that it inherited. Yet, Conservatives still hold to the view that deficits are a profoundly evil economic undertaking and claim to remain committed to the ideal of a consistently balanced federal budget. Reconciling this inconsistency in Conservative philosophy versus policy presents a challenge to true Conservatives.

Conservatives are right in stressing that deficits do matter. What they do not seem to understand, however, is that they matter in how and why they come into being in the first place. *Some deficits matter much more than others.*

Putting the Size of the Debt in Perspective

The recent focus on the deficit has been stimulated by public concern for both the absolute size and the rate of growth of the public debt. However, it is important to understand what the numbers really say. As Table 3.1 indicated, the *real* (or constant dollar) growth of the debt before its explosion during the Reagan years was substantially less than its *nominal* (or current dollar) growth. In constant dollars, the debt was less in 1980 than it had been at the end of World War II. As a percent of GDP, total debt was vastly smaller in 1980 than in 1945. Thus the argument that the growth of the debt was altering the American economic landscape is not very convincing, since the so-called spendthrift 1960s and 1970s did not have any impact on the real (as opposed to the nominal) level of federal debt.

The other misplaced emphasis of the Conservative argument, with regard to pre-Reagan debt accumulations, is to view the debt as a cause rather than the result of general economic conditions. *The simple fact is that a troubled economy produces deficits, not vice versa.*

Understanding the Cause of the Debt

Conservative analyses of deficits make little effort to distinguish among different sources or causes of a given deficit. Actually, two major but quite different causes for the federal government's running a deficit are identifiable. First, there are deficits that are directly the result of a general economic slump. When recession strikes, government revenues decrease as taxable income falls, but expenditures rise automatically as more people qualify for unemployment benefits and various other transfer payments (including subsidies to business). Even if additional expenditures were not made, a gap between revenues and expenditures would develop since government outlays were planned before the slump and were based on anticipated revenues. This is called a *cyclical budget deficit.* It is estimated that every time the unemployment rate rises by one percentage point in a recession, the loss of revenues and the automatic rise in outlays create a $40 billion to $50 billion revenue-expenditure gap.

A second, and quite different, source of debt growth may come from a *structural budget deficit.* Structural deficits arise from some discretionary redirection of fiscal policy—the passage of a tax cut (decreasing revenue collections) or the introduction of a huge public works or military spending program (increasing outlays), for instance. Structural deficits may develop as the result of either wise or unwise policy making. They may also result from external conditions over which policy makers have no control (or very little), as in the case of World War II, Vietnam War spending, or the emergency relief associated with the World Trade Center and Pentagon disasters and the costs of waging the subsequent war.

With a little reflection, it should be obvious that it is essential to know whether a given deficit is the result of cyclical or structural events. Clearly, an attempt to balance a budget in a period of cyclical downturn—either by raising taxes or by reducing governmental outlays to the needy—is both economic and political foolishness that could make downturns worse and destabilize political institutions. In failing to distinguish between types of deficits and persistently calling for a constitutional amendment requiring a balanced budget, Conservatives are proposing the most destructive possible approach to government budgeting.

While Conservatives oppose all deficits, it is obvious that most of their attack is directed against structural deficits because they feel any manipulation of government revenues and expenditures for the purpose of demand management is wrong. Their conclusion is easily stated: Deficits, purely and simply, cause inflation and discourage investment. That judgment, however, is not unequivocally supported by theory or empirical evidence.

Consider an economy that has entered a recession. A structural deficit acquired when an economy is undergoing a cyclical downturn or when substantial underemployment of available resources exists need not create demand-pull inflation. The expansion of total demand resulting from a consciously developed structural deficit under these conditions can put the unemployed back to work and reemploy unused productive capacity without excessively bidding up wage and resource prices. This was the case in the early and mid-

1960s. The moderate deficits of the Kennedy and Johnson years (before Vietnam War spending generated demand-pull inflation pressures) lowered unemployment and stimulated the economy without pumping up prices. Moreover, most of the inflationary pressure that built up in the late 1970s came from supply-side shocks and cost-push inflationary effects, not from the demand side and government deficits. The Conservative view that all inflation results from excess demand and that government deficits are the primary source for excess demand is just not supported if the events of the 1970s are honestly reported and evaluated.

Structural deficits do not necessarily and under all conditions discourage or crowd out private investment demand that might otherwise be forthcoming. If crowding out exists at all, it can take place only when an economy is near full employment and is utilizing most of a fixed stock of investable funds. At any point below this level, "crowding in" is a much greater likelihood, with private investment rising as expansionary fiscal policy puts unemployed resources back to work. As output rises, new investment opportunities develop; they do not disappear.

Conservative logic is empirically contradicted by recent events when Conservatives were having their own way with budget making. Following Conservative reasoning, the enormous deficits following their so-called "supply-side" tax cuts in 1981 that were not matched by spending reductions should have generated enormous inflationary pressures. With the largest structural deficits in American history, we might also have expected the greatest price inflation. In actuality, prices did not rise very much. As any good Keynesian would have predicted, the economy expanded, and the cyclical deficit actually shrank.

Given an understanding of the foregoing points, Liberals are not about to cave in to Conservative and popular pressures and dispatch deficit spending to the junkyard of ill-conceived economic policies. Quite to the contrary of Conservative allegations, Liberals have always believed that deficits matter. When well planned and executed, they provide an important tool of economic management. However, Liberals also believe that deficits matter when they are piled up as the result of badly executed policies. The defense of deficit spending under certain conditions can in no way be extended to defend the deficits of the Reagan years. Likewise, the deficit-inducing policies of the present Bush administration defy convincing justification.

The Reagan Debt Failure and the Balanced Budget Argument Examined

The loose fiscal policy of the Reagan years did not reflect a very rational approach to macroeconomic management. The near tripling of the federal debt over eight years did power the economy out of the 1981–82 recession, but unevenly and with lingering, troublesome side effects. Reagan's fiscal policies lacked a clear focus and were uncoordinated with monetary policy. As the federal budget was hemorrhaging from supply-side tax cuts, the administration encouraged a tight monetary policy to keep down the expected inflationary pressures. The effect was a bit like driving a car by depressing the accelerator and the brake at the same time. The car might move with some degree of control, but the equipment is being worn out. Suddenly it became apparent that as the recession lifted and prices held steady, a new problem had arisen. The higher interest rates resulting from the tight money policy had created a very strong dollar (that is, the high return on U.S. dollars put the dollar in great demand relative to other world currencies). As other currency values fell relative to the dollar, dollars bought more foreign goods, and domestically produced goods, denominated in dollars, cost more when sold overseas and paid for in cheaper foreign currencies. (We shall examine this problem in more detail in Issue 7.)

Conservatives maintain that the high-interest-rate policy was the direct result of deficits and deficit-inspired inflation. That is true only insofar as high interest rates were the ill-chosen Conservative reaction to the nonexistent problem of deficit-induced inflation. Conservatives had themselves to blame for a strong dollar and the resulting damage it caused to the economy. Ironically, under Conservative mismanagement, the nation succeeded in acquiring two very large deficits—the exploding federal debt and an international trade deficit. Paradoxically, the latter deficit served to negate many of the potentially positive effects of the former. The gains of an expansionary fiscal policy (even if it was a fiscal policy Conservatives did not want or understand) were offset by demand leakages resulting from a flood of foreign goods into American markets.

Whether the Conservative deficits were well planned or not is, of course, not the critical question. Nor is it really the first question we should ask. The question that reveals the truly important differences between Liberal and Conservative approaches to deficits is: Why would

Conservatives, who advocate budget balance, ever become associated with the greatest debt explosion in American history?

To unravel the question we need only remember the sources of the expanding deficit, the sequence of events that produced it, and the ultimate objectives of Conservative macroeconomic policy. The source of the Reagan deficit is no mystery. It resulted from two developments that were a critical part of the Conservative program and, when put in place, were bound to create a highly irrational fiscal strategy. As noted earlier, structural deficits could result from well-conceived programs or from wrong-headedness. In the case of the Reagan program, the wrong-headedness is abundantly clear.

The first part of the Reagan fiscal policy produced the personal and business tax cuts of 1981–83 and a gaping hemorrhage on the revenue side of the budget. The second part of the strategy was the incredible expansion of federal outlays resulting from a 50 percent or greater annual increase in military spending. Although social spending and entitlement programs (for example, Social Security) are usually singled out as the cause of growing debts, the charge obscures the fact that these programs, under the heaviest budget-cutting pressures, had shrunk as a share of the federal budget.

But was the deficit-expanding effect of cutting taxes and rising spending not understood? The answer is yes. It appears that the deficits were acquired by design. Only by making deficits and the size of the debt obnoxious would it be possible eventually to cap deficit spending with a balanced budget amendment. The sequence of events leading to $3 trillion of red ink should be understood. First, the tax cuts were obtained. Second, in the name of defense, military spending was increased. Third, growing deficits were accomplished. By giving people something good first—a tax cut and an improved defense posture—it became obvious that the only way the good things could be kept and not have the bad effects of deficits was to cut deeply into government social programs.

Some will say this is ascribing too much perversity and manipulation to Conservative politicians and economists. But it is the only explanation that makes sense if ultimate policy goals are to both shrink the size of government and neutralize fiscal policy by requiring a balanced budget. In other words, the Reagan red ink was not accidental or inherited but purposely created to frighten the nation into accepting a smaller, neutralized role for government in the economy.

The administration of President George W. Bush repeated this strategy in 2001. The comfortable position of budget surpluses made it relatively easy to gather popular and political support for a titanic $1.5 trillion tax reduction under the guise of letting people keep more of their own money, tax relief for marriage and children, and elimination of the estate tax. The passage of additional tax legislation in 2002–3 cut the tax rate on capital gains and dividends as well as granting businesses a significant increase in depreciation expense for equipment purchases.

The record deficit of 2003 vindicated the Liberal concern that President Bush's tax cuts have caused a return to mounting deficits. The events of September 11, 2001, only heightened such concerns: Necessary increases in government spending to cope with the aftermath of the terrorist attacks have only accelerated the transition toward deficits. Despite this fact, opinion polls in the past have indicated strong public support for a balanced-budget amendment. Immersion back into the sea of red ink, no matter how well justified, might prompt serious consideration of the amendment's adoption as the only way to tame the fiscal excesses of government. Yet, the expectation of a lengthy and protracted "War on Terrorism" as well as the massive cost of occupying and reconstructing Iraq suggests that the Bush administration must continue to use deficit financing to pay for tax cuts and foreign policies.

Fiscal mismanagement has once again set the stage for the neutralization of fiscal policy and renewed calls for a balanced-budget mandate. A constitutional law to balance the budget would require government to pursue policies that would worsen the business cycle. Taxes would rise and government spending would fall precisely when demand increases would be needed to offset a slump; and it is possible that an economic expansion could become an inflationary episode as increased tax collections are used to finance greater-than-needed public expenditures. For most Liberals, a legally required balanced budget is a leap back in time to an earlier era of failed economic thinking.

THE RADICAL ARGUMENT

As we discussed in the previous two issues, the current stage of capitalist crisis may be distinguished from previous crises by the central role government has come to play in the economy. The other side of the past six decades' efforts to use government both as an agent to make up chronic deficiencies in the demand for goods and to lower business production costs has been the steady increase of government deficits. The current deficit crisis and the problems it imposes serve as a measure of the failure of the belief that the normal stagnation tendencies of capitalism can be corrected by government actions.

Reaching the Outer Limits of Policy Management

Keynesians, as we have seen, perceived that the capitalist system could continue to obtain profits only as long as the demand for goods was sustained at high levels. Doubters simply disappeared as the levels of demand were pumped up first by World War II deficit spending and later by the deficits of the 1960s. Rather than competing with the private sector, as classical and neoclassical theory held, government spending (by all levels of government) reduced the pressures of chronic unemployment and excess capacity. It absorbed output and made the private realization of surplus value possible. As Table 3.2 shows, both the absolute magnitude of this spending and government outlays as a share of GDP have continued to grow. Amounting to a mere 7.4 percent of national output in 1903, government spending is now nearly one-third of the GDP. As we saw in the previous two issues, the expansion of government spending did slow the system's deterioration into crisis for a while, and although it seemed to work, no one talked much about government deficits. But by the late 1970s, deficits were seen as a source of trouble.

Of course, the trouble is that government spending in general and deficits in particular increase demand but at the same time raise costs to businesses, squeezing their profits. As we saw in the last two issues, the expansionary fiscal policy of the 1960s triggered upward pressures on the prices of resources and on wages. The present Conservative effort (and the efforts of some Liberals) to focus on these bad effects of activist fiscal policy and its resulting deficits merely reflects a redirection of American policy thinking away from the "demand solution" toward searches for a "cost solution" for sustaining profits. It does not represent a theoretical breakthrough for capitalism.

During the past two decades, neither demand-oriented policies of the Keynesian era nor supply-side solutions have benefited the vast majority of working Americans. If anything, the supply-side approach is simply a bold and naked effort to pick up the pieces of the demand-side failure. Indeed, the bulk of government spending largely benefits the upper classes in the form of lucrative contracts and subsidies. Meanwhile, the share of federal income taxes paid by corporations is at an all-

Table 3.2

Government in the Economy

Year	GDP* (billions of dollars)	All government spending (billions of dollars)	Government spending as a percentage of GDP
1903	23.0	1.7	7.4
1913	40.0	3.1	7.8
1929	103.4	8.0	7.7
1940	101.4	15.0	14.8
1950	293.8	59.3	20.2
1960	526.4	122.9	23.3
1970	1,038.5	294.8	28.4
1980	2,789.5	842.8	30.2
1990	5,803.1	1,872.6	32.3
2000	9,817.0	2,886.5	29.4
2002	10,480.8	3,224.0	30.8

Source: Bureau of Economic Analysis.
Note: GDP = gross domestic product.
*Figures prior to 1939 are gross national product (GNP).

time low. Accordingly, it is the American working class whose tax burden continually rises in order to pay off the wealthy owners of government bonds. Stagnant family incomes have necessitated an increase in personal debt just to maintain living standards. Since fiscal expansionism is no longer a meaningful political option for realizing surplus value, the accumulation of private debt by the working class has become critical for the continued viability of the system.

The supply-side actions to cut social spending and to end heavy taxation of the rich and the giant corporations are nothing more than efforts to maintain corporate profits by reducing the well-being of practically everyone but the very wealthy. The supply-sider wants not only to reduce taxes and social spending but also to roll back wages, permit monopoly power, and end consumer, job, and environmental protection. All such programs, it is argued, interfere with businesses' ability to invest, expand, and make profits. Of course, the supply-siders are right: Business does need greater freedom (read: ability to exploit) if it is to survive the growing profit squeeze. But if business survives this way, many people will not.

Yet there remains an irony in the supply-side emphasis on the cost effects of maintaining high levels of aggregate demand. Like a junkie hooked on drugs, giving up government deficits for good is difficult, probably impossible, regardless of the degree of human discomfort we are willing to impose on the general population. The fact is that enormous amounts of government spending are not demand-based at all but are directed toward the cost side. Spending has grown in a number of ways that are clearly aimed at lowering business operating costs and expanding profits. Since 2000, defense spending increased from about one-fifth to about one-quarter of all federal outlays. As the cost-overrun scandals by Haliburton and Brown and Root clearly show, defense expenditures are nothing less than a huge subsidy to very large American corporations. With America now deeply immersed in a protracted war on terrorism, the defense budget will continue to take an ever greater share of national income. Indeed, the stock prices of the large military contractors soared during one of the worst weeks for the stock market following the September 11 attacks. Meanwhile, building highways, subsidizing education, and even taking up most of the costs of maintaining adequate retirement and health programs for the elderly, which firms might have to pay for if Social Security did not, all have the effect of lowering business costs. Thus even Conservatives committed to balanced budgets have little real-world success in lowering government expenditures and balancing budgets. To make the irony a bit clearer: Like a junkie, the economy needs fiscal fixes to get high, but it also needs them just to stay even.

The Misplaced Focus on Federal Deficits

The attention directed by both Liberals and Conservatives to the size and growth of the federal debt, predictable as it may be, obscures the real problems of the system, of which the debt, like the growth of government in general, is only a symptom.

By looking only at the federal deficit, we are deflected from looking at other types of borrowing. The result is a misleading impression because the federal debt amounts to only a small part of total borrowing in the United States, which includes consumer debt, mortgage debt, corporate debt, and state and local government debt. In fact, by 2000, federal debt, even with its explosion in the 1980s, amounted to only about 19 percent of all outstanding domestic debt. Since borrowing by consumers, businesses, and other government units has precisely the same result as federal borrowing in powering demand, the emphasis on the federal share of debt is especially myopic. More to the point, between 1960 and 1980, the period most frequently cited by Conservatives as that in which federal debt expansion first created and then fueled a destructive inflationary spiral, the federal debt grew more slowly than any other component of the nation's total debt. While Conservatives are essentially correct in arguing that borrowing means too many dollars chasing too few goods and thus, sooner or later, creates inflationary pressures, they focus on only one small slice of the debt pie. Even with the federal budget in balance, the debt-driven growth of demand has not been halted.

The Conservative view that federal deficits must be brought under control (a position also supported by many Liberals—though usually for quite different reasons) focuses only on the "too many dollars" aspect of the problem. These theorists do not understand that doing the reverse of what seems to cause inflation or raise interest rates will not necessarily result in relatively falling prices and interest rates. The fact is that tightening up on debts (federal as well as other kinds) will reduce the number of dollars chasing goods. However, as we saw in the late 1970s and early 1980s, it does not necessarily reduce price pressures. True, rising demand may bid up prices initially, but prices may stay up as a result of businesses continuing old and inefficient (high cost per unit of production) operations. After all, reducing demand by lowering federal deficits will not necessarily signal to business an impending improvement in general economic conditions. It will not induce them to modernize their production operations and lower their costs by taking on additional investments. There would be little point in adding plant and equipment that might not be used precisely because demand was being restricted. Only by bringing the economy virtually to its knees, through a deep recession that created enormous excess capacity, was the strong upward pressure on prices halted in the early 1980s. When few dollars are chasing whatever goods are available, it is elemental that prices must and do come down.

Government, with its persistent expansion of debt, must be seen for what it really is—simply one aspect of the fundamental contradiction that challenges a capitalist, production-for-profit economy. The recurring crisis of production outstripping consumption has not ceased in our time. This tendency has merely taken new forms, with the contradiction manifesting itself in the battle over government budgets and fiscal and monetary policy. Indeed, the modern capitalist state is a proxy for capi-

Table 3.3

Outstanding Domestic American Debt, 1980–2000 (in billions of dollars)

Year	Consumer debt	Mortgage debt	Corporate debt	State and local government debt	Federal debt	Total debt	GDP
1980	358.0	932.0	909.1	344.4	735.0	3,957.9	2,789.5
1985	610.6	1,449.3	1,615.5	677.9	1,589.9	7,132.3	4,220.3
1990	824.4	2,504.1	2,533.1	992.3	2,498.1	10,849.6	5,803.1
1995	1,168.0	3,344.3	2,909.6	1,045.0	3,636.7	13,673.8	7,397.7
2000	1,719.0	4,837.4	4,538.8	1,192.3	3,385.1	18,098.8	9,817.0
Change (in percent)							
1980–1990	130	169	179	188	240	174	108
1980–2000	380	419	399	246	361	357	252

Source: Federal Reserve Board, "Flow of Funds," Table D.3, May 2004; *Economic Report of the President* (Washington, DC: Government Printing Office, 2004).
    Note: GDP = gross domestic product.

talism itself. The state budget is the battleground among contending groups in the capitalist economy.

Yet it is a battleground on which victory is unobtainable. We have learned over the past seven decades that when overproduction appears (or demand lags), as it periodically does, we may offset it by increasing demand (through government and private borrowing). Indeed, a measure of our reliance upon debt to "float" the economy is illustrated in Table 3.3: Nearly every category of debt, public and private, has grown faster than national output (GDP) since 1980. We have also learned that increasing demand raises costs to firms by stimulating wage and resource price increases. The so-called cure for the resulting inflation is a full-blown economic slump that will force wages and costs down, and this slump would very likely be deeper and more protracted than the downturn that would have occurred if demand had not been stimulated in the first place.

In conclusion, then, Radicals are not confused about what federal deficits are or what they can and cannot do. First of all, deficits are not the problem. Second, and herein resides an important irony, neither deficits nor budget balancing offers any long-run solution to the chronic problems of a production-for-profit economic system.

Unemployment

Is Joblessness an Overrated Problem?

Once I built a railroad, made it run
Made it race against time
Once I built a railroad, now it's done
Brother, can you spare a dime?
                    —*Popular song by Jay Gorney, 1932*

Capitalism forms an industrial reserve army that belongs to
capital quite as absolute as if the latter had bred it at its
own cost. Independently of the limits of the actual increase
of population, it . . . creates a mass of human material
always ready for exploitation.

                    —*Karl Marx, 1867*

Outsourcing is just a new way of doing international trade.
More things are tradable than were tradable in the past and
that's a good thing.
          —*N. Gregory Mankiw, Chair, President's Council of
                              Economic Advisors, 2004*

They've delivered a double blow to America's workers,
3 million jobs destroyed on their watch, and now they want
to export more of our jobs overseas. What in the world are
they thinking?
          —*Senator John Kerry, Presidential Candidate, 2004*

The Problem

In the United States, episodes of high unemployment are not unlike a serious flu epidemic. When the flu is raging out of control, whether one is actually suffering from the disease or merely watching others suffer, the debilitating symptoms are a frightening thing to ponder. But when the epidemic recedes, so too does most popular recollection of the anxiety and genuine pain it earlier caused. Most citizens' reaction to an epidemic of joblessness is very much the same. When it is happening, the worst economic scenarios all seem possible to a fearful and worried public; when it has fallen to merely "normal" or "below normal" levels, it is hard for those not still suffering from the malady to recall the earlier uncertainties. By mid-2004, with unemployment rates holding stubbornly in the range of 5.5 percent or more, the U.S. economy had shown few convincing signs that low unemployment rates would be visited upon the U.S. labor force in the near future.

In point of fact, though, American attitudes toward unemployment have undergone a long process of evolution. Before the Great Depression of the 1930s, joblessness was generally understood as a personal problem and not a matter of public policy concern. Given the cyclical nature of general economic conditions, employment prospects were understood to be governed by the ordinary ebb and flow of the economy. Losing one's job from time to time, while certainly a matter of bad luck and often an event individuals could rightfully get angry about, was part of the normal course of economic life for great numbers of Americans.

Between the 1930s and the late 1960s, this outlook changed considerably. In the emerging "New Economics" of John Maynard Keynes, it was no longer necessary to accept the capriciousness of the business cycle with passivity. Public policy could be constructed to roll back hard times and regenerate employment. Accordingly, the notion that, through a variety of fiscal policy actions, government could maintain full employment became a matter of widely accepted economic belief. From the passage of the Employment Act of 1946 down to the passage of the Humphrey-Hawkins Full Employment and Balanced Growth Act of 1978, full employment, officially at least, was the goal of macroeconomic policy making.

However, even before the Humphrey-Hawkins Act was passed, it was apparent that the nature of American unemployment was changing. It was no longer only a cyclical event stemming from slowdowns in the general level of economic activity. Even during good times, by the 1970s unemployment rates stayed above the generally accepted 4 percent level then associated with "full employment." As Figure 4.1 indicates, between 1974 and 1991, unemployment fell below 6 percent only four times and never below 5.2 percent. What was becoming evident was that joblessness for great numbers of Americans was not a function of cyclical economic conditions at all.

Increasingly, it was evident that structural shifts in the American economy—how, where, and what goods were actually being produced and distributed—were permanently eliminating many jobs, while regional economic shifts, new skill and educational requirements, and perhaps even certain patterns of social outlook (racism, for instance) were making many would-be workers unemployable.

Public policy efforts to reduce unemployment were reoriented to improve the education, mobility, and flexibility of older workers as well as new workforce entrants and seemed to take on a special urgency. However, the new initiatives had their detractors. Some felt that the government efforts were too little too late. Others saw them as an enormous and unnecessary bureaucratic boondoggle and that a better cure in the end was simply to be patient as labor markets and individuals came to respond to the new employment realities. Some, especially those looking at the 4 percent unemployment rate attained in December 2000, argued that "full employment" actually had been obtained and worried aloud that, given the demographics of the American economy (with great numbers of baby boomers facing imminent retirement), labor shortages, not unemployment, were the real problem.

In fact, the U.S. economy tilted into recession in March of 2001 and suffered additional setbacks from the terrorist attacks of September 11, 2001. Though the recession was brief with the bottom of the downturn reached by November 2001, resumption of economic growth was reminiscent of the aftermath of the last recession of 1990–91: *a jobless recovery*. Structural changes in labor markets, largely associated with the long-running transformation of the manufacturing sector, appeared as accelerating outsourcing of jobs to foreign nations. To many Americans, diminished job opportunities and unemployment became a matter to be taken much more seriously than just a few years before.

Synopsis

Conservatives see the present unemployment problem as largely the result of government efforts to manage labor markets. They therefore advocate

Figure 4.1   **Employment and Joblessness in the United States, 1950–2003**

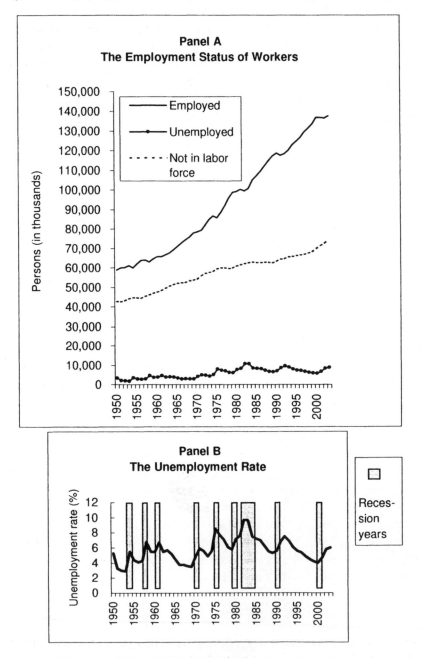

Source: Data from the Bureau of Labor Statistics.

minimum government involvement as the only long-run solution to joblessness. Liberal arguments hold that much of our current unemployment is beyond the reach of usual stabilization policy tools. Thus new and enlarged job programs as well as curtailing the transfer of jobs to other countries is necessary to compensate for the structural limitations of the economy that have created chronic unemployment. For Radicals, unemployment is characteristic of capitalism, a natural outgrowth of the system's tendency to produce surplus labor.

Anticipating the Arguments

- How, according to Conservatives, have government actions increased unemployment?
- What do Liberals mean by structural unemployment, and how would they cure it?
- Why do Radicals believe that high levels of unemployment are characteristic of a capitalist system?

THE CONSERVATIVE ARGUMENT

From the Conservative point of view, unemployment is logically unnecessary. In an economy left to its own devices, involuntary unemployment can result only from short-run market readjustments. Over the long term, as prices, wages, and output adjust, there is work for all at wages commensurate with their productive contributions. Individuals who value their labor higher than the market does or higher than its actual contribution to output, or who simply prefer leisure to work, may be jobless; however, their unemployment is voluntary and not a fundamental problem demanding policy makers' attention. At least, this would be the situation if labor markets were free of the interventions or stickiness and inefficiencies that abound in a world of Liberal social engineering, powerful labor unions, big government, and popular expectations that individuals have the right to a certain level of wages irrespective of these individuals' actual contributions to production.

A Rising Natural Rate of Unemployment

At all times, a natural rate of unemployment exists in a free market economy. By definition, this natural rate approximates the sum of frictional unemployment (voluntary joblessness as workers move from job to job) and structural unemployment (joblessness resulting from changes of skill-level demand and the willingness of workers to accept wage offers) in the economy at any particular time. It is the minimum unemployment level consistent with price stability. Any effort to lower the natural rate of joblessness would trigger inflationary wage and price pressures (because efforts to raise demand for workers will not create jobs for the frictionally or structurally unemployed but *will* bid up the wages of those presently employed). This concept of a natural rate of unemployment is associated with what economists call the *nonaccelerating inflation rate of unemployment* (NAIRU). NAIRU is defined as a rate of unemployment that is sustainable without generating acceleration in inflation.

Looked at from a slightly different perspective, the natural rate of unemployment—what some economists consider "full-employment unemployment"—is principally determined by structural conditions within the economy that affect the matching up of labor demand and labor supply. Of course, in an idealized economic world, in which wages and prices are perfectly flexible and workers are perfectly free to go wherever they desire in search of work, the natural rate would always tend to be near zero.

The natural rate of unemployment has been falling over the past ten years. The decline reflects the best operation of our economic system, while the periods when the natural rate rose were the product of a variety of measures originally intended to improve on the market economy's performance. The natural rate of unemployment rose because prices and wages were not flexible and because labor was not very mobile.

The lack of wage flexibility and labor mobility is the result of past Liberal efforts to intervene in the economy. However, presently concerned about rising "chronic" unemployment, they propose elaborate solutions that will guarantee greater unemployment and greater resource misallocation. To see the point, we need only examine a few of their past efforts.

The Record of a Failed Employment Policy

To understand how labor markets have been made less mobile and less flexible and therefore characterized by a rising natural rate of unemployment, consider four areas of Liberal tinkering: support of unions, social legislation, antidiscrimination efforts, and actions to offset technological displacements.

Liberal support for labor unions in this century, while benefiting some workers, has cost many their jobs. Unions, by instinct and design, seek to restrict the number of jobs in order to force wages up for their members. The older craft unions specifically used this tactic to raise their members' wages. By having long periods of apprenticeship and limiting the number of apprentices, unions in the building trades, for instance, purposely reduced the supply of available labor. This maintained wages for carpenters, masons, and hod carriers, but it also kept large numbers of would-be workers out of the labor force. Large industrial unions also reduce employment. By imposing on management an industry wage that is higher than would otherwise prevail in a free labor market, the industry's total demand for labor is reduced. The union succeeds in keeping the wages of its members high, but unemployment—among both union and nonunion workers—is increased.

Legally mandated social legislation also depresses employment. Ironically, many of those programs aimed specifically at the poorest and least secure workers have worsened rather than improved their lot. For instance, Liberals invariably cite the passage of minimum-wage laws as one of their greatest triumphs; yet such laws have probably had the largest negative impact on employment of all of their social engineering endeavors. Setting minimum-wage rates above a market-determined wage has two immediate effects. First, more individuals enter the labor market, now willing to work at the higher wage, whereas before they opted for leisure. Second, the number of jobs available is reduced because employers cut back their hiring. Liberals have defended minimum-wage legislation as a boon to less-skilled workers; it has actually had the opposite effect. The least-skilled jobs, those with the lowest marginal contribution to a firm's earnings, must be the first eliminated in response to raising the minimum-wage floor. Thus part-time employment for teenagers and unskilled factory work for women and minorities has declined as the minimum wage advanced.

Two other popular pieces of social legislation—unemployment insurance and Social Security—illustrate various ways that well-intended efforts to benefit workers raise the natural rate of unemployment. With more generous unemployment benefits, the pain of joblessness is cushioned. However, the benefits also serve to subsidize, and therefore extend, the period of search for a new job. They also invite entry of some workers into the labor force purely to obtain the benefits. Social Security, meanwhile, works in a slightly different way to increase joblessness. With employers required to pay half of the contributions, Social Security amounts, from an employer's point of view, to a job tax and a hiring disincentive.

Discrimination may exist in the larger society, but competitive markets are the ultimate destroyers of such a practice. The reason is simple: Employers who discriminate, thereby excluding certain elements of the work force (minorities or women, for instance) from certain jobs, reduce their level of employment and, therefore, output compared to nondiscriminatory employers. This diminishes their profitability. The market takes no prisoners when irrational choices lead to noneconomic outcomes.

The fourth area to consider is Liberal tinkering to cushion job losses from technological progress. Periodic and quite natural shifts in the economy's structure produce short-run unemployment from time to time. Buggy makers do not become autoworkers overnight, and autoworkers cannot immediately be transformed into computer specialists. However, it is possible to make a temporarily bad employment situation permanently worse. Recent declining employment in the old, moribund basic industries—steel, automobiles, and farm machinery, for instance—has encouraged Liberals to call for special aid programs for the hard-hit industrial centers of the Northeast and Midwest and for direct aid to the old, failing industries. Such assistance may in fact lower unemployment for a time, just as aid to buggy makers would have softened the unemployment effects of Henry Ford's Model T production. But it also has the socially undesirable effect of halting economic change. By subsidizing antiquated, inefficient industries, we must tax the vital sectors in the economy. Detroit and Gary, Indiana, are kept afloat, but jobs are reduced in the high-tech centers of Texas, California, and Massachusetts.

Recently, Liberals have become fixated on losses in manufacturing employment caused by outsourcing. Some of these job losses are attributable to transferring production tasks to foreign locations and employing lower cost foreign workers. Other losses attributed to outsourcing are not losses at all; they merely reflect increased efficiencies obtained through business practices that rely more on contracted temporary workers. It is important not to confuse "doom and gloom" predictions about widespread job losses with the truth about manufacturing and service sector employment. Gains in output per worker in manufacturing have outpaced the economy as whole. This, combined with changing consumption patterns and businesses routinely seeking lower cost locations and production techniques, has indeed caused employment in textiles, apparel, primary metals industry, leather goods, and petroleum and coal products to contract. Yet, employment gains in retail and wholesale trade, business services, health services, and finance, insurance, and real estate have more than offset the losses—and generally at better levels of compensation than those offered in declining manufacturing industries.

Liberal proposals for special job programs, protection from foreign imports, and restrictions on outsourcing to deal with structural unemployment traceable to technological progress and other structural changes in the economy are both unnecessary and counterproductive. Despite more than four decades of federal expenditures for the education of young people, the retraining of older workers, and elaborate public service programs, as well as affirmative action programs to increase the employment of minorities and women, there is virtually no evidence that significant numbers of would-be workers have been helped. In fact, the tax bill for funding and operating these programs has probably had a negative impact on jobs because private-sector funds were diverted to these ineffective programs.

If Americans find the present natural rate of unemployment to be higher than they would like, we possess the means to lower it. Freeing up labor markets, reducing union power, eliminating costly and counterproductive social engineering programs, and letting the chips of technological change fall where they may would go a long way toward ending the present mismatch between labor demand and labor supply.

The Unemployment Problem Is Overstated

The level of joblessness is overstated rather than understated. The overreaction to unemployment statistics has also directed attention away from recent positive employment developments. Even during periods of high unemployment in the recent past, the number of employed workers grew steadily. Since World War II, the market economy has exhibited less volatility and longer periods of expansion, thereby diminishing the severity of cyclical unemployment (Issue 1). In fact, since 1982, the American economy has experienced the longest, and second longest peacetime expansions on record. Likewise, unemployment resulting from structural changes has tended to be temporary, while the employment gains induced by such shifts in technology and patterns of production have surpassed the losses.

Finally, demographics have contributed to a lower natural unemployment rate. The Baby Boomers—who in sheer numbers contributed to a higher natural unemployment rate—are reaching retirement. The number of new entrants to replace these workers is comparatively small, and there are no signs that this trend will soon change. Already serious labor shortages are apparent in many regions of the country. These labor shortages will continue as the years pass. Indeed, a fair number of economists are arguing that policy makers and the public have the entire employment problem backward. The nation's long-term employment difficulties will be a matter of insufficient numbers of potential workers, not insufficient jobs. Lest this state of affairs be taken as a cause for rejoicing, we should remember that a smaller labor force, *ceteris paribus,* would also mean a smaller national output. Rather than worrying about how we can absorb the presently unemployed, we might be better served by figuring out how in the near future we intend to produce more with less labor.

THE LIBERAL ARGUMENT

Liberals also know that a natural rate of unemployment exists. To be precise, there is some level of unemployment that corresponds with a nonaccelerating inflation rate of unemployment (NAIRU). If the economy pushes beyond this level of unemployment, the demand for labor produces wage-rate increases in excess of productivity gains, and the general price level begins to rise. While the concept of NAIRU makes considerable sense, we are left with much uncertainty about what might be the precise level of unemployment that conforms to price stability. For example, in 2000, NAIRU was (by then at least) much lower than the near 7 percent many economists agreed upon in the early 1990s. Prices rose at an annual rate of 3.4 percent in 2000 (in other words, this was an acceptable, nonaccelerating price increase), but the unemployment rate had fallen to 4 percent, a thirty-one-year low. By the 2000s, revised estimates of NAIRU were in the upper 5 percent range. Unemployment in 2003 spiked at 6 percent while consumer prices had ebbed to a mere 2.3 percent annual rate, worrying policy makers that unemployment was too high and prices were not rising fast enough. Clearly, gravitating to some "natural state" for unemployment and inflation rates is less elusive in theory than it is in practice. Natural rate theory has been a lousy source of guidance to policy makers for more than a decade.

On the issue of unemployment, Conservatives continue to advance the argument that "everything works well so long as it works well and when it doesn't, don't do anything about it." Having argued earlier (in Issue 1) that cyclical (lack-of-demand) unemployment is self-correcting and unworthy of economists' attention, Conservatives continue to repudiate the available empirical evidence by contending that structural unemployment is also self-correcting. Such slavish commitment to the principles and processes of laissez-faire markets was perhaps possible a century ago. Yet, optimistic theorizing about ridding the economy of the adverse effects of policies to deal with unemployment caused by cyclical downturns, structural dislocations, labor market discrimination, and outsourcing is difficult to reconcile with the real distress imposed by the experience of unemployment.

The High Cost of Joblessness

In human terms, chronic unemployment erodes morale and self-esteem. Studies indicate that periods of prolonged unemployment destroy incentives and interest in work, even when the worker is later reemployed. Without employment, personal behavior patterns become erratic, leading to increased marital and family problems and greater child abuse. Unemployment also increases morbidity, mental illness, and crime. According to one study, a 1 percent increase in the unemployment rate will be associated with 37,000 deaths (including 20,000 heart attacks); 920 suicides; 650 homicides; 4,000 state mental hospital admissions; and 3,300 state prison admissions.* While it may be difficult (but not impossible) to put precise price tags on these human costs, we can measure the external or social costs of unemployment that result from (1) reduced tax collection, (2) rising unemployment insurance outlays, and (3) forgone production and sales. When all of these costs of permitting chronic unemployment are considered, the costs of special job programs to eliminate or reduce unemployment become insignificant.

A Historical Overview of Structural Unemployment

To understand the importance of structural unemployment, we need to put it in historical perspective. Beginning in March 1991, the American

---

*Barry Bluestone, Bennett Harrison, and Lawrence Baker, *Corporate Flight: The Causes and Consequences of Economic Dislocation* (Washington, DC: Progressive Alliance, 1981), 20.

economy underwent an unprecedented 120-month expansion. Unfortunately, unemployment rates rose after the recession ended and remained
high through 1995. A similar "jobless recovery" pattern has characterized the most recent recovery, which began in November 2001. Nevertheless, in both cases, unemployment was not the result of insufficient
demand; rather, it was the result of subtle institutional changes in the
American economy. The problems of unemployment require a new approach. Not only do we need policies to cure joblessness inflicted by
recessions, but we must recognize that some unemployment is a chronic
problem induced by a host of structural changes in the economy.

Since World War II, the American economy has enjoyed, with a few
brief interruptions, phenomenal economic growth; however, the expansion has produced important technological changes and regional economic shifts that have contributed to unemployment. Rising globalization
of industrial production aided by rapid growth in inexpensive information systems has given rise to the phenomenon of outsourcing jobs. The
demand for older jobs and skills has declined as new goods and production techniques have revolutionized labor. At the same time, the geographic distribution of manufacturing has been altered. Meanwhile, the
old employment bulwarks—steel, autos, and construction, for example—
are undergoing a deep structural decline, both as employers and as contributors to the nation's output, with no prospects for reversal. The result
has been to change the structure of labor markets.

Following are some examples of these structural shifts:

1. The continued decline in agricultural employment as farm production was increasingly mechanized.
2. The greater use of increasingly sophisticated technology in industrial production, thus reducing the relative demand for industrial labor in general and unskilled labor in particular.
3. The migration of many businesses and factories from the inner
cities to suburban locations, and out of the country.
4. The greater concentration of economic activity in large metro-
politan areas and the decline of employment in smaller cities.
5. The shift in the geographic location of industry to the West and
South as new industries grew up in these areas and old plants
left the industrial Northeast.
6. The sectoral shift in employment patterns as service industries and the government increased employment and the old

employers—in manufacturing, mining, and construction—declined. (In 1959, manufacturing, mining, and construction employed 36 percent of the workforce; by 2003, these industries employed less than 17 percent. Over the same period, service and government employment grew from 64 percent to over 83 percent of all employment.)

Across the nation, chronic structural unemployment was rooted in insufficient skills. Economic expansion or pumping up aggregate demand would not have much effect on an unemployed railroad worker in Altoona, Pennsylvania, an out-of-work miner in West Virginia, or an ex-steelworker in Gary, Indiana.

Changes in the composition of the labor force have added to the structural problems. Beginning in the 1960s, larger numbers of women began to look for work. Most of these new entrants possessed minimal skills and took, when they could get them, low-paying jobs in the service sector with little employment security. Many of the female job seekers were extremely immobile. Many were wives and mothers who had to seek work near their homes, which added a further restriction to their general lack of skills in obtaining work. Meanwhile, the entrance into the job market of the large number of people born in the post–World War II baby boom increased unemployment. As with women, many of the youthful job seekers did not meet the new employment demands. For urban, primarily black, youths, there were virtually no jobs at all. They had no desired skills and did not live near or have access to the few unskilled jobs available. As Figure 4.2 shows, the gap between blacks' and whites' employment opportunities has remained wide.

Automation, Outsourcing, and the Demand for Labor

The adverse impacts of inexperience, immobility, race, and sex upon labor markets diminished by the 1990s. Nevertheless, since then, the twin structural forces of automation and outsourcing have significantly changed the demand for workers in both manufacturing and the broader service sectors. In manufacturing, the basic "problem" is that very strong productivity growth has allowed American firms to produce more and more goods with fewer and fewer workers. Since the fourth quarter of 2001, manufacturing productivity has averaged almost 6 percent per

Figure 4.2   **Profile of the Nation's Unemployed, 1978–2003**

Source: Data from Bureau of Labor Statistics.

quarter (nearly twice the 1973–2000 average of 2.9 percent) while the high-wage jobs in manufacturing have steadily declined since 1998. The service sector has undergone similar transformations because of computerization, automation, and general technological change.

Since the end of the 2001 recession, much has been made of the growing threat to workers from "outsourcing," that is, the threat of job displacement emerging not from technology, but from the movement of jobs overseas. Global enterprises had long sought low-cost manufacturing havens in foreign nations. Job losses in the garment industry, television and electronic manufacturing, automobile assembly, motorcycles, household appliances, steel production, and much of the goods-producing sector of the economy set in gradually over decades. The pace of change in information technology blindsided many workers who had recently acquired what appeared to be highly valued skills in computing and management information systems during the technology boom from about 1993–2000.

Many back-office database management tasks and telemarketing projects among other things proved ripe for not just automation, but outsourcing to cheaper temporary workers, domestically and in other countries where the supply of workers possessing information systems skills is high and wages are low. Easy transmission of digitally encoded material has also made possible the outsourcing of medical diagnostics to freelance physicians around the world to read x-rays, examine slides of tissue samples, and offer consultative opinions. Even highly skilled, specialized service jobs can now be outsourced. The actual amount of employment that has migrated overseas is thus far a small fraction of the nation's 130 million jobs. But this ominous trend demands government policies that can provide for stable employment and income in the face of structural adjustments that continue to undermine good employment opportunities and confer joblessness on American workers.

A Liberal Program

As we have noted, structural unemployment and joblessness resulting from changes in the composition of the work force are not responsive to efforts to pump up aggregate demand. Instead, specific job-creating programs and protection for American workers are necessary to provide full employment. However, unlike the make-work measures of the past (such as the Works Progress Administration in the 1930s), these programs should not be mere Band-Aids. Since lack of skills is the primary cause of chronic unemployment, federal programs should be constructed to improve the employability of would-be workers.

Getting the jobless back to work through retraining and job-incentive programs produces real social savings. Initial program costs are quickly offset by the taxes the newly employed pay and by the reduction of social outlays directly related to their unemployed condition (that is, welfare and unemployment compensation). As demographic evidence indicates, the workers are needed to offset a serious shortage of labor in the not-too-distant future. Accordingly, it becomes all the more important to provide the training and discipline required for the chronically unemployed to become employable.

The Workforce Investment Act of 1998 represents the most recent variation of training and job-incentive programs. It is focused upon assistance to disadvantaged individuals, dislocated workers, and youth. The act ties grants for work investment programs to the establishment of "one-stop delivery systems" in local areas. These one-stop career centers consolidate information and core services of numerous governmental programs to provide counseling, job search assistance, training, performance appraisals of training programs, and other resources. Unfortunately, funding and operations are highly dependent upon state and local governments, a pattern reminiscent of the 1996 welfare reform. Consequently, the federal government is devolving a big part of its responsibility for implementation of employment policy onto the state and local levels. Liberals are concerned that this is yet another wrinkle in the Conservative strategy to shrink central government while gradually abdicating its obligation to full employment. Renewal of the Workforce Investment Act in the form of the Workforce Reinvestment and Adult Education Act of 2003 languished in a Senate committee into mid-2004. The 2003 bill also contained the Adult Basic Education Skills Act to continue state-sponsored adult education programs, and a reauthorization of the Rehabilitation Act of 1973 to help improve the employment prospects for disabled individuals.

Several job programs offer real opportunities for the so-called unemployables to join the labor force: youth programs, public service jobs, and wage subsidies.

Youth Programs

With unemployment among teenagers the highest of all groups (17.1 percent among white teenage males and 36 percent among African American or black teenage males,* compared to an overall 6 percent rate in 2003), youth unemployment demands special attention. The problem has grown worse since 2000. Teenagers account for about 14 percent of all the unemployed. Most teenage unemployment, especially among African Americans, is found in urban areas. Also, among the teenage unemployed there is a high educational dropout rate. Thus, employment programs for this group should be urban in focus and organized to encourage completion of public education. While learning useful skills, many youths will learn the workplace discipline that is necessary for retaining employment. A long-run improvement of youth unemployment problems is fairly certain as the past decade's declining birth rate makes itself felt in labor markets. The Department of Labor's Employment and Training Administration is charged with operating rather modest job programs to combat youth unemployment. Much of the effort is oriented at managing grants distributed to states to deal with improving employment prospects for youth. How well this has worked is unclear in the performance appraisals issued by the government. Combined with quite limited funding, one can conclude that commitment to addressing this problem is low.

Public Service Jobs

Beginning in 1973, the Comprehensive Employment and Training Act (CETA) instituted federal funding for local government hiring of public workers for limited employment periods. Rather than creating an overloaded federal bureaucracy, this approach allowed local communities to set and meet their own public service needs. Workers, meanwhile, obtained important on-the-job experience before their CETA employment ended in 1982.

By contrast, the Workforce Investment Act reoriented public policy in the direction of making the prospective trainee an informed "consumer" of training services with the hope of maximizing a successful transition to a good job. While laudable, this would be more effective if combined with on-the-job experience that could be supplied through greater availability of public service jobs. Unfortunately, the concept of publicly provided employment opportunities has fallen into disfavor. Customer service to the unemployed seems to have become the main

---

*Data represent changes in classification from "black and other" to "black or African American," reflecting changes in the Bureau of Labor Statistics data series beginning 2003.

priority of government agencies whose mission weighs more heavily on supplying information, cutting costs, and constructing performance indicators. A pleasant experience with the agency seems to have greater importance than actually reducing the unemployment rate.

Wage Subsidies

A third approach to chronic unemployment is to subsidize private sector employment of the unskilled. The bonus paid to private corporations is intended to offset the expected lower productivity of workers in this program. Somewhat paradoxically, Columbia University economist Edmund Phelps, credited with the development of natural rate theory, endorsed wage subsidies in his 1997 book *Rewarding Work.** The argument is that economical social engineering is obtained by "mainstreaming" the unemployed into the world of work through wage subsidies. In turn, the social costs of crime, drug abuse, welfare, medical care, and other burdens associated with unemployment are reduced by more than the expense of the subsidies.

THE RADICAL ARGUMENT

Both Conservatives and Liberals misunderstand the role of unemployment in a capitalist society. To the Conservative advocating a free market economy, there would be virtually no unemployment if the market were to work freely, that is, unimpeded by government action, labor unions, and so on. To the Liberal, unemployment is at least a periodic, and perhaps chronic, condition of capitalist economies, but it can be controlled by "enlightened" public policy. Neither position sees unemployment as central to capitalist organization, as necessary to the actual functioning of the system. The simple fact is that capitalism, regulated or unregulated, cannot help but create unemployment.

Unemployment: Capitalism as Usual

As capitalists accumulate and successfully translate past labor into what they see as profit-producing capital and investment, the need for an ab-

---

Edmund S. Phelps, *Rewarding Work: How to Restore Participation and Self-Support to Free Enterprise* (Cambridge, MA: Harvard University Press, 1997).

solute or growing volume of labor diminishes. This must be true by simple definition. The object of capital development is to increase production without increased (or with decreased) costs. Labor-saving machinery is cost-saving machinery only because labor is paid less per unit of output. More output can be obtained by employing more capital and less labor. Thus increased capitalization and technological growth, all things being equal, must produce growing surplus labor. This is the historical tendency of capitalism that is even confirmed in the official productivity and unemployment statistics over the past couple of years.

The growth of unemployment tends to be in recessionary clusters rather than in a steady, unbroken upward movement; however, the official unemployment rate has been trending upward over a long period (only recently and mildly reversed during the Clinton-era boom). Since the mid-1950s we have seen the official unemployment rate (itself a statistical understatement of the problem) move relentlessly higher even in comparatively good years. In other words, the percentage of the labor force in what Marx called "the reserve army of the unemployed" is constantly expanding. No doubt this unemployment would have been even higher in the past had government not pursued the expansionary policies. In fact, the situation has been getting progressively worse despite elaborate governmental efforts to hold down unemployment. Neither the free market nor Keynesian tinkering halts this tendency.

The failure of expansionary fiscal policy to deal with the problem of chronic unemployment is particularly evident if we go back to the tax cut of 1964. This was perhaps the first self-consciously Keynesian effort to use fiscal policy to reduce unemployment (then at 5 or 6 percent). The $11 billion Kennedy-Johnson tax reduction did spur business investment and increase national output. Between 1964 and 1966, investment increased by more than 22 percent—more than twice the rate of the previous two years. The gross domestic product (GDP) grew by 13 percent during the same period, compared to a growth rate of less than 10 percent in the earlier period. However, reported unemployment fell by only 900,000 between 1964 and 1966, despite the fact that government alone increased its payroll by 1.7 million persons. Thus any real reduction in unemployment came not from tax cutting à la Keynes but from good old government hiring.

An additional case against the supposed effectiveness of "full-employment" fiscal policy is the hyperexpansion of government spending that took place during the Vietnam War. Although government policy during the war may now be represented by Liberals as unintended and undesired (in other words, determined on political rather than economic grounds), it did not result in the employment growth that modern Keynesians associate with expansionary fiscal policy. Between 1966 and 1969, during the height of war appropriations, unemployment fell by less than 100,000. Meanwhile, direct government employment added an additional 1.6 million workers to public payrolls. Direct government hiring, not private sector job growth, brought unemployment rates down during the middle and late 1960s.

The point of these examples should not be misunderstood. Fiscal expansionism does create demand for workers. After the 1964 tax cut, during the Vietnam War boom, and after the 1981 Reagan tax cut, unemployment rates did fall a bit. But in each case, normal unemployment (what Conservatives euphemistically call the natural rate of unemployment) leveled off at a higher level: 3.5 percent in the mid-1960s, 5 percent in the early 1970s, and 7 percent or more in the mid-1980s. What was happening was that "full employment" was being achieved at successively higher levels of normal unemployment, with the pressures of an expanding economy having no useful effect on many workers who were falling out of the employable labor force altogether. Meanwhile, as we shall see below, the "improving" unemployment rates of the 1990s are a massive deception.

Capitalism Benefits from Unemployment

Political rhetoric to the contrary, the fact is that capitalism benefits from surplus labor—at least to a certain degree. Surplus labor usually forces wages downward or at least slows upward pressures. Workers compete with one another, and employers have a pleasant buyer's market. Even the prospects of important union wage gains are diminished by the competitive threat of the swelling ranks of unemployed. Recently, corporations have shamelessly used the specter of growing unemployment to force the labor union elite of the working class to sign new contracts with "givebacks." Wage gains and fringe benefits struggled for in the past were wiped out as rising unemployment weakened the unions' bargaining position. The old-line management bargaining tactic of "take it or leave it" was once again successful.

The declining rates of reported unemployment in the 1990s, at first glance, seem to suggest that the long upward trend in unemployment has been arrested. This is not so. First of all, the rising levels of employment mask the fact that a very large number of relatively high-paying jobs were lost in the 1970s and 1980s. Automation, downsizing, and the overseas flight of firms and jobs cut deeply into premium employment opportunities. The fact that average real wages in the United States are still below their 1974 levels illustrates the effect of such employment losses. Indeed, if a greater number of Americans are actually working (and we will address this data manipulation question shortly), a very large proportion of them are working at lower wages, and not uncommonly at more than one job. Ironically, on the same day in early 1998 that the Bureau of Labor Statistics reported a low 4.6 percent unemployment rate, the nation's largest charitable hunger relief agency released a study showing it had distributed food to 21 million needy individuals in 1997 and that 39 percent of these recipients were employed—about half of them working at full-time jobs.

Celebration of a lowering unemployment rate is a silly undertaking if reductions in joblessness have been accomplished through "spreading the work around" by dint of driving wages down and using part-time employment. Having a job one cannot survive on is cold comfort indeed.

Understating the Problem

Radicals are always amused by conventional economists' use of data in support of their ideological outlook. Perhaps no important set of statistics is more misleading than the official data that are released on American employment and unemployment. After figuring out how the employed and the unemployed are counted, one can see that official statistics always understate the size of the unemployment problem, whatever the general conditions of the economy.

Bad as it appears to be, our unemployment problem is really much worse than we realize because we understate the number of unemployed in at least three ways. First, the average annual rate does not show the number of people affected by some type of annual unemployment. For instance, in 2001 at least 16 million Americans experienced some involuntary unemployment during the year. Looked at this way, unemployment touched at least one in every ten American workers during the year. Even if an unemployed worker suffered only a week or two of lost labor, the effect on savings, retirement plans, and the educational hopes of the worker's children could be devastating. Second, our statistics tend to overestimate the actual number employed. In 2003, the "employed" included 24 million Americans who worked only part time. Such calculations expand the total employed category but do not show how slight their employment is. Third, official statistics do not indicate those who are socially underemployed from the standpoint of earnings. At least 6 million full-time workers earn wages below the official poverty income level. Fourth, the "unemployed" category does not include people who want a job, but have given up looking or made few attempts to find a job. No precise measures are available, but it is estimated that if this group were added to our known unemployment, actual unemployment in 2003 probably stood at about 7 percent rather than the reported 6 percent.

Deeper structural problems continue to plague the economy. Since the end of the last recession in November 2001, the official unemployment rate has fallen from about 6.3 percent to 5.5 percent. Unfortunately, the labor market remains in a severe slump as a result of an unprecedented two and half years of job losses despite positive GDP growth. Additionally, the lack of job growth combined with an expanding working-age population has created an employment deficit of about 7 million jobs.

It is important to understand not only the real size but also the composition of unemployment in the United States. Clearly, job possibilities are poorer if one is black, female, or young. This discrimination in employment is not surprising. It reflects the general contraction of labor markets and the resulting exclusion of newcomers. On one hand, such discrimination has served the system well, because many of the unemployed are not visible but hidden away in the ghetto or home. On the other hand, obvious discrimination of this kind creates considerable political development among the affected groups, who quite consciously and correctly see themselves as an exploited class. Liberals, aware of this tendency, have proposed make-work and on-the-job training programs aimed at quashing the discontent of the hard-core unemployed. But such programs have no long-run effect on improving employment. Undaunted by failure, still weirder twists in employment policy such as requiring the Employment Training Administration to devise ways to spend a portion of its budget to improve employment opportunities within the context of "faith-based initiatives" have emerged.

There is obviously a limit to how large the surplus labor army can grow—not just an economic limit but also a political one. Unemployment breeds contempt for the existing order and sows the seeds of revolution. Therefore, capitalism faces the constant problem of devising expensive legitimization schemes. Ironically, given our "soak the poor" tax structure, employed workers are increasingly burdened by taxes to support unemployed workers. This situation has so far only set workers against nonworkers, rather than uniting all against the system that oppresses them.

In any case, modern public policy can do little or nothing about the significant increase in the duration of unemployment, especially among older and higher educated workers. In 2003, about 22 percent of all unemployed workers had been out of work more than six months—a worse situation than in the previous four expansions. The blight of long-term unemployment took an unusual toll on two groups that should be prime workers in the labor force: college graduates and workers over forty-five years of age. Instead, they have been the most vulnerable with college graduates constituting 20 percent and workers forty-five years of age and older accounting for 35 percent of long-term unemployment. Thus, membership in the reserve army of the unemployed is not evaded because of skills, education, or even a proven track record in the job market.

Short-run manipulation and trade-offs with inflation (see the following issue) are possible, but the structural foundations of capitalist unemployment remain. Nor do special job-creating programs for the chronically unemployed offer a long-run solution. At best, they only buy a little time through deceptive but unfulfilled promises of future jobs. Small wonder that officials have no wish to tabulate all the unemployed. But their statistical manipulation does not change the historical tendency of capitalism.

Inflation

Can Price Pressures Be Kept Under Control?

The recognition that substantial inflation is always and everywhere a monetary phenomenon is only the beginnings of an understanding of the cause and cure of inflation.

—Milton Friedman, 1979

Future price levels and, hence rates of inflation should be reasonably predictable, a pattern that in practice requires the average rate of inflation to be low.

—Robert Barro, 1996

Thus inflation is unjust and deflation is inexpedient. Of the two perhaps deflation is, if we rule out exaggerated inflations such as that of Germany, the worse; because it is worse in an impoverished world to provoke unemployment than to disappoint the rentier.

—John Maynard Keynes, 1923

Prices are thus high or low not because more or less money is in circulation, but there is more money in circulation because prices are high or low. This is one of the principal economic laws, and the detailed substantiation of it based on the history of prices is perhaps the only achievement of the post–Ricardian English economists.

—Karl Marx, 1859

Lenin was certainly right. There is no subtler, no surer means of overturning the existing basis of society than to debauch the currency. The process engages all hidden forces of economic law on the side of destruction, and does it in a manner which not one man in a million is able to diagnose.

—John Maynard Keynes, 1919

The Problem

Inflation is understood by economists as a sustained rise in the general (or average) level of prices. For the uninitiated, such a phenomenon may not seem to be a particularly threatening event, especially if such a rise in prices is at least offset by an equivalent or greater rate of increase in personal incomes. In that kind of situation, *real income* (a person's price-adjusted purchasing power) is unaffected or even possibly rises, with the net result that no decline takes place in most citizens' standard of living.

Yet in the deeper recesses of accumulated human intellect, there abides a profound fear about inflation and its possible consequences. Possibly our receptivity to such recurrent anxiety goes all the way back to a more primitive time in human development. No worry could have been greater among our cave-dwelling ancestors than the possibility of some unpropitious event—bad weather, depredations by wild animals, invasions by hostile fellow humans, or similar occurrences—that denied cave dwellers access to their regular source of food supplies and also destroyed the family larder. In more modern times, humans have learned that price inflation under certain circumstances can produce precisely the same kind of personal predicament. When inflationary rates continue to rise rapidly, displaying runaway or hyperinflationary characteristics, they can quickly surpass any wage gains and wipe out family savings (the larder), producing destitution as great as any unfortunate cave dweller ever experienced.

Happily, the occurrence of such extreme inflationary episodes is not common, but these events are not easily forgotten either. For instance, the hyperinflationary episode that gripped Germany immediately after World War I (1918–23) still haunts European economic consciousness.

The German hyperinflation was brought on by the impact of the war and war-induced price increases, defeat and the imposition of war reparations, and finally a bankrupt central government that—unable to pay its own bills—resorted to turning on the printing presses and daily issuing (by the tons!) ever larger denominations of increasingly worthless, paper currency. The proportions of the hyperinflation that resulted were staggering and are difficult to grasp: Between peacetime 1913 and the armistice in 1918, the value of the German mark fell by 3,400 percent. Thus, it took 34 marks in late 1918 to purchase a commodity that sold for just 1 mark five years earlier.

By mid-1922, as inflation began to accelerate, the same 1913 product would have required an outlay of 24,000 marks. By the middle of 1923, six months before the collapse and reorganization of the German currency and financial system, it would have commanded a price of 1.4 billion marks. The astronomical rate of increase was, of course, somewhat cushioned by the fact that wages also increased at extraordinary rates, but not nearly as swiftly as prices advanced. German workers, paid no longer in pay envelopes but in cartons filled with bricks of paper currency, saw their real (inflation-adjusted) wages fall to about one-third of their prewar level by 1923. Near the end of the hyperinflationary experience, banks were paying 18 to 20 percent interest *per day* on savings accounts, but that was scarcely half the average daily inflationary rate.

The episode came to an end in late 1923 with the reformation of the German banking and monetary system, but not until most Germans had lost their savings and were forced to accept a drastically reduced standard of living. A few benefited from it all: Large landowners paid off their mortgages and industrialists their debts in inflation-devalued paper money and reconsolidated their power over the German economy. And, of course, the residual legatee of greatest gain during those awful years was Adolf Hitler and his Nazi Party, first gaining support from many Germans with their promise of building a "new order" in Germany and finally foisting on the world the pain and cost of Germany's hyperinflation in the form of humankind's bloodiest of wars (World War II). Small wonder that Europeans have a special fear of inflation.

While the American economy has never experienced anything like the European hyperinflation of the 1920s, persistent increases in prices remain a central concern of economic policy makers. Fifty years from now, when economic historians look back on the American economy of the late twentieth and early twenty-first centuries, they will surely remark on the great effort expended to both understand and control inflation. Taking a longer-term view of the problem, the thoughtful reader should recognize that persistent inflation has *not* been the norm in the long sweep of American economic development. In fact, *deflation*, or a fall in the overall level of prices, occurred during most of the nineteenth century and during the Great Depression of the 1930s. Nevertheless, the consequences of a systematic rise in overall prices are easy to grasp: Inflation reduces the purchasing power of money and the value of any financial asset that yields a fixed return. Moreover, inflation generally causes interest rates (the "price" of money) to increase as lenders try to hedge their losses by reducing their supply of loanable funds. With a reduction in the supply of bank loans, businesses find it more expensive to finance new plants and equipment; consequently they cut back on employment and output. In this way, inflation can have a very deleterious effect on the economy because it discourages investment and savings and introduces great uncertainty into the decisions of both firms and households. Thus, the problem of maintaining a stable price level has been a long-standing concern of both private and public policy makers. However, as with other economic phenomena, widespread observation does not imply a consensus as to its ultimate cause and cure. Before we explore the different explanations for inflation, it is important to grasp some of the patterns regarding long-term price fluctuations.

Looking back over the past two hundred years of American economic history, it is possible to identify specific periods when the rate of change in the aggregate price level fell (deflation), rose (inflation), or slowed (disinflation). Figure 5.1 shows how the aggregate level of retail prices—as measured by the consumer price index (CPI)—has performed.

Generally, stable or falling prices prevailed into the early part of the twentieth century. There was a notable acceleration in prices from 1911 to 1920, mostly associated with the inflation caused by World War I and the demand for military goods. Yet this was followed in the Roaring Twenties with a reversal in price movements.

The decade of the 1930s is mostly remembered for the protracted decline in national income, output, and employment, but it also was a time of falling prices. While a stable price level became a primary concern of the governments in most advanced industrial nations, one of the leading economists of the time, John Maynard Keynes, cautioned against the effects of persistent deflation. Prior to Keynes, conventional economic doctrine assumed that flexible prices would automatically cure any imbalance between supply and demand in particular markets or for the economy as a whole. Keynes opposed the logic of this argument by claiming that deteriorating economic conditions in the advanced industrial economies of the 1930s were not going to reverse themselves. If the capitalist system was going to survive the Great Depression, government actions that superseded the market—such as deficit spending to raise national income—were absolutely essential.

Government efforts to increase aggregate income through deficit financing have been widely credited with rescuing the stagnant capitalist economies of the 1930s. However, since the 1930s, price stability has been an elusive achievement for macroeconomic policy makers.

The great ungluing of the American economy after 1966 was due to a confluence of both domestic and international political economic forces.

136

Figure 5.1 **Consumer Price Index, 1800–2003**

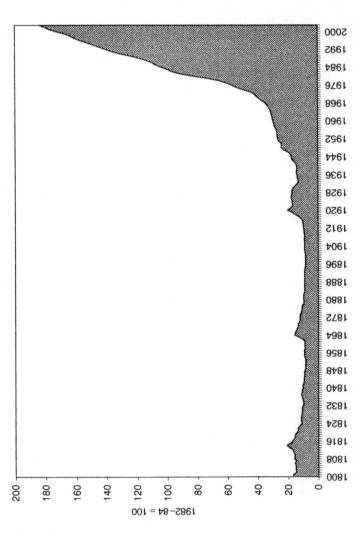

Source: U.S. Bureau of the Census, *Historical Statistics of the United States, Colonial Times to 1970* (Washington, DC: Government Printing Office, 2003) and data from the Bureau of Labor Statistics.

The persistent and accelerating rise in overall prices posed profound questions for conventional explanations of inflation. While it was generally believed by Keynesians that government tax and expenditure policies could always ensure a stable balance between inflation, employment, and output growth, by the mid-1970s the tried-and-true tools of macroeconomic policy had broken down. The unprecedented inflation of the late 1970s and early 1980s generated a backlash against Keynesian demand-side macroeconomic policies. America seemed demoralized by the lack of resolve on the part of policy makers to bring down inflation. Paul Volcker, chairman of the Federal Reserve, had spearheaded the attack on inflation by raising short-term interest rates to an unprecedented 19 percent, which induced one of the worst downturns in economic activity since the Great Depression of the 1930s. Volcker's strategy was to accept an economic slowdown as the price for bringing inflation under control.

Since the mid-1980s, inflation has been on a steady downward trajectory. Over the past decade, inflation has averaged about 2.5 percent, a trend that had not been experienced by Americans since the mid-1960s. History will judge whether this portends a return to the long-term tendency of only gradual increases in the overall price level, interrupted by short intervals of significant inflation. Currently, while measured inflation is low, there are several potential risks on the horizon, including the significant increase in oil and raw material prices that are by-products of both the Iraq war and China's demand for raw materials. The current challenge is to understand how recent experiences with inflation have shaped the logic of the different paradigms.

Synopsis

Inflation, from the Conservative perspective, is caused by a combination of government interference in the market and misguided attempts by the monetary authorities to manipulate the money supply over the business cycle. According to Conservatives, inflation can best be contained by eliminating excessive regulations, which raise the costs of doing business, and by keeping money supply growth at a pace commensurate with the long-run trend in output.

Liberals interpret the inflation record of the past quite differently, pointing out that random shocks over which economists had little or no control were largely responsible for the high inflation of the 1970s. The record low inflation rates of the past several years support the Liberal contention that responsible regulatory and fiscal policies, combined with a reasonably flexible monetary policy, will provide the economy with a solid foundation to ensure steady growth in output and employment.

For Radicals, inflation partly reflects the chaotic and uncontrolled nature of capitalist production itself, and the inherent conflict and struggle between capital and labor over the social surplus. Radicals recognize that while inflation can quickly destroy the livelihoods and savings of workers, current macroeconomic policies to control inflation are having the same effect. As long as the banking and financial system is controlled and run by the capitalist and rentier classes, workers will be forced to accept lower wages and living standards in the interest of achieving price stability.

Anticipating the Arguments

- Conservatives maintain that inflation is primarily caused by discretionary actions by the monetary authorities. Why do they claim that such policies are inherently inflationary?
- Why do Liberals believe that it is more important to maintain low interest rates than to worry about actual or expected inflation?
- Why do Radicals claim that financial institutions and finance capital will always try to keep inflation low at the expense of the working and lower classes?

THE CONSERVATIVE ARGUMENT

Americans learned a very costly lesson from the failed Keynesian fiscal and monetary policies of the 1960s and 1970s: Long-run prosperity cannot be ensured by government interference in the economy. Moreover, attempts by the Federal Reserve to manage the supply of money to accommodate a particular rate of gross domestic product (GDP) growth are destined to fail. What the 1980s amply demonstrated was that a sound monetary policy and reduced government regulations could yield strong growth, with low inflation and a rising standard of living for all.

Producers and consumers understand that government expenditures can result only in a higher level of prices because those are largely unproductive expenditures that do not contribute to the accumulation of profits. In addition, borrowing by the state to finance such spending *crowds out* private consumption and investment from the market. As we first learned from Adam Smith, profits are the source of new capital investment, which in turn determines an economy's rate of growth and standard of living.

While it is true that government spending programs can provide the economy with a temporary stimulus (e.g., hiring unemployed workers to clean streets), over the long run these activities do not add to national wealth. Finally, even public works programs to build bridges and schools must ultimately be funded by taxing businesses and workers.

A second lesson to be learned from the economic history of the past twenty-odd years is that government deregulation policies have had a salutary effect on price levels. Lower prices for airplane tickets and phone calls and higher rates of return on consumer bank accounts are just some of the benefits derived from deregulation efforts. Free and unfettered global competition has also been directly responsible for lowering resource prices, which has translated into lower prices for consumer goods. This has been a great benefit to consumers, equivalent to a significant tax reduction. However, low or zero inflation will become a permanent feature of the American economy only when *all* prices are allowed to be determined in free and open markets. Government can ensure a steady price level if it continues to encourage price competition and permits the market mechanism to be the final arbiter of the allocation, distribution, and production of goods and services.

On the other hand, government interference in a dynamic market economy will result in the inefficient allocation of scarce resources, which is the basic cause of inflation. For example, when the public sector either purchases goods or services and/or hires workers, it bids up the cost of land, labor, and capital. Similarly, any attempt by government to obtain loans to finance its deficit can only result in bidding up interest rates. Furthermore, when government engages in expensive and unnecessary construction and social welfare programs, it also drives up the price for scarce commodities and services. In this way the government sector "crowds out" private investment and spending and causes a general rise in the price level. Inflation and the expectation of further price increases (due to more public spending and debt issuance) become embedded in product, labor, and financial markets so that prices rise in anticipation of actual changes. This sets the stage for an upward spiral in prices that threatens to undermine the market system.

At this point it should be quite evident that price stability is also contingent upon limited government involvement in the economy. Just as important, most Conservatives believe, is a policy that only permits the money supply to grow at a constant rate. This principle, known as *monetarism,* presumes that there is a stable and predictable relationship between the amount of goods and services in the economy and the amount of money and credit required to produce, circulate, and consume them. Since a capitalist economy has a natural tendency to grow, persistent inflation must result when the money supply expands faster than real economic activity. Obviously, short-term disturbances in the production process, such as floods, droughts, and other weather-related factors, can cause a temporary rise in prices. Nevertheless, free markets have a profound capacity to adjust to such sudden shocks by eventually bringing supply and demand back into balance. Crucial to the maintenance of this balance is the one factor that should be controlled by government— the supply of money and credit.

Lessons from the 1980s

Inflation is one of the most regressive and punitive taxes because it reduces the purchasing power of those who are least able to resist or bear its effects: wage earners and retirees on fixed incomes. More than his program of tax cuts, Ronald Reagan probably will be most remembered for breaking the back of the high inflation that had gripped the American economy prior to his election in 1980. How did Reagan do it? By adhering to the basic tenets that undergird any successful free market economy: a sound monetary policy and reduced government interference in markets. Voters responded to the clarity and success of Reagan's inflation-fighting program by electing him to two successive terms. In the broadest sense, Ronald Reagan understood that attempts by governments to interfere in the economic decisions of private individuals would serve to distort the price system and bring on inflation.

Figure 5.2 shows that the policies of the Ronald Reagan and George H. Bush administrations were quite successful in fighting inflation. From 1982 to 1992 price increases averaged 4.0 percent, compared to 8.1 percent over the prior ten years. Thus, supply-side economic policies to deregulate the economy were quite successful in reducing persistent inflation and high interest rates. Conservative policies also provided a stimulus to the economy that far exceeded what could have been expected from a Keynesian tax-and-spend program. With many years of low inflation behind us, businesses are now more secure about future costs and revenues. Companies are able to operate at higher rates of capacity utilization and lower rates of unemployment relative to the 1970s because they are confident that inflation will remain sub-

Figure 5.2 **Measures of Inflation**

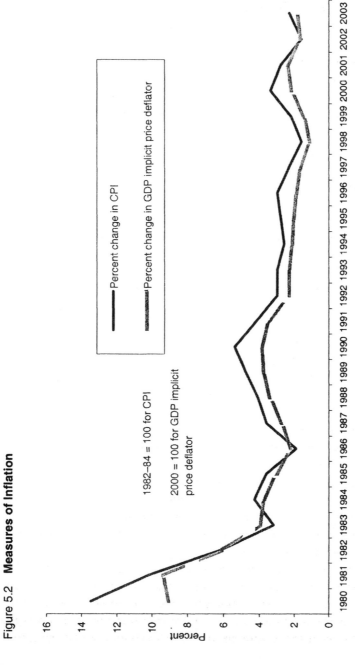

Percent change in CPI

Percent change in GDP implicit price deflator

1982–84 = 100 for CPI

2000 = 100 for GDP implicit price deflator

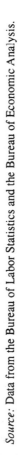

Source: Data from the Bureau of Labor Statistics and the Bureau of Economic Analysis.

dued. Moreover, lower interest rates were brought about by restrictive monetary policies to permanently wring inflation out of the economy. The resurgence in American manufacturing productivity has largely been due to cheaper long-term financing for new plants, property, and equipment.

Consumers and workers also have benefited greatly from the low-inflation policies of the previous decade. Housing is much more affordable because banks are once again comfortable with underwriting long-term mortgages at fixed rates of interest. There is also much less fear in the broader financial markets that inflation will eat away at the fixed stream of earnings from bond or mortgage portfolios. A low inflation environment has brought strong earnings growth to many corporations, and the surge in the rate of return from holding U.S. stocks is also largely due to the persistence of stable prices since the mid-1980s. In addition, the decline in interest rates on consumer loans to finance purchases of automobiles and consumer durables has been a key factor in maintaining overall growth. Once again, a stable price environment has allowed both lenders and borrowers to engage in profitable transactions that have facilitated consumption and increased the pool of private investment capital.

Keep the Lid on Inflation

Since the end of both the 1990–91 and 2001 recessions, there have been calls for a relaxation in the Federal Reserve's vigilance against inflation. While it is true that employment growth lagged behind other postwar recoveries, this was primarily because of fundamental changes in the structure of production and demand, which could not be easily influenced by changes in economic policy. For example, the globalization of production, foreign competition, and technological change have permanently changed the demand for labor in the U.S. economy. On balance, however, these changes are likely to keep the overall level of domestic price inflation low. This is because increased foreign competition from overseas workers is likely to restrain the growth in U.S. wages and salaries. Employment costs—which are generally a firm's largest expense—will also be tempered by rising labor productivity in the service sectors. For example, consumers are paying less for many services because the transaction costs of those activities have dramatically fallen over the past decade. Banking, insurance, retail, convenience food, and many other labor-intensive services have experienced notable improvements in the quality of delivery and production because of the widespread adoption of computers and new information technologies. Since the service sector now employs the vast majority of workers, the fight against wage-driven inflation will become increasingly dependent upon additional productivity-enhancing automation.

Finally, there is much evidence that historical price inflation—as measured by the government's Bureau of Labor Statistics (BLS)—has been greatly overstated. A couple of problems associated with the construction of the index are worth noting. First, the CPI was subject to a *substitution bias*—that is, it was not adjusted to reflect the fact that consumers could switch to lower-priced, substitute goods if the price of a particular product rose. In fact, the BLS used to *exclude* cheaper generic drugs from the calculation of the CPI although most health insurance programs required their customers to buy generics. Thus, price increases for pharmaceuticals propelled the entire CPI upward despite the fact that consumers might be able to dodge the higher prices by switching from brand-name medications to generic substitutes. Indeed, it is not possible to build a perfect CPI that will account for people switching to cookies if the price of doughnuts rises or resorting to video rentals if movie theater ticket prices increase.

Second, the CPI tracks the prices of a market basket of goods in a base year period. The quality of this market basket of goods can change considerably. Additionally, the actual market basket of goods varies as new products are introduced. For example, analog stereos progressed to superior multichannel digital systems, personal computers (once not even imagined as occupying the consumer's basket of goods) became faster, medical care improved, automobiles sport global positioning systems, and so forth. In short, it is difficult to tell if increases in consumer prices that are captured by the CPI reflect improved product quality or pure inflation. Given general improvements in product quality and changes in the composition of consumption purchases because of new and improved products, one can safely conclude that the CPI has tended to exaggerate inflation.

Relying on the CPI, the government overstated inflation in the past and at considerable cost to the economy. Wages, other resource prices and contracts often are tied or indexed to the CPI. In addition, taxpayers are burdened with unjustified cost-of-living increases for Social Security and other public sector expenditures that are also linked to overall change in the CPI.

Recognition of the defects in computing the CPI has prompted the development of adjustments to the CPI to correct for some of the substitution bias and account for the effect that improved quality has upon product prices. Conservatives agree with advocates who favor alternative indices, such as the GDP implicit price deflator shown in Figure 5.2, as better measures of the general level of prices and the pace of change in prices in the economy.

In sum, the Conservative program to fight inflation—deregulation of the economy and a responsible monetary policy—has proven to be quite successful. Critics would be well advised to reflect on the changes sweeping the world that favor free markets and reject government-dominated economies. Underlying the discontent with centrally planned socialist economies was recognition of their inability to maintain a reasonable standard of living for the common person. Out-of-control inflation during the early years of Russia's transition to capitalism is the most dramatic example of the fundamental failure of an economy previously organized along collectivist ideas. On the other hand, countries that rapidly embraced capitalist economic principles, such as the Czech Republic, Poland, and Hungary, experienced a dramatic decline in inflation and a simultaneous rise in per capita income. The emerging economic leaders of tomorrow realize that stable prices are essential for prosperity, and have readily adopted Conservative policies to ensure political and social success in the future.

THE LIBERAL ARGUMENT

It has become quite fashionable in recent times to lay the blame for most economic problems at the doorstep of Keynesian economics. With respect to inflation, most Conservatives argue that demand-side economic policies have an inflationary bias because they ignore microeconomic and monetary factors. It is further claimed that policies developed in the 1930s to fight economy-wide deflation, falling income, and output are no longer relevant or useful for a modern, globally oriented capitalist economy. According to the Conservative paradigm, inflation is mostly a monetary phenomenon that is best controlled by steady growth in the money supply.

While it is true that Keynes's economic policies were unquestionably influenced by the conditions of the Great Depression, Keynes never denigrated the importance of a stable price level to ensure growth and prosperity. Having observed the German hyperinflation of the 1920s, Keynes was well aware of the relationship between monetary factors and prices. It should also be remembered that Keynes had experience as both an academic and government economist, as well as serving as the president of a life insurance company. Thus he clearly understood the adverse impact that inflation has on financial assets with fixed returns. Indeed, Keynes was so concerned about understanding the interrelationships between production, finance, and money that he titled his most famous book *The General Theory of Employment, Interest, and Money.*

Since that book's publication in 1936, the advanced industrialized nations have had to grapple with numerous changes in the performance and structure of their respective economies. As we have seen, persistent gains in the overall price level did not become a widespread problem until the late 1960s. Prior to that time, the inflation record of demand-side policies compared rather favorably with the experience of the so-called supply-side era. For example, the average change in the CPI between 1961 and 1969 was 2.4 percent compared to the supply-side era's 4.0 percent. While Conservatives blame the expansionary fiscal policies of the Democratic Johnson and Kennedy administrations for stimulating inflation, it was during the Republican Nixon and Ford regimes that price controls were imposed in an unsuccessful attempt to suppress inflation.

Random Shocks and Structural Changes

The eruption of inflation during the 1970s and early 1980s was not, in fact, due to the failure of Keynesian stabilization policies. Rather, it was the result of a series of random events and structural changes that built an inflationary bias into the economy. For example, between 1971 and 1973, the Nixon administration attempted to devalue the dollar to ease worsening U.S. balance-of-payments problems (which were caused mostly by our Vietnam War spending). While American goods were more attractive in foreign markets because of devaluation, foreign goods became expensive to U.S. consumers. The result was that domestic prices of imported goods went up. In October 1973, the United States exported 19 million tons of wheat to the Soviet Union, substantially reducing American supplies of grain, resulting in higher food prices, especially for bread. Beginning in the 1970s, the oil-producing nations banded together in a cartel that effectively raised crude oil prices from less than

$2 per barrel in the early 1970s to nearly $40 by 1981, forcing all prices upward. Inflationary pressures were also being generated by the slow-down in labor productivity as a result of lagging investment and the influx of a growing cohort of younger and more inexperienced workers into labor markets.

These inflationary shocks and pressures created a general inflation-ary psychology: Since people *expected* prices to rise, they quickly bought up currently available goods in the market. This had the effect of *realizing* those expectations. Each event seemed to support the view that prices would continue to go up. These expectations of future in-flation induced both labor unions and businesses to act to protect them-selves from future inflationary shocks. Wages and prices began to go up even faster than the rise caused by the random inflationary events. The effect of this general inflationary increase, which caused the CPI to more than double between 1970 and 1980, was to lower consumers' real purchasing power. The "inflation tax" reduced the spendable in-come of ordinary consumers and businesses, and aggregate demand fell. With falling demand and slowing economic growth, there was an accompanying rise in unemployment.

To many Liberals, the situation called for capping inflationary in-creases by some use of price controls while maintaining employment and growth through appropriate fiscal policy. This was not to be the case. Democratic president Jimmy Carter's efforts at voluntary wage-price guidelines, in 1978 and 1979, were a complete failure. At the same time, expansionary efforts to reduce unemployment were blocked by Conservatives who had decided that inflation was the biggest problem and who wrongly concluded that inflation was the result of past fiscal policy excesses.

The Monetarist Program of the 1980s

The central disagreement that Liberals have with Conservatives regard-ing the attainment of a stable price level involves two distinct issues: the role of monetary policy and how to cope with the changing structure of the economy. First, the Conservative fixation on steady and predictable growth in the money supply to guarantee a stable price level will be shown to be without merit. Second, the traditional relationship between inflation and unemployment has also been undermined by recent eco-nomic history, as steady declines in real average hourly earnings have not brought the economy to full employment. Indeed, technological change, global competition, and greater income inequality have exerted powerful downward pressures on prices, wages, and income. With fiscal policy paralyzed by political gridlock and an unreasoned fear of federal deficits, the responsibility for macroeconomic coordination lies squarely in the hands of the chairman of the Federal Reserve Board (the Fed). Nevertheless, the preoccupation of the monetary authorities with fighting *past* bouts of inflation has led to its imposition of unnecessarily high interest rates. This policy of *tight money* continues to act as a powerful restraining force on aggregate growth.

The Conservative program for maintaining a stable price level assumes that economic growth is primarily determined by the growth in the money supply. That is, the central bank should fix money supply growth at a rate that is consistent with the economy's long-run potential for growth. Milton Friedman, who has been the foremost proponent of monetarism, has argued that we should eliminate the Fed and replace it with a computer that allows the money supply to grow at a fixed rate. By 1980, with inflation raging, monetarism was given a perfect opportunity to rescue a stagnant and listless economy. Ironically, during the 1980s, when inflation was being subdued, money supply growth was accelerating into the double-digit range. While monetarism has not been totally discredited, no less an authority than the Federal Reserve Bank of New York acknowledged the breakdown in the relationship between the growth in the money supply and the rate of inflation.

While one might have thought that the 1980s would have settled the question of the best monetary theory and policy, unfortunately political and economic realities interfered. The basic political problem confronting Reagan's administration was how to pay for promised tax cuts, increase military spending, and balance the federal budget. In order to carry out his program, Reagan needed the Fed's cooperation. At that time, the Fed had been pursuing an extremely tight monetary policy, which caused interest rates to rise while output and employment declined. The recession of 1982 quickly quelled inflation, but the unemployment rate reached nearly 11 percent, a level not seen since the Great Depression of the 1930s.

With the nation in deep recession in late 1982, Reagan sought to jump-start the economy by increasing defense expenditures and reducing taxes. The tax cuts, combined with very strong money supply growth (courtesy of the Fed), stimulated economic activity and set the conditions for a recovery. Monetarist theory notwithstanding, interest rates continued to move downward through the mid-1980s, precisely as both the money supply and the federal deficit were exploding. While monetarist theory would have predicted severe inflation, perhaps even hyperinflation, disinflation (a slowing in the growth rate of overall prices) actually persisted while employment and output proceeded to expand until mid-1990. As the economy moved into the mid-1980s and beyond, it became evident that there was little relationship between money supply growth and retail inflation (as measured by changes in the consumer price index). Moreover, by the late-1990s inflation exhibited an *inverse* relationship to money supply growth.

For all of his Conservative beliefs and contrary to the picture that Conservatives portray, Ronald Reagan followed a textbook Keynesian policy of *easy money* and tax cuts to move the economy out of a recession. Had the Fed's monetary policy not been as "accommodating" (letting the money supply expand to absorb the demand generated from a rising budget deficit), it is doubtful that Reagan's fiscal policies would have provided enough stimulus to prevent a recession. Moreover, the Reagan administration's approach of very rapidly growing the federal deficit was a crucial, yet unheralded, component of its political success. Thus, it is clear that monetary and fiscal coordination between the government and the Fed often plays a vital role in determining the macroeconomic performance of the U.S. economy.

Managing Inflation in the Here and Now

Monetary policy has drifted away from targeting the money supply. In recent years, the Federal Reserve seems to have aligned with, but does not formally acknowledge the use of, the "Taylor Rule." Conceived by Stanford University economist John Taylor, short-term interest rates are the principal focus. They are manipulated to achieve a desired balance, or acceptable trade-off, between full employment and long-run inflation rates. This view operates from the perspective that *some* level of inflation is both a normal and necessary characteristic of an expanding economy. Policy makers are spurred to raising short-term interest rates when existing rates entice borrowing that threatens to allow inflation to exceed an estimated target that is consistent with full employment. On the other hand, if actual GDP were falling short of the potential GDP (full employment), monetary policy makers would pursue a lower interest rate strategy as long as it is consistent with the long-run inflation target.

The fact that some variant of Taylor's Rule seems to guide policy making is not really a revelation to anyone's thinking about how short-term interest rates might be altered to fight inflation or to counter an economic slump. The key is that the Conservative-favored monetary rule does not dominate the scene when it comes to managing inflation in the real world. Analysis of modern policy making acknowledges that policy makers form preferences about how much deviation in inflation and output will be tolerated before they *act* to counter an ominous turn in economic conditions. Thus, the "rule" of contemporary monetary policy is really a matter of when to exercise discretionary intervention, not a matter of avoiding intervention.

While the American economy faces potential inflationary pressures, it is unlikely to accelerate to an unacceptable pace. The globalization of production, increased energy efficiencies in both homes and businesses, and productivity gains from the widespread use of computers have helped and will continue to help, keep inflation in check. On the other hand, the record of the Fed has not been good in promoting balanced economic growth over the past several years. The Fed increased the short-term interest rate on lending between banking institutions (the federal funds rate) to 6.5 percent throughout 1999–2000 based upon what proved to be an unfounded fear of potential inflation. However, with unprecedented speed the Fed resorted to a striking reversal of policy when confronted with the very real prospect of recession, the destabilizing impact of the terrorist attacks of September 11, and a growing fear of *deflation*. Thirteen successive interest rate cuts dropped rates to 1 percent by June 2003. The federal funds rate remained at a 45-year low, which helped to lower mortgage costs and fuel the rapid rise in home ownership. By June 2004, the Fed raised short-term rates by 1/4 percent, thus beginning another round of successive rate increases to stave off inflation. Much to the chagrin of Conservatives, activist policy is alive and well.

THE RADICAL ARGUMENT

Central to Marx's economic critique of capitalism is his perception of the inherent tendency in capitalism toward ever greater instability. Marx expected violent fluctuations in output, employment, and prices to be the necessary outcome of increased competition and struggle between firms. Driven to realize ever-greater amounts of profit on an ever growing scale of production, businesses must employ any means necessary, including price cutting, price gouging, sabotage, and fraud, to destroy their competitors. Persistent intra- and interindustry warfare results in greater macroeconomic instability. For Radicals, the historical record of price movements in the United States reflects both the incredible development of the forces of production and their growing incompatibility with the needs and social relations of working people. As we have seen, Conservatives and Liberals view the recent success at fighting inflation to be the result of decisive Federal Reserve actions, deregulation, increased foreign competition, and technological change. In contrast, Radicals would argue that the persistence of high *real* interest rates and a declining *real* wage lie at the core of capitalists' macroeconomic policy efforts designed to achieve price stability on the backs of the working people in America.

Inflation versus Unemployment: The False Trade-off

Rather than being simply a macroeconomic goal, Radicals argue that the traditional means employed by both Conservatives and Liberals to fight inflation have ended up destroying the livelihoods and living standards of the vast majority of workers. Bankers and financiers understand price stability to mean *no* increase in the overall price level (literally, 0 percent inflation). To ensure this goal, a nonelected body of elite managers of the monetary system—the Federal Reserve System—is granted nearly total control over the economy. This group is not concerned if their policies require interest rates to rise and stay at levels that result in high unemployment and falling wages. Their sole objective is to make sure that prices do not rise so that they might preserve the value of bond and mortgage portfolios held by financial institutions. To do this, the Federal Reserve had to maintain high inflation-adjusted interest rates throughout the 1980s and 1990s.

The destruction of America's industrial heartland and, with it, thousands of high-paying manufacturing jobs was largely the result of Conservative policies to reduce inflation through tight monetary policies and an avowed antiunion stance. The data convincingly demonstrate the "success" of the supply-side programs of the 1980s, which brought about unprecedented high real interest and thus destroyed the manufacturing sector and its workforce. This period also began with Reagan's busting of the air traffic controllers' union (PATCO), which not only set the tone for future labor relations but also was hailed as the first victory by Conservatives over inflation.

Of course, the broader objective was to reduce overall labor costs by breaking the power of unions to impose wage demands or to organize and bargain in a collective fashion. This is particularly important to capitalists as they invest in new service-based sectors where labor expenses make up a relatively larger share of total production costs. Although services are also generally much more labor-intensive than manufacturing industries, they have proved to be rather susceptible to productivity gains from automation and mechanization. Given these structural changes in the economy, it is no wonder that Conservatives believe that price stability can be achieved only by repressing labor costs and pursuing virulent antiunion policies. In fact, the recent official government data on falling unit labor costs confirm the success of these policies. Furthermore, it is essential that advanced capitalist economies maintain what Marx termed a "reserve army" of unemployed workers who are always willing to work at wages below prevailing norms. While Liberals may say they wish to return to the full-employment/high-wage era of the mid-1960s, Radicals realize that this is impossible under the present rules governing our economic system. What's more, even though the U.S. economy experienced unprecedented low unemployment during the late 1990s, real average hourly wages have continued to decline. Unlike the prediction of supply-and-demand theory, an increase in the demand for labor has not been accompanied by a concomitant rise in the real wage. Finally, while the Fed is obsessed with peremptorily restraining wage growth, it will do nothing to stop a real inflationary threat: the 20 percent gain in corporate profits over the past two years. This only further confirms the inherent class bias in monetary policy in the service of corporate and banking interests.

Even if workers are able to exert political pressure to restore some of their lost earnings (e.g., by increasing the minimum wage), their efforts are likely to be overwhelmed by the efforts of government and corporate leaders to maintain a stable price level by exposing American workers to greater global competition. Radicals clearly recognize that free trade agreements such as the North American Free Trade Agreement (NAFTA) and the globalization agenda of the World Trade Organization (WTO) seek to encourage capital mobility across borders. While supporters of increased foreign competition claim that it will make American industry more competitive and efficient, the effect on workers will only be lower wages and fewer jobs. Importing cheap foreign goods may serve to check inflation, but the continued globalization of domestic production will lead to a reduction in the standard of living for most wage and salary earners.

Inflation, the Fed, and Class Interests

Capitalism's past and recent experiences with inflation have not been good for the vast majority of working people. As has been noted, high rates of inflation create a sense that the economy is out of control. This undermines confidence in politicians and political institutions. During such periods of turmoil, people often become willing to accept reactionary or authoritarian regimes that promise to get inflation under control. Imposing harsh reductions in government services, employment, and social spending, combined with "sound" (i.e., tight) monetary policies that create high interest rates and result in high unemployment, is the typical means used by repressive governments to bring inflation under control. Chile, Argentina, Brazil, and Poland have all employed such tactics with the active support of the World Bank and the International Monetary Fund. While these actions hurt the working poor and middle class the most, political elites, foreign creditors, and upper classes generally applaud these oppressive measures.

Inflation was not a threat in the 1990s, but the Fed aligned monetary policy with the interests of banks and the financial services industry by keeping real interest rates high to maintain the incomes of creditors and speculators. The high costs of borrowing increasingly burdened working people to the point where bankruptcies and nonperforming loans produced a worrisome state of affairs. Not until the stock market began to exhibit clear signs of downturn in 2000, jolting the intoxicated casino mentality of the financial elite, did the Fed act to lower interest rates. Financial institutions, brokerage firms, mutual funds, and globalization advocates applauded the aggressive interest rate cutting undertaken by, the Fed through the spring and summer of 2001.

Then came the terrorist attacks on New York and Washington on September 11, 2001. On the heels of a slowing economy, Wall Street reacted as if the events were nothing less than catastrophic and the plunge in the stock market spurred the Fed to action with more interest rate reductions. Ironically, the economic calamity facing working people for the preceding decade had received no attention from the Fed. Interest rates were held at unnecessarily high levels to fend off inflation. Only when the financial sector began to have trouble did the Fed forsake anti-inflationary regimen.

Long-term price stability should be an important part of the Radical economic policy agenda. Liberals are soft on fighting inflation because they instinctively associate its cure with the repressive policies of Conservatives. They miss the point that a more humane program must be offered. The core of such a program would seek to change the balance of financial power in the American economy away from large creditors such as banks and insurance companies and toward workers and small businesses. Put simply, since bankers and bondholders prefer slow growth and tight monetary conditions to fend off any hint of inflation, they will always endorse central bank policies that result in unnecessarily high real interest rates and unemployment. What's more, bank presidents also sit on the board of directors of most of the twelve regional Federal Reserve banks and their views strongly influence Fed policy. Thus, the goal of a Radical program for stable prices should seek to create a single worker-controlled and state-owned bank, the nationalization of financial markets, and the mandatory distribution of equity rights in all corporations to workers.

Equity and Price Stability

Ensuring a stable price environment cannot be left to the unelected monetary authority of the Fed, the financial markets, or politicians. As the industrial and financial structure of the American economy becomes increasingly concentrated and centralized, the threat of increased inflation because of monopoly pricing power intensifies. Currently, there is no governmental or public institution exerting a meaningful challenge to the growing economic and political power of large financial corporations. As their power and influence grow, the monetary and political authorities will continue to bend to the dictates of financial capital. Furthermore, the current structure of the Fed provides negligible oversight from Congress: Its budget is immune from congressional appropriations and its primary decision-making body—the Federal Open Market Committee (FOMC)—is vested with too much power over the lives of Americans.

While reforming the Fed would be an important first step, a more important change would be to abolish the distinction between commercial and central banking so that a worker-controlled state-owned bank could be responsible for all banking transactions. Such an institution would be first and foremost concerned with the social consequences of fighting inflation, and represent the interests of average Americans and not bankers and their wealthy constituents. A central bank operated and controlled by working people would allocate investments where they are most needed—low-income housing, day care, and child health care facilities—and away from unproductive activities such as speculation in commercial real estate and the stock market. Moreover, various groups devoted to community purposes could be organized around local branches of publicly owned banks. These local and regional banks would take in all deposits and make low-interest loans to enterprises in their respective communities.

Finally, in order to guard against excessive asset inflation, financial markets would have to be nationalized and heavily regulated. In addition, there would have to be a mandatory distribution of equity rights to all employees. This would have the effect of redistributing ownership and power to workers and making sure that their interests were considered before the narrow interests of corporate managers. With a democratized financial structure, the investment environment would be much more conducive for long-term investments in productive ventures that provide the goods and services needed by the vast majority of people while simultaneously employing large numbers of workers.

In sum, inflation must be understood as the natural outcome of the irrationality of an economy organized along the principles of capitalist competition. Inflation, whether generated by price gouging, financial speculation, or the production of socially useless goods, is part of a broader economic logic that subordinates the needs of people to profit and greed. The continuing decline in real wages demonstrates that inflation is *not* the result of overpaid workers, although workers are sure to suffer if inflation flares up again. To that end, price stability can be assured only if the operations of the financial system are directed by public institutions that are accountable to the working people of America. Furthermore, there must be a radical reorientation of both private and government resources into investments that will raise the living standards of average wage earners.

The New Population Problem

Can We Save Our Social Security System?

Among our objectives I place the security of men, women
and children of the nation first. . . . Hence I am looking for
a sound means which I can recommend to provide security
against several of the great disturbing factors in life—
especially those which relate to unemployment and old age.
—President Franklin D. Roosevelt, June 8, 1934

All in all, Social Security is an excellent example of
Director's law in operation, namely, "Public expenditures
are made for the primary benefit of the middle class, and
financed with taxes which are borne in considerable part by
the poor and the rich."
—Milton Friedman, 1980

Cutting back on benefits will undermine people's faith in the
integrity of the whole system—they will feel double-crossed.
—Wilbur J. Cohen, former Health, Education,
and Welfare official, 1981

The retirement of the Baby Boom generation will double
the number of retirees. . . . The timing of their retirement
will affect the composition and the productivity of the
workforce. The increased number of retirees will have an
impact on the costs of entitlements, including increased
retirement benefits, and a labor shortage with fewer
workers to fill existing positions.
—Patricia P. Pine, Ph.D., New York State
Office for the Aging, 2004

The Problem

Among the first macroeconomic concerns pondered by economists was the possible connection between the size of a nation's population and the general well-being of its people. Looking at the world at the end of the eighteenth century, the great British economist, Thomas Malthus (1766–1834), concluded that population growth would sooner or later impose important restrictions on human progress. Based on available evidence, Malthus and his disciples concluded that starvation would be a permanent and ultimate check on population growth and the fortunes of most of the human species.

This was so because populations had the capacity to expand geometrically (1, 2, 4, 8, 16 . . .) while agricultural output (food) could only expand arithmetically (1, 2, 3, 4, 5 . . .). In point of fact, the dark Malthusian world never materialized. To be sure, starvation indeed would raise its ugly head across the globe from time to time but according to evolving economic wisdom, such events were local concerns and nothing that a rapid increase in agriculture productivity could not cure.

In a mostly unexpected way, however, the contemporary American economy finds itself confronted with a new population problem. The dilemma does not arise out of the sheer numbers of its population, but rather from the numbers of that portion of its population that have entered, or are about to enter, their postemployment years. Put simply as a question, the problem is: How and what resources can be provided for sustaining the increasing proportion of the society that, by virtue of age or disability, no longer contributes to national income?

Long an institution and a federal budgetary outlay that has enjoyed immense popularity, America's Social Security system is on the verge of becoming an enormously divisive issue that pits the younger working population against a growing population of elderly citizens. To understand the roots of the generational crisis that promises to threaten the American program of Old-Age, Survivors, and Disability Insurance (OASDI), it is perhaps informative to tear a page from natural history before turning to concrete political and economic realities.

The North American beaver is a prolific and industrious mammal that lives in highly social communities. "Busy as a beaver" is a well-known euphemism, the roots of which acknowledge the fact that this single-minded and disagreeable little animal stands second only to human beings among warm-blooded creatures in its physical alteration of the natural landscape.

Like human beings, beavers are also subject to aging and infirmity and the probable accompaniment of diminishing capacity for work. Accordingly, a situation develops in which the old beaver's output—measured in cutting and collecting sapling boughs and carrying on maintenance of the dam and the lodge—is less than the inputs needed to sustain the oldster. The growing gap between the old beaver's contribution to the colony and the colony's cost in sustaining the old fellow becomes immediately apparent when the food supply (for whatever reason) dwindles to the point where the young beavers and the community itself are in danger of starvation. The oldster is driven out, and the old beaver swims downstream. If lucky enough to reach a river or a lake, he will take refuge in an abandoned burrow and spend his remaining time gnawing on the very tough trunks of large trees and on freshly fallen branches until extinguished by starvation or a predator.

The *beaver solution* represents one social and economic approach to the process of aging. Brutal as such a solution may seem to contemporary human beings of civilized pretensions, the beaver solution remains the only sure-fire cure for societies suddenly overwhelmed by age-based dependency problems. *And* it is a model to which human cultures have turned from time to time if the community itself was to survive.

The urgent demographic problem of the United States (and a great many other countries) and the urgency for coming to terms with the costs that an aging population imposes on the larger society simply cannot be ignored. Failure to tackle this problem in humane and rational ways means that some variation of "the beaver solution" will (must) inevitably evolve.

Until the twentieth century, the existence of a large elderly and postemployment population was rarely viewed as an economic problem. The principal reason was not a matter of voluntary charity but rather reflected mortality statistics. As late as 1920, the average life expectancy at birth in the United States stood at 53.6 years for men and 54.6 years for women. It is no overstatement to say most of the population "worked until they died" and the handful of others who survived a few years between work and death passed their time in a relative's home or in sordid public facilities. From the perspective of public policy, America had no program for the elderly other than individual adaptations of the beaver solution.

In the 1930s, however, the problem of the dependent elderly could no longer be ignored. People were living longer and well past the years where they could find, given their accumulating disabilities, employment. A few industries, such as the railroads, had been forced by labor unions to provide retirement benefits, but most American retirement programs were developed long after the creation of the Social Security system.

In any event, when the bottom fell out of the American economy after 1929, unemployed old folks with few or no sources of income (since their kids were out of work too) were finally recognized as a social and economic problem that was not going to go away even after the Great Depression. In 1935, at the urging of President Franklin D. Roosevelt, Congress passed the Social Security Act.

In truth, the original act was not a particularly grand commitment. It compared poorly with old age and disability plans in place in most western European nations, some of which had been operating for forty years or more. Under the 1935 act, eligible workers would contribute to a fund one-half of 1 percent (matched by an equal employer contribution) of the first $3,000 of annual earnings. It was estimated the first wave of recipients would receive from $10 to $85 per month from the Social Security Administration upon reaching age sixty-five (which was three years beyond the then existing life-expectancy of males). From the beginning, the OASDI program was not an insurance program at all. It was, and never really changed from, a "pay-as-you-go" financing arrangement. When OASDI went into effect in 1938, only about 42 percent of American workers qualified for participation—modest beginnings, indeed, for the most popular social welfare program ever introduced in the United States.

Over the years OASDI grew. In 1940, the 78,000 retired workers eligible to receive Social Security checks got an average $22 per month; 30,000 retired workers "with aged wife" averaged $36 per month and widows with children under age fourteen got checks averaging $35 per month. By 1950, the average monthly benefit check climbed to $59, reached $125 in 1970, and shot up to $382 by 1980. In 2003 the average monthly Social Security check was $922. If adjusted for inflation, the increase in benefits-paid tarnishes a bit, but not enough to dim the fact that great numbers of older Americans enjoy a standard of living scarcely dreamed of a half century or even a quarter century ago. With the addition of Medicare, to cover a substantial share of seniors' medical costs in the mid-1960s, it was evident America had abandoned the beaver solution.

However, an increasingly important question remained to be answered: Could the nation pay for its beneficence to its elderly? There was, after all, the enormous generation of Baby Boomers (over 70 million of them) who would start drawing on their Social Security benefits somewhere around

2010. By the 1980s, a lot of economists and politicians began to argue that the Social Security system had serious long-term funding problems, and, in 1984, some modest but important changes in the administration of system accounts deferred (but did not eliminate) doomsday scenarios.

By 2003, a number of Bush administration studies "proved" (at least to the administration's satisfaction) that short of *immediately* raising the federal income tax rate by 69 percent, raising payroll taxes (OASDI contributions) by 95 percent, cutting Social Security benefits by 45 percent, *or* some combination of the preceding, *and* holding the line on these changes through 2075, OASDI insolvency was a long-term certainty. Interestingly though, fully 80 percent of the $45 trillion "fiscal gap" (the difference between projected outlays and projected Social Security receipts) that would pile up by 2075 if no action were taken, would come directly from projected Medicare outlays. For the record, $45 trillion is "serious money"—about equal to the private net worth (assets minus liabilities) of all Americans, about seven times the size of the present federal debt, or four times as large as 2004 gross domestic product (GDP).

The fact that so much of the fiscal gap derives from Medicare reveals a problem not much considered until recently: More people are getting older . . . and older. Average life expectancy at birth today is seventy-six (it was sixty-two in 1935 and sixty-eight in 1945, about the time the Baby Boomers started arriving). But once you reach considerable age, modern medicine—at considerable cost—continues to increase life expectancy. Between 1985 and 1995, the death rates of those aged eighty to eighty-four fell by 8 percent.

In any event, America is a swiftly aging society in which maintenance of the elderly will lay an increasing claim upon national output. Presently, Social Security and Medicare outlays amount to 7 percent of GDP. Even after placing a freeze on benefits, a recent Congressional study estimates, this share will rise to 15 percent by 2037 and to 22 percent by 2075.

The problem is not one without solutions, but no solution is painless:

1. increase the eligibility age for benefits
2. increase the Social Security tax burden on those paying into the system
3. increase general (income) tax collections to fund pay-as-you-go outlays
4. lower the outlays paid to Social Security recipients
5. drop the system as it exists altogether and fashion something new.

The nation faces some tough choices.

Synopsis

Conservatives maintain that the defenders of the Social Security system have fraudulently promised elderly Americans a retirement income that simply cannot be afforded by the nation. Meanwhile, the very concept of an "involuntary" Social Security program erodes individuals' rights and operates as a drag on the entire economy in its discouraging of private savings. Liberals respond that Social Security is both a solemn promise and the only protection that many have from abject poverty in their declining years. Liberals also maintain that the fear of the Social Security system going bankrupt is a pure scare tactic used by its opponents. Radicals see the eventual sacrificing of Social Security as an illustration of the fiscal crisis confronting government—an inability to provide both outlays that benefit capital and expenditures for people's needs. Thus, Social Security and other social outlays must be constantly reduced.

Anticipating the Arguments

- On the basis of what evidence do Conservatives maintain we cannot "afford" the Social Security program?
- How do Conservatives and Liberals disagree on the question of an individual's responsibility and choice in the matter of providing for retirement?
- Why do Radicals believe that the growing attack on the Social Security system really masks a fundamental problem in state financing? What do they see as the cause of this problem?

THE CONSERVATIVE ARGUMENT

As with most social programs, Social Security is an excellent example of how Americans have been deluded and manipulated since the incipient drift toward welfare statism began under Franklin Roosevelt. Ironically, most Americans simply do not understand that Social Security and other "giveaway" programs are pushing the national economy to the brink of disaster. It is not simply a "type" of program that Conservatives oppose for philosophical reasons. The opposition is based on simple economic sense: There is no such thing as a free lunch. And the cost of the Social Security banquet, despite its immense popularity, is prohibitive.

Myth versus Reality

The managers and political supporters of the Social Security system have created a number of self-serving myths about their programs that persist in spite of common sense and overwhelming evidence to the contrary. Perhaps the most enduring myth is that Social Security is merely a pension program, in which government holds tax payments in a pool and then pays them out on an actualized basis, just as a private pension insurance company would. Even a catchy and inventive TV commercial on behalf of the Social Security system a few years ago perpetuated this belief when it announced: "It's your money!" Nothing could be further from the truth. The insurance-fund approach to the Social Security system was abandoned long ago. What remains of the old funds (Old-Age Survivors Insurance Trust Fund, Disability Insurance Trust Fund, and Medicare Trust Fund) will be exhausted in the near future. The fact is that Social Security is operated on a pay-as-you-go basis; consequently, next to nothing is accumulated. Any surplus funds must be used to purchase U.S. government securities, which, because the securities are issued to finance the federal deficits, amounts to a backdoor means of taxation. No investments are made in the usual capital markets patronized by private pensions that result in accumulation of dividends and interest—things that, after all, make it possible for private pension insurers to operate not only with solvency but with profitability.

A pay-as-you-go system means it is not "your money" when you retire, but someone else's. Your money, meanwhile, is—or will be—going to support someone else. On the surface that may seem fair enough, as long as someone else's money is available to finance retirees' needs. Most recipient's retirement benefits (skipping the various nonretirement programs of Social Security) are paid out of current taxes *and* exceed the actual contribution of the retiree (because benefits tend to grow much faster than contributions). Retirees are receiving more than they paid into the system. In other words, they are receiving transfer payments from those who are productively at work. The simple fact is that a Social Security pensioner is just as certainly on welfare as is a mother supported by Temporary Assistance to Needy Families or a food stamp recipient.

This leads to a second myth: Retirement monies, whether provided by insurance or a welfare system, will be ensured upon retirement. It seems fair that if you pay for someone else, someone should pay for you. However, this is possible only by a relentless increase in the contribution rate. The current demographic profile of the population makes it a certainty that the number of recipients will grow faster than the number of contributors. The situation is a bit like the old pyramid game or a chain letter: Those near the bottom of the list have to muster a far larger money contribution or required number of letters over those higher on the list. But like the pyramid or chain letter, the burden for those on the bottom sooner or later becomes too great compared to the estimated rewards, and the link is broken. It is a simple political fact that the relative level of benefits for Social Security retirees will not be continued when contributors are faced with an excessive burden and little hope that they will ever get back anything close to their contributions. There is no economic "proof" that workers in the year 2050 will not pay 30 to 50 percent of their salaries in order to sustain retirees at present standards, but it seems likely that such demands on workers will be unacceptable.

Meanwhile, the immense popularity of the Social Security system, as well as its economic difficulties, stem largely from another myth: Social Security was intended to provide all with a comfortable standard of living upon retirement. Even by Franklin Roosevelt's liberal standards, Social Security was only supposed to provide "safeguards from misfortune." Framers of the act did not have in mind sending New York retirees to Florida condos to bask in the sun. Social Security was intended to protect the very poor and elderly from total destitution. It was, for the more fortunate, to be a small bonus to their personal retirement savings. Except for the very poor, benefits were to equal what the individual had paid in, which in the 1930s and 1940s was not very much. All that has changed today. Many Americans see their Social Security benefits— which far exceed their contributions—as *their entire retirement program.* They believe that Social Security is both a substitute for savings and a reason not to save.

Undesired Effects

Because of the persuasiveness of the mythology, there is practically universal acceptance by Americans of the Social Security system. People who might grumble about "welfare queens" driving Cadillacs and who would never accept food stamps, accept Social Security payments without a second thought. Moreover, senior citizens see Social

Security as a right and are quite willing to vote against any honest politician who has the audacity to question either the philosophy or the economics of the system.

Older citizens act as a powerful political lobby through organizations such as the American Association of Retired Persons (AARP). They make ending the system impossible and reducing the system's actual benefits practically impossible. As a result, this political lobby of kindly but uninformed older citizens keeps pushing Social Security and ultimately the entire economy down the road to disaster. Only a serious reeducation effort can halt this trend.

One of the first steps is to see that the Social Security system is a badly designed tax system. Both Social Security and Medicare are financed through the imposition of a constant tax rate imposed on employees and employers. Currently (2005), the Social Security tax is 12.4 percent, split between employee and employer at 6.2 percent on the first $90,000 of income. Medicare is also equally split at 1.45 percent apiece but on *all* earned income. The effect of this rate structure is to burden low-income earners more than high-income individuals. The irony is that low-wage earners, who most desperately depend on Social Security in retirement, have all their labor income subjected to the Social Security tax, while higher incomes, particularly those above the $90,000 base, experience less of an impact.

Another disadvantage of this method of taxation is that it discourages job creation. Because employers are required to match the employee's contribution rate, employers find it advantageous to hire fewer workers. This may occur in one of two ways. First, each worker represents a hidden tax payment because employers are required to match employee contributions. By keeping numbers of workers down, taxes and costs are lowered. Second, where employers are already paying the maximum tax because workers are at their maximum wage for paying Social Security contributions, it is desirable to require more work from present workers (and pay more in wages) than to hire new workers and pay the additional employment tax. The outcome of such a tax system is to reduce employment, but Liberals rarely come forth to criticize these arrangements.

The distortions caused by the Social Security tax are accompanied by an inequitable scheme of benefits payments. Payments are determined neither by the amount paid in nor by the individual's needs. While some limits to benefits are set according to lifetime contributions to the system, the benefit schedule is connected only loosely to actual contribution rates. To a considerable extent, conditions totally unconnected to either need or contributions determine payments to the Social Security recipient. Married persons receive greater benefits than the unmarried because a spouse who never worked qualifies for an amount equal to half the benefit received by the retired working spouse upon reaching full retirement age. Dependent children also make families eligible for additional benefit payments. A widow or widower who never worked is able to get the late spouse's pension.

Perhaps the greatest inequity is imposed upon low-income workers who never exceed Social Security's taxable income base and out of economic necessity must continue to work beyond the full retirement age. Consequently, all of their income is subjected to the Social Security tax while those whose incomes exceed the taxable income base experience a lower effective tax rate. High-income individuals are more likely to have private pensions and other assets that allow them to retire early or at least stop working when they reach Social Security's demarcation of full retirement age. The size of the monthly benefit check is determined by the years of highest earnings so the regressivity of the tax is reinforced by the regressive distribution of benefits. To make matters worse, low-income earners have shorter life expectancies than high-income earners. In short, low-income workers are taxed hardest, receive the least, and find they are literally working to death for the Social Security system.

Part insurance in philosophy and part welfare, the benefit program is both unfair to the needy and inequitable to the contributor. Welfare to the truly indigent is perfectly acceptable to a Conservative. Even a system by which a contributor received benefits equal to his or her contribution can be defended logically (so long as the contributions are voluntary). However, we have neither.

An undesirable macroeconomic outcome of the Social Security program has been its impact on savings. As we noted before, the initial object of Social Security was to provide a bare cushion for those who lost their savings in the Depression years. However, as the coverage and benefits of the program—not just old age benefits but everything from educational to health benefits—has grown, Social Security has increasingly been treated as a substitute for personal savings. According to respected estimates, Social Security depresses personal savings by 30 to 50 percent. The Social Security "contributions" collected by the government are not saved but rather spent on a pay-as-you-go basis. Thus government-forced saving (in withheld contributions) does not replace lost personal savings. The macroeconomic effect of dwindling savings rates is not difficult to estimate. In particular, it denies the nation the fund of savings that would otherwise be available for expanded investment. More consumption and less savings mean less capital. Accordingly, with investment lowered, employment is lowered and unemployment increased. The negative macroeconomic effects of Social Security cannot be overlooked in their impact. Martin Feldstein (chair of the President's Council of Economic Advisors in the Regan administration) and others have estimated the drag on the GDP to be very great. National output may be reduced by as much as 15 to 20 percent as a result of Social Security's discouragement of savings.

An Intermediate Solution

Conservatives understand that reforming Social Security cannot take place overnight. Americans need to be weaned slowly from Social Security dependency. The goal for OASDI reform, of course, must be to transform the existing bureaucratic system through successive increments of privatization.

As a simple matter of fairness, those now collecting Social Security benefits should be able to continue to do so. And, those near retirement age and who have already made their retirement plans should have access to existing options. Yet, even these groups must understand that future increments of government largess will be small and infrequent. In other words, effective caps on present giveaways must be put in place, and put in place in such a way that they are not subject to political change of heart. After all, Hell knoweth no fury like that of a senior citizen politically scorned.

For those who are some distance from retirement, a privatized alternative to the present system should be established. Workers would be able to direct all or a portion of their Social Security contributions into a private—essentially personal—account, which they or their agents will invest so as to maximize accumulations when retirement age is reached. It should go without saying, that—over time—no investment alternative outperforms equity markets. Ideally, no restrictions should be placed on the account holder's range of choices. However, as a practical matter, it would be unwieldy to allow frequent transactions among a wide array of investments for so many personal account holders with initially small balances. Additionally, a substantial share of the participants—if not the vast majority—will not have enough expertise to assess risky investment opportunities. A limited list of funds and some restrictions on the number of exchanges among funds would be necessary to hold down transaction costs and curtail foolish speculation that would reduce accumulations for retirement. Yet, transition to a private system will cause people to realize that this time it really is *their money*.

The contributions to, and earned accumulations of the account, will be exempt from taxes in the accumulation years. Upon reaching retirement age, they shall be taxed as ordinary income once the recipient starts drawing down the account. Moreover, and in a decided improvement over the unfairness of the present system, early death will not cut off the recipient's heirs or designees from access to the accumulated funds, regardless of whether the recipient has actually reached retirement age.

With respect to funds already paid into the system (before the privatization strategy is enacted into law), a change in benefit calculation should be introduced. With respect to existing Social Security accumulations, rather than basing future payout benefits according to the recipient's wages (as exists presently), future benefits would be indexed to price changes. In other words, benefit payments obtained up to the time privatization is introduced would be fixed in their real dollar value and would never grow because of increases in earnings. If it is clear that accumulated benefits will not increase (legally speaking, *cannot* increase), the "bounce effect" of political tinkering will be eliminated. And, it is the only fair thing to do.

Obviously, prudent workers will move as quickly as possible to privatize their future Social Security contributions—perhaps even rolling over past fund accumulations into their personal account (but only on the basis of a "real dollar" adjustment to determine the real value of current fund accumulations). Over time, workers will recognize that the market, not government bureaucrats and politicians, will provide the better long-run return from payroll deductions. With a little more time, and the introduction of an investment option, most will recognize they would be better served by not being compelled to pay "payroll taxes," and can opt out of the intermediate Social Security system altogether. When we reach that point, "Amen" can be said to the biggest political boondoggle America has ever contrived.

THE LIBERAL ARGUMENT

Conservatives are correct when they assert that the Social Security system is the showpiece and the keystone of American social legislation. They are dead wrong, however, when they claim it "proves" the foolishness of government efforts to maintain minimum social welfare conditions. The Conservative allegation with regard to the "bankruptcy" of Social Security financing and their charge that we simply cannot afford the excessive benefits of Social Security are misrepresentations of the facts.

The differing perspectives of Liberals and Conservatives should be evident by this point. However, it needs to be pointed out that no issue so clearly sets out the differences in our respective ideologies than the matter of how the nation's elderly citizens should be treated. Central to the Conservative faith and its approach to the Social Security question is the notion that people do not count; only markets do. Liberals, on the other hand, approach every economic policy matter with a basic standard in mind: *What is the fair outcome?* The dismantling of Social Security or its eventual privatization is decidedly *unfair.*

The Importance of Social Security

Steeped as it is in the philosophy of voluntarism and individualistic social behavior, the Conservative argument preaches that it is each person's responsibility to provide for his or her old age or illness. Their arguments, however, fail to point out that this was precisely the kind of social philosophy that prevailed before the New Deal era and before Social Security. Such an individualistic approach to national social welfare was found wanting at that time and nothing has happened to change the situation. Even in the best of times, the average industrial worker had only the most limited opportunity to set aside a "nest egg" for his or her retirement years. Indeed, most workers in the pre–New Deal era worked until they were physically unable to go on any longer or, more likely, until bosses interested in hiring younger, more productive workers fired them. The "declining years" of an elderly worker were often spent in the back bedroom of a son's or daughter's home. This extended family condition has received praise from Conservative social theorists who emphasize the values of family and togetherness. Reality was usually different. Having an old person live with you meant, sooner or later, increased medical bills for the family and almost always long hours of tending the elderly when they became bedridden. Not many who had to go through this sort of thing—neither the old parent nor the children—found life quite so idyllic as modern exponents of the extended family make it seem.

For other poor workers, without savings *and* without family, there was the grim prospect of wasting away in a public institution. "Going to the poorhouse" was not just gallows humor among workers; it was a very real possibility. Usually located on the outskirts of a city, "county homes" and "state homes" had an exquisite institutional ugliness. Workers usually lived dormitory-style; thus husband and wife were separated save for an occasional walk on the premises. The food was of equal quality and quantity to the fare offered at the county jail. There were few social programs for residents to enjoy, just utter boredom until the end.

While Conservatives anguish over the adverse effects of Social Security on private savings habits, their concerns overlook the fact that few American workers were able to save anyway. After the introduction of the Social Security system, saving was not only possible but also required, as workers and their employers put income aside in trust funds.

For those workers who did succeed in putting away some savings for their later years, the Great Depression of the 1930s demonstrated that there was little virtue in voluntary frugality. As the stock market crashed and banking and financial institutions went under, the elderly of the era watched their savings vanish. Practically overnight, the diligent citizen who had planned ahead for retirement was no better off than the poorest worker or the most profligate. This was the situation when the Social Security Act was passed in 1935. Far from being a destructive "giveaway," it was a very modest attempt to pull millions of elderly Americans out of the terrible insecurity of economic dependency. Conservatives represent Social Security as a step into the collectivist state; the irony is that it returned many elderly people to a condition of economic self-sufficiency and individualism.

As the years passed after 1935, the Social Security system was broadened. First, many additional workers and their dependents came to be covered under the law. Second, Social Security was extended to provide health and disability benefits. Third, the payments under Social Security provisions were enlarged. As a result, Americans came to rely on Social Security to handle the economic problems of their retirement years. It became part of a new social contract between government and its citizens, and it is almost universally popular.

It would be wrong to conclude, as Conservatives suggest, that we no longer need Social Security, that the modern-day affluence of Americans would allow a private and voluntary accumulation of savings that would be a "better deal" for workers than the Social Security system. Comparisons with private pension programs are downright misleading. No private insurance company can offer—regardless of the price— a retirement package that includes a pension, health insurance, disability, and life insurance where the benefits are protected from inflation and are largely tax free. Not only is no better plan available, but also many workers simply cannot be certain of meeting their payments for a private program. Thus they would run the risk, if jobs and income decline, of forfeiting their retirement plan. Very quickly, Americans could return to the cruel economic conditions that beset the elderly before 1935.

The "Dependency Ratio" Myth and the Need to "Grow" the Economy

Among the favored Conservative devices to discredit the existing Social Security system is to maintain that the increasing ratio of retired workers to employed workers will soon reach a level at which those working simply cannot—without impoverishing themselves—sustain the existing number of Social Security recipients. The argument frequently takes on tangible form as illustrated in Figure 6.1. The dependency ratio projections rest on existing demographic projections with respect to life expectancy and on the assumption that currently available benefits to Social Security recipients will remain (in real terms) constant.

Figure 6.1 charts the present and projected ratio of Social Security beneficiaries per one hundred workers from 2003 through 2080. The dependency ratio rises from about thirty in 2003 to about forty in 2020 and on to fifty-five in 2080. The gray line depicts the Conservatives' projection of how the rising dependency ratio drags up the benefit outlays that must be paid by working Americans. Social Security payouts amount to about 11 percent of workers' earnings in 2003, rise to about 13 percent by 2020, and shoot up to nearly 20 percent by 2080.

The data as presented are alleged to illustrate that a rising dependency ratio necessarily edges the nation toward a point where the existing numbers of workers will be unable—by virtue of insufficient numbers—to sustain, out of pocket, the transfers that are mandated to be paid to a grow-

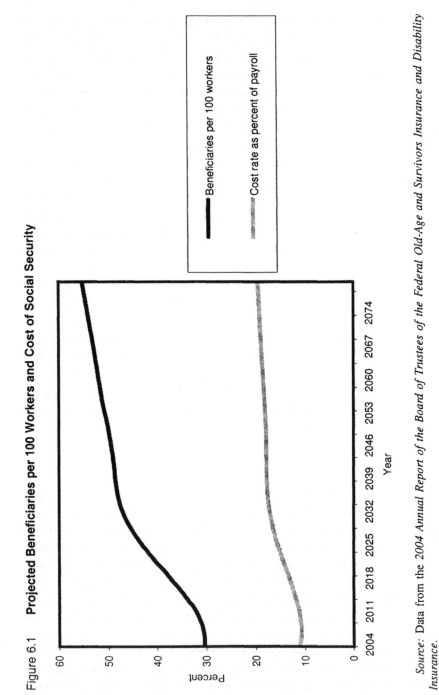

Figure 6.1   **Projected Beneficiaries per 100 Workers and Cost of Social Security**

Source: Data from the *2004 Annual Report of the Board of Trustees of the Federal Old-Age and Survivors Insurance and Disability Insurance.*

ing number of oldsters. Curiously, the argument takes on a vague Marxist preconception: that a nation's output value is simply equal to the labor value of those working—hence nonworkers are simply appropriating the fruits of workers' labor. The obvious fact that GDP (and hence GDP per capita) is not simply a function of numbers of people employed is completely missed. The entire concept of improving labor productivity and its effects receives no direct consideration in graphics dwelling on a "dependency ratio" that report the ratio of retirees to workers.

This assertion is easily proved by looking back to the late 1950s and using a slightly different dependency ratio that compares paid workers with nonworkers (retirees, the extraordinary numbers of young Baby Boomers and their nonworking Moms, as well as others not in the labor force). As a simple matter of "dependency," there were fewer workers in comparison to nonworkers (of all kinds) in 1960 than there will be (given existing demographic projections) in 2020 or 2050 or 2080.

However, the really important point to remember is that the high dependency ratio at the end of the 1950s in no way signaled impending stagnation. In fact, between 1960 and 1973, real GDP increased by 70 percent, which facilitated a 50 percent increase in employment, and a 44 percent increase in real median income (as well as a 43 percent increase in real outlays paid by the Social Security system). Not only is the whining about "dependency ratios" misleading, it evades the real problem: the currently slow rate of growth in GDP per capita—a matter addressed in Issue 2.

We Can Afford It

Before reform of the Social Security system in the mid-1980s, a convincing argument could be made for the fact that OASDI and Medicare were quickly going broke. However, the reforms have had a beneficial effect on all four of the system's trust funds. Between 1980 and 2003, the balance in the Old-Age and Survivors Insurance Trust ballooned from $22.8 billion to $1,355.3 billion, the Disability Insurance Trust balance grew from $3.6 billion to $175.4 billion, and the Hospital Insurance Trust went from $14.5 billion to $251.1 billion. Only the Supplemental Medical Insurance Trust remains grossly underfunded, scarcely holding its own in real terms with a current balance of less than $24.8 billion. Doomsday projections for Social Security funding are based upon rather low estimates of labor productivity, which, taken together with a rising dependency ratio, results in forecasts of depleted fund balances and high costs.

Indeed, the problems of the Medical trust fund are illustrative of the truly serious problem the system faces: exploding Medicare outlays. Even examination of the George W. Bush administration's generous overstating of the fiscal gap the Social Security system faces reveals that the real problem is rising medical costs. Of the $40 to $50 trillion gap they allege exists between estimated income and estimated outlays between now and 2075, more than 80 percent is the result of projected medical cost increases.

Quite simply, the fiscal gap disappears (or at least becomes small enough so as to be susceptible to disappearance with a little fine-tuning of income and outlays and a little more economic growth) *if we bring medical and hospital costs under control.*

In fact the medical cost problem is not just a Medicare problem. In league with the pharmaceutical companies and the HMOs, the Bush administration has shamelessly stood aside, as everyone's medical costs have increased at four or five times the rate of the consumer price index increases. With 44 million Americans of all ages not having any medical insurance coverage, rising medical costs are not just the problem of the elderly.

The simple fact is that the nation needs a freestanding national health insurance program that holds down medical costs and guarantees universal coverage, whatever one's income or age. With that in place, we could return Social Security to its original purpose: to make it possible for every citizen to be assured in their old age of a reasonably comfortable and independent lifestyle.

Alas, Conservatives do not want an affordable Social Security system. For that matter, they do not want a successful, freestanding national health insurance program either. In a highly calculated fashion, the Bush administration has done about everything in its power to eliminate the creation or enlargement of any government social program. The device for doing this: eliminate the availability of funds by driving up annual federal deficits. It was not by accident (or even a war) that a projected $5 trillion federal surplus between 2001 and 2015 was transformed into the currently projected accumulation of $5 trillion of deficits—mostly by way of excessive tax cuts that bestowed great rewards on the wealthiest of Americans.

This intentional creation of federal deficits has been—among the general population—a mostly unnoticed and quiet strategy aimed at convincing Americans we cannot afford *any* social outlay that requires increasing government outlays. However, paraphrasing President Lincoln, while it's possible to fool some of the people all the time and all the people some of the time, *it's not possible to fool all the people all the time.*

THE RADICAL ARGUMENT

The current crisis in the American Social Security system cannot be understood apart from the general fiscal crisis that grips the government budgets of all modern capitalist economies. From the Radical perspective, we must go beyond the narrow and partisan claims of Liberal and Conservative adversaries and look deeper into the fundamental relations of the state and capitalist enterprise. These real economic relationships, not merely political prejudices, set the actual limits to the growth and development of social spending.

The State Budget within Capitalist Economies

Within a capitalist economic system, the object is always to employ capital and to produce goods in such a way that profits (or surplus over the costs of production) continue to rise. It should be remembered that this is not an arbitrary and doctrinaire definition. Conservatives as well as Liberals know full well that "profit is the name of the game." Conservatives, of course, maintain that government appropriation of some share of production (government taxes and their budgetary allocations) comes *at the expense* of the private sector. In other words, what government takes and redistributes is a subtraction from what businesses would otherwise receive. Liberals, on the other hand, also see the government taxing and budgetary process as redistributive but defend it on the grounds that either such redistribution is socially desirable or that government spending in fact generates output that would not otherwise take place (see the Liberal argument in Issue 2). Both views, however, miss the important role played by government taxing and budgeting within the modern capitalist state because they fail to grasp the central place of the state in the process of accumulating capital *and* maintaining social and economic order. In consequence, neither understands the central issues involved in the political and economic struggle over social spending in general or the Social Security system in particular.

If we examine the taxing and budgeting activities of modern capitalist states, it becomes apparent that they pursue two basically different objectives: "accumulation" and "legitimation."* On one hand, the state undertakes actions that are aimed directly at stimulating economic growth and encouraging business profits (providing for capital accumulation). On the other hand, the state attempts to create and maintain general conditions of social harmony, thus legitimating the operation of a capitalist society.

If in fact the state could provide the desired levels of accumulation and legitimation at the same time, there would be no crisis. Nor, of course, would there be much reason to study economics because, in such an Alice in Wonderland world, scarcity would not exist. In the real world, however, these two objectives are competing uses for the state budget. Moreover, as we shall see, outlays for one purpose may be in direct contradiction to the goals of the other objective. The contradiction has become particularly sharp in our era of lagging capitalist growth. Presently, it is obvious that there are very real limits to the budgetary outlays that government can make in these two general areas without (1) raising to unacceptable levels the taxes on the society or on certain groups within the society or (2) generating excessive inflationary pressures (see Issues 2 and 3).

To see how the "accumulation" and "legitimation" functions of the capitalist state budget work, we need only dissect the budget according to these functions. First, there is a broad category of social capital outlays that either *directly* increase capitalist output (social investment) or *indirectly* lower the cost of capitalist production (social consumption). Social investment and social consumption spending add to the accumulation of capital in a variety of ways. Social investment includes outlays for roads, airports, and industrial parks, that is, outlays that increase private-sector output by having government pay for part of the investment cost. Social consumption expenditures such as education and unemployment insurance are useful to business *indirectly,* since the enterprise does not have to pay for training its workers or for sustaining them when economic conditions deteriorate. While social investment and social consumption spending primarily serve the accumulating function, it is obvious that they also work to legitimate the capitalist system. Meanwhile, certain other outlays, which we shall call social expenses,

---

*The following analysis adopts the terminology and concepts of the now classic work of James O'Connor: *Fiscal Crisis of the State* (New York: St. Martin's Press, 1973).

have not the slightest impact on accumulation and work only to achieve legitimation. This is the service performed by those budgetary outlays that commonly are called "welfare"—payments to the surplus or unemployed portion of the population for the purpose of bribing them into complacency and political acceptance of the economic order.

The categories may seem confusing, and in truth the confusion is heightened by the fact that some government outlays serve both accumulation and legitimation ends. Social Security, for instance, lowers the production cost of employers (by having government provide pension funds) and legitimates by sustaining otherwise "useless" workers. Nevertheless, with a little reflection it is possible to categorize government outlays according to how they serve one or both of these basic functions. Such an approach is important because it demystifies the otherwise obscure organization of the government budget. We can begin to see just what certain spending categories are intended to do.

The Growing Fiscal Crisis

Viewing the budget according to the categories of accumulation and legitimation ties together nicely the Radical critique offered in the earlier issues dealing with stabilization policy, unemployment, deficits, and even international economic policy. By looking at how the government budget is constructed according to the conflicting demands of accumulation and legitimation, we can gain insight into the problems of modern macroeconomic policy making. The issue of Social Security becomes understood in the context of a much larger political and economic crisis.

The general fiscal crisis of the modern capitalist state (within which the Social Security crisis is but one small element) can be put simply enough: There are rising demands for government outlays and a dwindling capacity or willingness to pay for such outlays through taxes. Thus the crisis takes a number of forms. First, there is the problem of rising accumulation and legitimation demands. In a period of economic stagnation, business (in particular the big business or monopoly sector) requires greater outlays (or what amounts to the same thing, tax cuts) to lower production costs and facilitate capital accumulation. Thus, farm subsidies and business "investment credit" programs have continued to expand. Some direct aids to business—such as the "enterprise zone" concept—have been presented inaccurately, as if they were really aid to the unemployed worker. Meanwhile, there has been a rise in legitimation claims, more so in an economy deeply committed to rising levels of mass consumption.

Second, with claims rising, there has been a steady pressure for tax increases. In the 1980s, this stimulated a considerable number of tax-payer revolts such as California's Proposition 13 and dozens of similar efforts to force down taxes. The victory of Ronald Reagan in 1980, perhaps more than anything else, signaled a popular reaction among taxpayers to hold down spending and even to cut it back. Yet when we look back at the fiscal restraint actually produced by the tax revolts and by Reagan's victory in 1980, we find that few ordinary people have benefited.

The budgetary cuts forced by the fiscal crisis have come primarily from the "legitimation" activities of government. In other words, using Marxist terminology, the budget has become increasingly an instrument of class oppression and domination. Thus budgetary actions that primarily benefit big business and the upper-income groups' abilities to accumulate profits and capital have been protected or have actually expanded, while budget items aimed at maintaining a minimum level of personal well-being have been sacrificed. Quite simply, it is a matter of profits for General Motors and Microsoft *first.* Conservatives, with their supply-side and trickle-down theories, have been surprisingly honest in putting forth this objective. Even more surprisingly, people who have nothing to gain from such an approach have accepted this nonsense, but only up to a point. Social Security is a good example of how the fiscal crisis can explode into a serious political crisis.

Social Security and the Fiscal Crisis

The recent shrinkage of purely "legitimation" outlays within the budget, while painful to welfare recipients, never held out much possibility for solving the fiscal crisis. Quite simply, our outlays for the poor always have been too small to provide a significant amount of savings that can be transferred to needed accumulation activities. Moreover, even the wildest-eyed Conservative knows at heart that literally starving the poor to death would bring more political chaos than the system could handle. After all, some minimum outlay must be made for legitimation. To state the matter bluntly, "the beaver solution" is not a policy option in a capitalist order that seeks to sustain its political viability.

Social Security, with its $471 billion in outlays each year, is certainly an attractive area from which to obtain some accumulation gains. Since "everybody" pays into Social Security and receives its benefits, the class nature of raiding Social Security is not so immediately obvious. If we look beneath the surface, however, we find that the Social Security crisis is an illustrative case showing the basic class nature of government spending and taxing.

On the revenue side, Social Security taxes are collected only on earned income. No taxes are paid from income received from rents, interest, and dividends. Thus the owners of wealth and property are exempted from any payments. Second, the payroll tax itself is regressive, with a constant percentage levied from the first dollar up to a maximum earned-income level. The result is that low-income groups must pay a higher portion of their income in Social Security taxes. Currently these people are told that Social Security can be saved only by making the tax more regressive, that is, by raising the percentage contribution (and modestly expanding the taxable income level) or by taxing the benefits actually received. This regressive tax structure is encouraged by the fiction that Social Security is self-funding, or that you get according to what you pay in. By keeping the self-funding myth alive, workers are told simply that they can get only what they pay for. If the funds go bankrupt, contributions must increase or benefits must go down. This successfully evades the whole question of guaranteeing minimum retirement benefits irrespective of contributions and allows us to avoid the question of establishing minimum welfare standards for the elderly and the ill. It maintains the capitalist faith that we are responsible only for ourselves and not for others.

Class bias also appears on the benefits side of the Social Security system. Proposals to lengthen the period for retirement eligibility work against the low-income production worker whose ability to work productively is diminished by the physical demands of his or her job. Being forced into early retirement because of health means accepting greatly reduced benefits for the rest of one's life. Meanwhile, well-to-do professionals, who do not suffer from health-damaging employment, are permitted to collect benefits *and* earned income after retirement age has been reached.

The assault on the Social Security system reveals much about capitalism in general and specifically about the current (but well-disguised) crisis of the capitalist order. First, by attacking Social Security as well as such traditional "legitimation" functions as welfare spending, the defenders of capitalism reveal just how far and how deep the fiscal crisis has developed. The trade-off between accumulation and legitimation activities by the state has become quite severe, a much greater problem certainly than well-meaning Liberal defenders of Social Security understand. Second, both the attack on Social Security and the proposed efforts to save it amount to a new "disciplining" of the working population. Even with its many flaws, Social Security has been an important social welfare program and has been immensely popular with most Americans. Its promise far exceeded its delivery, but it did create a widely held belief that society would indeed protect individuals. Reneging on Social Security sends the signal that this commitment will no longer be honored. Whether Americans are willing to accept a new discipline of reduced social welfare remains to be seen, but the old Liberal program for a system that delivered both accumulation and legitimation is being undone, even if this fact is not reported by the media nor understood by ordinary citizens.

Meanwhile, the reader should put in the context of capitalist needs and habits the likelihood of the geriatric-care industry receiving a serious "spanking" such as Liberals propose. Similarly, the plausibility of the long-term Conservative plan to get rid of Social Security must be weighed against the political disorder that would surely arise thereafter. From a Radical perspective, Conservatives and Liberals, as usual, are offering cures upon which they simply cannot deliver because capitalists will not allow it. Recognition of this reality goes a long way to clear the head of self-mystification about what American macroeconomic policy making *is* and *is not* about.

International Economics

Where Does America Fit into the New World Order?

Under a system of a perfectly free commerce, each country naturally devotes its capital and labor to such employments as are most beneficial to each. This pursuit of individual advantage is admirably connected with the universal good of the whole.

—David Ricardo, 1817

If nations can learn to provide themselves with full employment by their domestic policy . . . international trade would cease to be what it is, namely, a desperate expedient to maintain employment at home by forcing sales on foreign markets and restricting purchases which if successful will merely shift the problem of unemployment to the neighbor.

—John Maynard Keynes, 1936

On the whole, capitalism is growing far more rapidly than before; but this growth is not only becoming more and more uneven in general, its unevenness also manifests itself, in particular, in the decay of countries richest in capital.

—V.I. Lenin, 1916

We live in a global economy that is characterized by free trade in goods and services and even more by the free movement of capital. As a result, interest rates, exchange rates, and stock prices in various countries are intimately interrelated, and global financial markets exert tremendous influence on economic conditions everywhere. Financial capital enjoys a privileged position. Capital is more mobile than other factors of production, and financial capital is even more mobile than other forms of capital.

—George Soros, 2000

The cranes on the docks of Shanghai, Hong Kong, and Tianjin are not simply loading containers for export to the United States. They are also unloading huge amounts of American machinery, American farm products, American aircraft, and American electronics.

—Robert Zoellick, U.S. trade representative, 2004

The Problem

Until comparatively recently, Americans have not paid much attention to international economic affairs. From the end of World War II to the 1970s, the preeminent position of America in both international trade and finance was pretty much taken for granted by Americans (and by most of the rest of the world too), very much as we took for granted our international political preeminence. Unlike many nations whose very existence depended on foreign trade and commerce, American imports and exports of goods had never been very large, not amounting to much more than 6 percent of our gross domestic product (Figure 7.1). As one economist observed of the American tendency to worry little about matters of foreign trade and finance, to do otherwise "would be to let the tail wag the dog."*

To understand how we have moved away from our earlier insular, unconcerned attitude about the rest of the world and toward pondering the impact of international events on the domestic American economy, we need only look at the following chain of representative events over the past three decades:

- In early 1987, the United States becomes the largest debtor nation in the world, largely attributable to an uninterrupted string of annual trade deficits since 1976.
- In 1989, the United States and Canada (America's most significant trading partner) sign a free trade agreement.
- In 1991, the European Community leaps beyond free trade with the Treaty of Maastricht, establishing a plan for political and economic unification.
- In 1991, the United States leads a coalition of many nations to reverse Iraq's occupation of Kuwait, which ends in a smashing military success. The cold war era ends in the same year with the dissolution of the Soviet Union into fifteen independent states.
- By 1993, Mexico (America's third-largest trading partner), Canada, and the United States enact the North American Free Trade Agreement (NAFTA). Thereafter, efforts begin in earnest among many North, Central and South American, and Caribbean nations to create

*Campbell R. McConnell, *Economics: Principles, Problems, and Policies*, 7th ed. (New York: McGraw-Hill, 1977), 918.

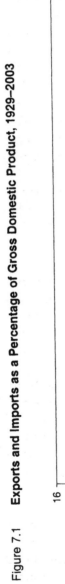

Figure 7.1　**Exports and Imports as a Percentage of Gross Domestic Product, 1929–2003**

Source: Data from Bureau of Economic Analysis, National Income and Product Accounts.

a hemispheric free trade zone under the Free Trade Agreement of the Americas (FTAA).

- In 2001, the nation reels from the collapse of a long economic boom and the bursting of a stock market bubble, and finds itself involved in a "war on terror" after September 11.
- In 2003, the United States and the United Kingdom along with a relatively small group of cooperating allies initiate a second Gulf War against Iraq and quickly dislodge the government of Saddam Hussein. More than a year later, the battle drags on in the streets of Iraqi cities. International support wears thin, oil prices skyrocket, and the U.S. trade deficit continues to grow.
- By early 2004, a component of a hemispheric trade initiative emerges in the form of the Central American Free Trade Agreement (CAFTA). Separately, the United States and Australia sign a free trade agreement in May of 2004. The U.S. zeal for free trade is shadowed by its dependency on capital inflows from abroad.
- By 2004, the dollar's weakness against the euro and other major currencies seems like a permanent condition. Meanwhile, China's rising importance in international trade as well as the "outsourcing" of U.S. jobs impact the domestic political agenda.

These and other events show that (1) the long-held American economic and political preeminence in the world is in retreat; (2) America now depends more on the world for trade and capital, and also chronically buys more than it sells; and (3) the conditions of domestic well-being are intricately connected to the nation's international trade and financial condition. Alas, the tail *was* wagging the dog.

Understanding international interdependence and appreciating the influence of the country's international position requires comprehension of how international trade takes place. Although discussions of international economic issues invariably become quite complicated, mastery of the fundamental reasoning involved is easier than many noneconomists realize. The conditions affecting trade among nations are not very different from the conditions affecting trade among individuals in a simple market. Just as an individual's ability to sell his or her goods is basically determined by (1) the price of the goods and (2) the ability and willingness of buyers to pay that price, so it is with exports and imports. Whatever America or any other exporting nation is able to sell to the rest of the world is determined by the prices that must be charged for their exported goods and by foreign purchasers' willingness and ability to pay such prices. Similarly, the amount of goods we buy from abroad (import) depends on the prices we are charged and our willingness or ability to pay these prices.

Accordingly, it becomes obvious that the various factors that affect the prices of a nation's goods and the ability of world buyers to purchase the goods at the prices offered are the basic variables in determining any particular nation's export or import position. Some examples serve to make the point clearer. All things being equal, anything that might raise the price of American goods relative to the prices being charged by other (non-American) sellers of the same goods would obviously discourage foreign purchases of American products. Higher production costs, resulting from rising factor prices, various production inefficiencies, or domestic inflation would raise the prices of exports. And, so too could a situation where fluctuations in international exchange rates result in the exporting nation's currency becoming strong (high-priced) relative to importing nations' currencies.* These forces push export prices upward, which would likely lead to a decline of American exports. And what makes exports unattractive to foreigners usually makes imports attractive at home. When foreign goods are cheaper than American goods, American consumers would choose to buy foreign products. In other words, U.S. exports would be lower and imports higher. The opposite would be true if our prices were relatively lower than prices charged by the rest of the world (that is, our exports higher and our imports lower as a result of this type of price disparity).

However, even if U.S. prices were competitive with world prices (or were even lower), exporting goods and services would be difficult if the rest of the world was gripped by a serious recession that greatly reduced other nations' ability to buy imported products and services. On the other hand, the United States would expect to be able to sell more in the world— as long as its prices were attractive—if the world was enjoying prosperity.

---

*A strong (relative to other nations) currency will not necessarily work against a nation's exports and balance of payments. Other factors are important, such as the relative prices of goods in the first place. However, in the mid-1980s, high interest rates in the United States led to foreigners' seeking American dollars to purchase high-return American investments. The result was "an exceptionally strong dollar" even though the United States was already in a serious trade deficit situation. The higher-priced dollar meant that when U.S. goods were sold overseas, after the conversion of dollar prices to the local currency, they were priced quite high. The result was to depress American exports even further. Meanwhile, imported goods enjoyed, after price conversion into dollars, low prices that encouraged U.S. imports to soar.

This comparatively simple model of world trade, however, becomes more complicated when more than prices are at work. For instance, consider what will happen if American prices are relatively high compared to the rest of the world and the American economy is experiencing a modest expansion while most of the world is in an economic slump. U.S. exports will be relatively low because of higher prices *and* because of diminished worldwide ability to buy U.S. goods. Meanwhile, the United States imports more because its capacity to purchase is fairly high and foreign goods are cheaper than American-made products. Indeed, this was precisely the real-world situation in the mid-1980s as the United States began to run up very large trade deficits. A significant reversal in the early 1990s gave way to ballooning, followed by record-breaking, trade deficits.

The main influences upon exports and imports are rather easily explained, but greater complexity lurks beyond the basics. Explanations about the relative international trade and financial position of the United States are scarcely matters of universal agreement among economists. However, near unanimity exists on one point: *The U.S. economy is more interconnected with the rest of the world than ever before.* As a result, domestic economic policies—both in their immediate objectives and in their longer-term effects—must always be seen within the context of an international economy, not just the domestic economy. Other nations can surely be expected to respond to U.S. policy initiatives. Their actions in turn rebound on the United States, perhaps negating or distorting the outcomes we sought with our original domestic policy. For American economic policy makers, economic interdependence is a two-way street and the world has become a much smaller, more complicated place in the past few decades.

Synopsis

Conservatives argue that U.S. trade and currency problems are traceable to protectionism, pegged exchange rates, and ill-conceived domestic economic policy. Liberals oppose the Conservative remedy of free trade and floating exchange rates, maintaining that the cost in terms of jobs and industrial decline in the United States would surpass any benefits. They hold that only stimulation of the domestic economy will ensure international vitality. Radicals assert that the present international trade and finance problems are a gauge of the nation's decline from power and a further measure of the chronic capitalist crisis of production and distribution.

Anticipating the Arguments

- According to Conservatives, what particular economic problems are caused by protectionism?
- Why do Liberals believe that even worse problems would be caused by free trade and floating exchange rates?
- What do Radicals identify as the cause for recent U.S. balance-of-payments problems?

THE CONSERVATIVE ARGUMENT

Perhaps the severest test of personal commitment to a free and open capitalist economy arises with respect to international trade and finance. Economists, politicians, and especially business leaders who perceive the advantages of competition and the market and who ardently oppose any type of controls or intervention in domestic activities are tempted to abandon their philosophy at the nation's borders. Perhaps it is a narrow nationalism or a basic parochialism in economic thought, but the logic of free markets is too easily abandoned when international issues are raised. For the consistent Conservative, however, there should be no exceptions. Free economic arrangements are as crucial internationally as they are domestically.

The Necessity of Free Trade

The first requirement for free trade is the elimination of all tariffs, quotas, and bilateral or multilateral trade agreements that inhibit the free operation of international markets. Each nation must be free to sell its goods to any other, and each nation must be open to any other's goods. Regrettably, however, the desire for protectionism runs very deep among nations. This remnant of outmoded mercantilist philosophy persistently reappears when one nation gains a production or price advantage over another in a particular product or line of products. In the United States, it appears when firms or industries act as special-interest groups lobbying Congress to raise duties on hated imports or to set quotas on these imports. Supposedly, by limiting the ability of foreign firms to compete through price or other means, American industry's position is enhanced.

Conservatives acknowledge that part of society's difficulty in adhering to free trade is one of perception. The costs of trade appear in highly visible ways: displaced workers, bankrupted steel manufacturers, and prominent properties wistfully lost to foreign ownership. However, the benefits of trade in the form of lower prices to consumers, the redirection of resources to higher value purposes such as the manufacture of silicon chips instead of fueling blast furnaces, and the enjoyment of infusions of capital from abroad are easily lost on the ordinary person. Rarely does free trade receive credit for a birthday or Christmas being celebrated more fervently because the absence of trade barriers made it possible to buy twice as many goods. Nor do many people immediately acknowledge the technological and economic necessity of employment shifting from steel production to computer memory production. At the same time, shifting labor to chauffeuring luxury limousines from stagecoach driving is readily accepted as an improvement and no one would venture to assert that low-wage rickshaw drivers in Asia threaten the employment prospects of U.S. workers.

Ironically, labor unions in affected industries very often ally themselves with the corporation in their lobbying effort. For example, in 2002, the United Steelworkers joined with the majority of the steel industry to urge import tariffs on steel. President George W. Bush acceded to imposing the tariffs of 8 to 30 percent on various steel products for a period of three years. From the union's point of view, the object is always to protect jobs. The real outcome is quite different, however, for several reasons.

First, protectionism is costly. It raises the prices of imported goods for all consumers or artificially holds up the price of competing domestic goods. This may mean jobs and income for steelworkers and steel companies in Gary, Indiana, but it means reduced buying power and lost jobs elsewhere. Tariffs and quotas have not protected American earnings, but have merely redistributed income and jobs and raised prices for everybody.

Second, protectionism encourages inefficiency. Without the incentive provided by competition, neither business nor labor is induced to increase productivity or to modernize production techniques. In turn, consumers must pay for an industry's protected inefficiency, which can be quite costly over time because it tends to grow cumulatively. The limits on foreign competition are very often increased as production gaps grow between a vibrant overseas producer and a lethargic domestic industry.

Third, protectionism invites retaliation. Other nations will be induced to follow the same protectionist path if their goods are effectively priced out of our domestic markets. Thus we may find the threat of foreign steel eliminated at the cost of being unable to sell U.S. tractors in foreign markets. The result may be the end of trade altogether. Recognition of this fact arose shortly after the Bush administration imposed tariffs on imported steel in 2002. Outrage from foreign producers coalesced in a dispute mediated by the World Trade Organization (WTO). The steel tariffs were deemed unfair trade by the WTO and the United States faced $2.2 billion in retaliatory tariffs from the European Union. Rescinding the tariffs in December of 2003 averted a retaliatory response that could have impacted a whole range of American firms, not just steel companies.

Fourth, protectionism invites other undesirable tinkering with trade, exchange rates, and capital flows to effect political solutions to economic problems. For instance, Liberals would attempt to artificially improve our international balance of payments through a variety of interventions. Practically disregarding the favorable effect of inflows of foreign earnings by U.S. businesses on our balance of payments, many Liberals have incorrectly singled out the export of U.S. capital as a primary cause for balance-of-payments deficits. Their shortsighted cure is to restrict U.S. overseas investment. As with all protectionist actions, the effect has been counterproductive for the economy. American businesses are placed at a competitive disadvantage in world markets at precisely the time when they should be developing strength.

Free trade and free overseas movement of U.S. capital may indeed mean the end of some American industries and may throw some workers out of jobs. However, other production possibilities are opened. Let the Koreans concentrate on toy or textile production and the United States exploit its computer technology. Indeed, let each nation develop its comparative advantages so that trade between them is possible.

Milton Friedman has emphasized the significance of a commitment to free trade this way:

> There are few measures we could take that would do more to promote the cause of freedom at home and abroad. Instead of making grants to foreign governments in the name of economic aid—and thereby promoting socialism—while at the same time imposing restrictions on the products they succeed in producing—and thereby hindering free enterprise—we

could assume a consistent and principled stance. We could say to the rest of the world: We believe in freedom and intend to practice it. No one can force you to be free. That is your business. But we can offer you full co-operation on equal terms to all. Our market is open to you. Sell here what you can and wish to. Use the proceeds to buy what you wish. In this way co-operation among individuals can be worldwide yet free.*

The Necessity of Floating Exchange Rates

Despite the central importance of free trade policies in developing an efficient and mutually beneficial system of international commerce, free trade alone will not bring freedom to international markets. The other side of the free trade coin is the maintenance of freely floating exchange rates. Indeed, the two must proceed together.

To understand the advantages of flexible exchange rates, we need to see how they work and how pegged rates cause trading difficulties. Take two countries, the United States and Great Britain, for instance. Consider also a particular bundle of representative goods. In Britain, this bundle of goods can presently be purchased for £50, and in the United States an identical bundle costs $100. Accordingly, we can say that £50 buys $100 worth of goods, and vice versa. Thus we can conclude that in terms of a free or floating exchange, £50 = $100, or £1 = $2, or $1 = £0.5. Now consider that inflationary pressures develop in the United States, causing the dollar price of our bundle of goods to rise to $200. If the exchange rates are still floating freely, the new exchange rate will be £1 = $4. Inflation has reduced, both at home and overseas, the buying power of the dollar, which is exactly the effect we would expect of inflation. However, if the United States tried to maintain the old $2 = £1 rate, the official exchange value of dollars to pounds would be overvalued. The price of American goods in Britain would be artificially high. Rather than getting an equivalent bundle of goods for £50, Britons would get only half a bundle for their money if they bought American goods. Meanwhile, in the United States, British goods would be relatively cheaper than American goods. It would take only $2 to buy goods denominated at £1 rather than the $4 that would be required if we had a freely floating exchange rate reflecting the

---

*Milton Friedman, *Capitalism and Freedom* (Chicago: University of Chicago Press, 1962), 74.

actual 4 : 1 dollars-to-pounds ratio. It becomes immediately obvious that pegged rates that are either above or below the real purchasing power parity (based on our identical bundles of goods) make it impossible for stability to exist in international markets. Nations with currencies that are overvalued relative to those of other nations will actually encourage a worsening balance of trade as import prices are held down and export prices are held up. And so it was for the United States during the mid- and late 1980s as certain domestic economic policies tended to produce a strong and expensive dollar. Meanwhile—and this is a strategy not lost on most nations—undervaluation of a nation's currency tends to encourage exports and discourage imports.

From the end of World War II until the 1970s, the world used a fixed exchange-rate system. Under what was known as the Bretton Woods arrangements, the U.S. dollar replaced gold, the traditional international unit of account, as the instrument for measuring and making international payments.*

To oversee these international transactions, the International Monetary Fund (IMF) was created. The pound, the French franc, the German mark, the yen, and all other currencies were valued by the IMF against the dollar. (The franc and mark have since been replaced by the euro, the common currency of most member countries in the European Union.) Thus when a nation experienced domestic inflation that raised the price of its goods relative to those of other nations, it was obliged, for international money exchange purposes, to devalue its currency in relation to the dollar. If, for instance, the British experienced an inflation that doubled the price (in pounds) of British goods, the only way to bring the inflated British currency into proper balance with unchanged dollars (and other currencies) would be to devalue the pound by one-half. Each dollar would now buy twice as many pounds and twice as much British goods as was possible before the revaluing. If the British did not devalue their currency, trading nations would shun either their products or their currency, and the domestic crisis would be worsened. To forestall short-term shortages of funds for international payments and to avoid the anarchy of devaluation wars as

---

*Meeting at Bretton Woods, New Hampshire, toward the end of World War II, the Allied powers agreed to an "adjustable-peg" system. While exchange rates for individual currencies were pegged to the dollar, their value in dollar terms could be changed to reflect overvaluation or undervaluation.

each nation sought to gain a brief currency advantage over others, the trading nations maintained reserve balances with the IMF or could borrow from the fund. Meanwhile, the fund pegged currencies to the dollar, adjusting values from time to time as economic conditions within nations changed. So long as the dollar was sound, the problems of inflation or unemployment could be limited to the affected country. The system's weakness, however, was what everyone had thought to be its strength—the dollar.

During the 1950s and 1960s, the previously weakened European and Japanese economies strengthened precisely as the American economy slowed. For the United States, the pegged exchange rate meant maintaining an overvalued dollar. The result was a growing balance-of-payments deficit during the 1970s as overpriced American goods sold poorly in foreign markets while cheaper foreign goods flooded the United States. Under a pegged system, the only options to eliminate the balance-of-payment deficits were to (1) pay out gold to creditors (so long as we were on an international gold standard); (2) engineer a domestic recession to lower import demand and reduce the prices of exported goods (thus increasing export volume); (3) establish import controls; or (4) resort to an official devaluation of the nation's currency. For a variety of reasons, each of these options has such serious political or economic effects that the balance-of-payments deficit could not be eliminated. As a result, the worsening U.S. payments situation through the early 1970s was directly traceable to the Bretton Woods–IMF system of fixed exchange rates.

Furthermore, the flow of dollars into European markets and the effects of U.S. government efforts to impose exchange controls created extensive internal currency problems for all nations. The initial flood of U.S. dollars and the attempt to maintain the value of these dollars forced an unwanted inflation on many European nations as their central banks purchased all dollars presented to them. With foreigners now holding more dollars than they wanted—dollars that were believed overvalued by the old Bretton Woods pegging system—the United States was forced to take action. On August 15, 1971, President Nixon suspended the dollar's convertibility to gold. At the time, foreign dollar holdings were four times greater than the value of the U.S. gold stock, the price of which was then officially stated as $35 per ounce. Gold henceforth became a speculative commodity having no official role in international payments. It climbed to over $900 per ounce in 1980 before tumbling back to between $300 and $400 by the mid-1980s.

After the United States ceased gold conversion, there were periodic efforts to revalue the dollar under the old pegging system. However, even after several devaluations of the dollar, it became obvious that the era of fixed exchange rates was over. Each nation now let its currency "float" to whatever value the market established, and neither gold nor U.S. dollars served as the international currency. Instead, the IMF kept national payment accounts in order through a kind of "paper gold" (SDRs, special drawing rights) that were made available to members on a quote system. The value of the SDRs was based on an average of five leading nations' currencies.*

The drift toward floating exchange rates was a desirable development. If practiced honestly and without the slightest tinkering by governments, floating rates allow nations to trade goods based on their real values as opposed to the manipulated values under pegged rates.

Over the long run, flexible exchange rates eliminate balance-of-payments deficits and associated problems. The market forces of supply and demand for a nation's currency create an equilibrium. Assume that two nations are trading. An excess of imports over exports in nation A will bid up the price of the currency of the exporting nation B (or lower the value of the importer's currency relative to that of the exporter). The currency of importing nation A is now devalued. However, this means that its goods are now priced lower than before, and its exports to B will rise while its imports from B will fall until equilibrium between the two trading nations is reached.

From the point of view of most Conservatives, the abandonment of pegged exchange rates and the international gold standard has freed international trade from some of the tyrannies of the past. In theory at least, floating exchange rates can reflect increasingly the real value of a nation's currency against that of other nations. However, this latter situation has not yet been attained. The present managed float system still allows member nations great latitude in determining their own exchange rates and in taking individual actions to bolster their currency. Until exchange rates are freely flexible and until free trade prin-

---

*SDR valuation is now based on the euro, Japanese yen, pound sterling, and the U.S. dollar.

ciples are generally accepted, international trade and currency crises will continue.*

International Crisis as Failure of Domestic Policies

The creation of free trade and freely floating rates, desirable as they are, will not protect a nation that is hell-bent to cut its own throat. The recent exchange rate and trading difficulties of the United States are the direct result of foolish domestic policies. In particular, the expansionary fiscal and monetary policies of the 1970s triggered an inflationary situation that, to our benefit, did drive the price of the dollar downward, but also caused soaring product prices (relative to the rest of the world) that overwhelmed any exchange rate gains. The net result was a decrease in U.S. exports and a rise in U.S. imports. Moreover, in an effort to protect themselves from "importing" the American inflation, a number of our trading partners undertook contractionary economic policies at home. Correspondingly, as the German, Japanese, and other economies cooled down, the ability of the United States to sell in these nations was further reduced.

To prove the point once again that domestic policies are interconnected with international economic conditions, consider what the costs were in the 1980s as America came to grips with the chronic inflation that had gnawed deep into the economy through the 1970s. To halt the inflationary pressures, the Federal Reserve had been required to use a tight-money, high-interest-rate policy. However, the high American interest rates (and the relative stability of the United States as a place for investment) were attractive to foreign investors, who now sought dollars to buy high-yield U.S. securities. Their actions bid up the price of the dollar, and with its rise, the price of American goods rose relative to foreign goods. Soon an unfavorable trade balance changed sharply for the worse. It also produced a growing pressure to return to the bad old days of protective tariffs and pegged exchange rates. The old lie—that

---

*The argument on behalf of floating exchange rates presented here is the "traditional" Conservative view. It should be noted, however, that some Conservatives, led recently by Robert Mundell, favor a return to the gold standard. This view argues that tying the domestic and international monetary arrangements to a fixed gold standard will create greater stability, making it impossible for nations to export their domestic inflationary policies and to "manipulate" exchange rates to their own advantage.

trade balances and currency values can be manipulated as desired through public policy efforts—surfaced again.

Yet America's recent trade problems were not, at bottom, the result of flexible exchange rates and free trade, which were singled out as the culprits by some Liberals. The problems began with domestic inflation, and the problems would only ease by ending inflation—even though the means for fighting inflation might have to be even worse short-term trade deficits. At any rate, the lesson to be learned here is that we cannot separate the domestic economy, either in its general conditions or in the policies undertaken to correct these conditions, from the international economy. To avoid the spillover of domestic policy effects into world markets and back again into the domestic economy, the only certain strategy is to let domestic trends work themselves out naturally and to undertake a minimum domestic policy strategy because supposed public policy "cures" for macroeconomic problems only make the situation worse.

The Trend Toward Freer Trade

Fortunately, historical experience and a better understanding of the merits of free trade have moved trade liberalization to the front of both domestic and international agendas. The development of a North American free trade zone among the countries of Canada, Mexico, and the United States via NAFTA; the FTAA's progress in creating a free trade area throughout much of the Western Hemisphere; expansion of the European Union; the U.S.-Australia Free Trade Agreement; increased participation in the free trade agreements of the Association of Southeast Asia Nations (ASEAN); and the expanded role of the World Trade Organization in managing trade disputes, advancing freer trade, and promoting economic integration is refreshing. It is difficult to determine if this evolution truly represents a change in philosophy among policy makers who in the past have been beholden to Liberal or even Radical views about trade or if they have been overwhelmed by the inevitable failure of public policies designed to obstruct trade.

The Conservative position is absolutely clear with respect to efforts to set up trade barriers to protect American markets and to manipulate currency values to expand exports: All such interference with the market mechanism, despite the short-term painful effects of an unfavorable balance of trade, must be opposed if we are ever to obtain the benefits of free international trade. The negative numbers for the three major gauges of trade balances shown in Figure 7.2 are bound to be cited by Liberals and Radicals as cause for alarm and used as justification for a return to increased meddling with international trade and finance. In fact, recent trade deficits reflect the enviable strength of the U.S. economy. The flexibility of an open, market-based economy has allowed the country to assert its advantages in the production and export of capital goods, technology, and services. America should eschew protectionism and interventionism in favor of focusing on an agenda that can result in improved trade balances such as increasing the domestic saving rate and abiding by more disciplined monetary and fiscal policies (Issue 2).

THE LIBERAL ARGUMENT

Typically, Conservatives remain detached from reality and hopelessly utopian in their advocacy of free trade: the perfect solution for an imperfect world. Although there are, theoretically, greater long-run benefits to be obtained under free trade than under protectionism, Conservatives are calling for America to act as a free trader in a very unfree international economic environment. Playing by the rules while most of the rest of the world cheats has already cost us dearly.

A Background to the Trade Crisis of the 1980s

According to the Conservative scenario, free trade and floating exchange rates go hand in hand to produce harmony and equilibrium in international trade and finance. Quite naturally, they oppose any efforts at protection or manipulation of exchange rates. However, they do not seem to make any connection between their own domestic economic policies and the nation's recent trade deficits, preferring to blame it all on past Liberal economic policy.

In point of fact, the incredible decline of American exports and the even more incredible flood of imports after 1980 were the direct result of Conservative domestic policies that had adverse international effects for the United States *precisely because* we had followed a free trade, floating-exchange-rate path. The scenario went like this: The incorrect Conservative view that the inflationary pressures of the late 1970s were demand-based (too much spending by government, business, and consumers) led to the adoption of a tight money policy by the Federal Re-

196

Figure 7.2 U.S. International Transaction Balances, 1970–2002

Source: Data from *Economic Report of the President* (Washington, DC: Government Printing Office, 2004).

serve System. Consistent with our macroeconomic understandings, this led to rising real interest rates and eventually to a domestic recession. On the surface, the recession might have been expected to have a stimulating effect on exports as prices of domestic goods steadied or even fell a bit. However, this did not happen. Instead, in an economic world where exchange rates had become more flexible (after the collapse of the old pegging system), high interest rates in the United States suddenly became attractive to foreign investors. The demand for dollars (to invest in the United States) grew, and as demand grew, the price of the dollar rose. With the dollar now strengthening relative to other currencies, dollar-denominated goods became more expensive in foreign markets while goods denominated in yen, marks, francs, and other currencies became cheaper in the United States. The effect was to depress U.S. exports and invite an explosive increase in imports. The recession in the domestic economy, stemming as it did from the original tight money policy, was in fact worsened as many key industries were closed out of foreign markets precisely as they were being battered at home by imports.

It suddenly became apparent that domestic economic policies could have unintended international effects in a world of floating exchange rates and free trade. Of course, free traders will argue at this point that sooner or later the overvalued dollar will fall in value as exchange rates adjust. All this supposes, naturally, that exchange rates are in actual fact freely floating, and it presumes that an overvalued dollar will not continue to be propped up by a high-interest-rate money policy that is in place to fight domestic inflation.

While it is easy for economic theorists of any political preference to dismiss protectionism as "beggar thy neighbor" economic policy, the recent protectionist sentiment, from a Liberal point of view, is perfectly explainable and not entirely without justification. The lesson from the trade problems of the 1980s is that pursuit of free trade in a world where some nations practice free trade and maintenance of floating exchange rates while others manage their rates can lead to unacceptable economic costs. These costs materialize in the destruction of certain domestic industries and greatly increased American unemployment. Trade liberalization has encouraged U.S. firms to outsource operations and jobs to less-developed countries with fewer regulatory restraints and lower wages. In short, for all its theoretical attractiveness, free trade and floating exchange rates can, under certain conditions, deliver the opposite of what they promise.

The Case for Modified Protectionism

As Figure 7.3 shows, U.S. tariffs have fallen steadily since World War II and stand at historical lows. Duties collected amount to less than 5 percent of the value of imports. In the 1930s, duties stood at about 60 percent. Moreover, since the Kennedy years the U.S. government has conducted serious trade negotiations to reduce restrictive tariffs and import quotas throughout the trading world.

But reduction of trade restraints must be a two-way street. Reductions of restrictions on U.S. goods should be expected from nations desiring or obtaining benefits from the United States. Otherwise, the United States throws its doors open to foreign goods while its goods are effectively excluded from foreign ports. Nor are tariffs and quotas the only devices nations use for creating trade advantages. The Japanese, for instance, have provided extensive governmental subsidies for their manufacturers, thus creating artificially low prices. Legitimate health and safety concerns to prevent fire blight from being spread to Japan on American apples degenerated into overly stringent regulations that effectively bar most apple imports from the United States despite the fact that the apples are blight-free. Their notorious dumping of such under priced commodities as TVs, cameras, specialty steel items, and the like has provoked the United States to take restrictive trade actions.

The reality of contemporary trade arrangements is one in which the United States must frequently exert muscle through trade restrictions to respond to unfair tactics by other nations. As of February 2004, the U.S. International Trade Commission reported 358 antidumping and countervailing duty orders against 51 countries in retaliation for unfair trade practices. Some of these sanctions were imposed more than two decades ago and have been continued because the offending countries refuse to reform their trade practices.

When these real-world obstacles to trade are considered, it is apparent that the road to free trade is much bumpier than Conservatives admit. Apart from the difficulty of inducing all trading nations to accept the principles of free trade (which would be a minimum requirement even under Conservative logic), the serious domestic problems that might follow the hurried or reckless adoption of free trade must be considered.

First, the failure to employ protective tariffs might deal a deathblow to many American industries. Among these would be firms that are critical to the country's ability to defend itself militarily or to its continued eco-

Figure 7.3   Major U.S. Tariff Laws, Trade Agreements, and Level of Effective Tariffs

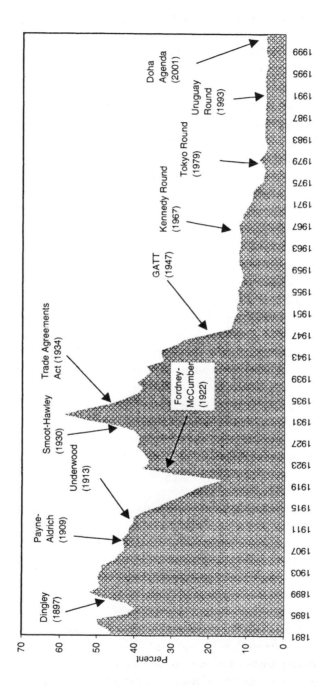

Source: Data from U.S. International Trade Commission.

nomic well-being if world trade is interrupted in the future. In brief, the military and political significance of self-sufficiency in certain goods and raw materials would outweigh the argument of greater efficiency resulting from free trade.

Second, concentrating production efforts only in industrial areas where a nation may have a comparative trade advantage would tend to create an undiversified and possibly unstable economy. As the domestic production mix became more specialized and concentrated, it would become more vulnerable (not stronger, as Conservatives argue) when there was any interruption in world markets. The serious impact that overseas shortages of critical goods might have domestically has been demonstrated amply by the crises caused by the OPEC energy cartel. Similarly, the United States might experience interruptions in the purchase of its specialized goods when buyers disappear. The result would be massive layoffs and recession at home.

Third, and closely associated with the first two points, free trade might have the effect of closing off the development of new (infant) industries. Established overseas firms would enjoy marketing and capital advantages that could not be overcome. Limited, industry-focused tariff protection would allow new industries to emerge and mature. The strategy of industry-focused protection can also be applied to provide "breathing room" for established industries that have been buffeted and smothered by fierce, and often unfair, competition from abroad. The steel tariffs of 2002 were conceived with the intent of providing breathing room for the steel industry to restructure and revitalize itself.

Fourth, American firms might be completely priced out of certain markets by cheaper foreign labor or by foreign dumping, causing massive domestic economic upheaval and unemployment. In the short run, free trade, without any quotas or restrictions, would probably produce massive unemployment in basic industries such as steel and autos, which would make our current unemployment problems in these industries look inconsequential. Even if, in the long run, new industries emerged to fill the employment gap, billions would be spent on unemployment insurance, welfare, and job retraining. Whole areas of the nation would be disrupted as our nation's production mix changed. Such costs would more than offset the efficiency advantages proposed by Conservatives.

Fifth, Liberals are not strictly obsessed with protecting the domestic economy from potentially adverse effects of international competition. The Generalized System of Preferences (GSP) allows developing countries duty-free sales to America for certain goods. This is less expensive than gifts of foreign aid as a way to help poor countries and certainly preferable to a noninterventionist stance of survival of the fittest, which would not allow such assistance.

The Need for Rules and Enforcement

Managing international exchange is nothing new and is practically unavoidable. Increasing *globalization* or *internationalization* of world markets has not been automatically accompanied by implicit rules of free exchange that all trading nations abide by and understand. Trade policy has been increasingly engineered by governments, especially since the inception of the General Agreement on Tariffs and Trade (GATT) in 1947 and its subsequent passage into the World Trade Organization. GATT began with 23 signatory nations and expanded to 147 countries under WTO, accounting for more than 90 percent of world trade. WTO supplies a mechanism by which countries can resolve trade disputes. America has its own antidumping statutes and trade laws that can be invoked in response to specific unfair tactics. The phasing in of free trade to allow time to discern the effect upon particular industries and allow time for adjustments among the signatory nations indicates that NAFTA, FTAA, the U.S.-Australia Free Trade Agreement, and other "free trade agreements" are inclined more toward managed trade than free trade.

Conservatives are correct in asserting that pegging international exchange rates by tying them to gold or the U.S. dollar is misguided. However, the period following the demise of the Bretton Woods system is not characterized by freely floating exchange rates. Central banks of the world and national government, principally of the G-10 countries,* are actively engaged in *managed float.* That is, they have adopted a policy of intervention in foreign exchange markets to maintain orderly market conditions. This vague wording is generally understood to mean offsetting disruptive, short-term variations in exchange rates.

---

*G-10 or "Group of Ten" countries included at the time the United States, United Kingdom, France, Germany, Japan, Belgium, Canada, Italy, Netherlands, Sweden, and Switzerland. The G-10 actually numbered eleven with the addition of Switzerland in 1984. A new forum called the G-20, was composed of big trading nations' finance ministers and central bank governors, and was formed in 1999.

In the 1970s, the United States worked in concert with foreign central banks to reverse the dollar's depreciation, which had been caused by oil crises, inflation, and trade deficits. Subsequently, recession and high interest rates sent the dollar soaring on foreign exchange markets. The Reagan administration was predictably noninterventionist in its first term. However, by the second term of the Reagan presidency the sustained and rapid rise in the dollar was constricting exports and enlarging the trade deficit. Collective action on the part of the major industrialized countries ensued in 1985 in a conscious effort to drive down the value of the dollar and marked the resumption of intervention.

The bottom line is that free trade and freely floating exchange rates are not really the exclusive coordinating mechanism in the world of international trade. For example, a country may attempt to drive down the value of its currency in an effort to offset a trade deficit, which may have been caused by the lowering of trade barriers. Unless the economic nationalism of states can be brought under control through international agreements that are vigorously enforced, the benefits of free trade will always elude those nations that maintain floating exchange rates and open markets.

Putting the International Economy in Perspective

Regardless of what happens in the development and enforcement of international "rules of the game," the United States cannot withdraw from the world economy. Probably the most significant problem posed by free trade and floating exchange rates is that the domestic economy is subordinated in international economic affairs. Policies aimed at correcting balance-of-payments and exchange rate problems may actually worsen domestic problems. For instance, unemployment in the United States would have to grow and an extended domestic recession would be required as the price of ending our international payments deficit.

Free traders may resolve this conflict between needed expansionary policies at home and the required contractionary actions to put international payments in balance by glibly saying, "We must bite the bullet." Matters are not that simple. Indeed, the contraction might be so unbearable as to trigger extensive political reactions in the United States that would destroy not only our political institutions but also the market economy so beloved by Conservatives.

The necessity for strong and enforced trading and exchange rules has never been greater. The American economy is no longer dominant, nor is it insulated from the rest of the world. With the continuing integration of the European economies, the United States will no longer be the largest of the world economies. Requiring that the rest of the world play by the rules of the trading game (and penalizing those who do not) is, after all, only fair. However, given the degree of cheating in the past, as well as our diminished stature in the world economy, the United States may have to act unilaterally to protect itself.

The real measure of a nation's strength in international affairs is the strength of its domestic economy. Accordingly, the United States may have to undertake limited protectionism and exchange rate intervention to shield itself. Such actions, of course, must be complemented by domestic microeconomic and macroeconomic policies to stimulate investment and productivity growth; otherwise, the Conservative scenario of a nation decaying behind its own protectionist walls is a distinct possibility.

THE RADICAL ARGUMENT

Although the Conservative and Liberal scenarios of international trade and exchange problems seem to be quite different, a closer examination indicates that they are similar. Both arguments accept as a matter of fact or "right" the continued dominance of the United States in world trade. The remedies that they suggest for current problems, whether the free trade approach of the Conservatives or the administrative emphasis of the Liberals, are intended primarily to restore and strengthen the American position. Moreover, their underestimation of the significance of international trade and finance and of the degree of crisis now existing in these areas is a dangerous error of judgment.

Capitalist nations do not trade and expand their international influence merely to improve efficiency or to benefit mutually from each nation's exploitation of its comparative advantage. Profit making, pure and simple, is the engine that drives overseas trade and investment. Indeed, the overseas search for markets, cheap resources, and profitable investment is absolutely essential for any capitalist system's continued expansion. Rather than trade and international economic affairs being mere aspects of capitalism, as Conservatives and Liberals suggest, they are the central features of modern production-for-profit economies. The international trade and exchange crisis is thus the result of the insatiable drive of individual capitalist nations to exploit the rest of the world for their own gain.

The Rise of the American Empire

Americans tend to think of themselves as reluctant internationalists drawn into world affairs only to save the rest of the world from itself. However, the facts support quite a different explanation. By the turn of the twentieth century, American capitalism had exhausted its domestic markets. The long decade of depression in the 1890s suggested to many the need for overseas expansion either to obtain markets for surplus goods or to gain access to cheap raw materials and foreign labor. The United States steadily enlarged its world trade between the 1890s and the 1960s, exporting ever-larger amounts of expensive manufactured goods and importing greater quantities of cheap raw materials. At the same time, to secure markets and assume control over raw materials, Americans exported vast amounts of capital (see Table 7.1).

The old trading powers of Europe exhausted themselves in two world wars—wars that had been fundamentally economic wars for trade supremacy—while the United States continued to expand its overseas sales, purchases, and investment. By the 1960s, the United States, in terms of comparative development, had reached the peak of its international economic power. The rise to this height and the later fall are important and instructive enough to examine in some detail.

In 1950, U.S. gross domestic output was about equal to that of the rest of the world combined. Great Britain's output was only 13 percent of America's, while those of France, West Germany, and Japan were 10, 8, and 4 percent, respectively. During World War II, the United States, as principal supplier of arms, had accumulated almost the entire world's gold stock, as well as many other overseas assets. Our exports accounted for about one-third of all the world's exports and more than one quarter of all manufactured exports.

Meanwhile, as a result of Marshall Plan aid and other dollar grants to noncommunist European economies, other capitalist nations fell into a client relationship with the United States. Dependent economically on aid and trade programs and militarily (in the cold war years) on America's armed forces and mutual defense treaties (such as NATO) that were dominated by the United States, the older capitalist nations became part of the American economic sphere. At the same time, the United States expanded

Table 7.1

Value of U.S. Foreign Investment, Selected Years, 1880–2001
(in billions of dollars)

Year	Direct investment abroad
1880	1.6
1890	2.9
1900	2.5
1914	3.5
1920	7.0
1930	17.2
1940	12.2
1950	19.0
1960	40.2
1970	75.5
1980	215.4
1990	620.0
2001	1,598.1

Source: U.S. Bureau of the Census, *Historical Statistics of the United States* (Washington, DC: Government Printing Office), *Economic Report of the President* (Washington, DC: Government Printing Office, 2001), and *Economic Report of the President* (Washington, DC: Government Printing Office, 2004).

its penetration into the Third World, establishing a new, informal colonial system. Within this imperial system, the resource-rich remnants of the former European colonial empire in Africa and Asia joined Latin America as part of the U.S. sphere of influence. Through development aid and especially through supporting friendly but repressive regimes with military assistance, the United States established a neocolonial system without resorting to the old tactic of territorial seizure.

By the late 1950s, the United States enjoyed virtually unchallenged economic hegemony over the noncommunist world, comprising the Western European and Japanese economies and much of the Third World. Supposedly international agencies such as the International Monetary Fund, the World Bank, and the United Nations became arms of American foreign economic and political policy. Under such conditions, it is small wonder that the American dollar became the international medium of exchange and that the international financial situation of the United States appeared so secure. We could virtually dictate exchange rates, and we could hide any balance-of-payments problem by compelling foreign governments to accept and hold dollars rather than demand gold. The ultimate fall from this pinnacle of international power was to be a terrifying experience for Americans.

The Collapse of the Empire

The fall from power was speeded by events overseas and at home. First, the Soviet challenge failed to disappear. The Soviet economy rose swiftly from the ruins of World War II. Despite the Korean War and dozens of other cold war confrontations, the power of cold war ideology in holding the American–Western European alliance together waned as Europeans reevaluated their position within the American empire. This, as much as anything, directed Europe to a more middle-ground approach.

Second, the European economies made their own rapid recoveries in the 1960s. By 1972, the combined gross domestic output of Western Europe and Japan exceeded that of the United States. Accordingly, the U.S. share of world markets declined drastically. Between 1950 and 1972, our share of passenger vehicle production fell from 82 to 29 percent; similarly, the share of steel production fell from 55 to 20 percent and that of energy production from 50 to 33 percent. At the same time, other industrial nations began to claim larger shares of the American market. Finished manufactured imports increased almost 300 percent between 1965 and 1970, while U.S. exports of manufactured goods grew by only 80 percent in the same period.

Third, U.S. domination of the Third World declined. Wars of national liberation and the emergence of new regimes committed to an independent political course eroded American influence. The failure of our effort in Vietnam to stem the tide of Third World nationalism only accelerated the decline of the empire. By 1973, the United States was helpless in dealing with the OPEC oil embargo. In 1979, it could only stand aside quietly as Iran, perhaps one of the most crucial parts of our earlier neocolonial system, threw out its pro-American government.

Fourth, the emergence of American multinational corporations further weakened the United States. The flight of U.S. capital overseas to the expanding economies in Europe and the Third World accelerated the decline of the U.S. balance-of-payments position. The multinationals' flight left investment and employment gaps at home, with which the nation was ill prepared to deal. By 1971, the United States registered the first trade imbalance in the century, as imports exceeded exports.

Global Competition and the Race to the Bottom

The 1990s ushered in a new era of heightened capitalist competition, where the needs and demands of giant multinational corporations are displacing the sovereignty of individual nations. Unelected bureaucrats at such supranational capitalist institutions as the World Bank, the International Monetary Fund, and the World Trade Organization are dictating the rules of world trade while preventing governments from blocking or restricting capital mobility. Corporations and their propagandists have mounted a ferocious campaign against those who challenge or suggest any alternative other than a model of so-called "export-led" growth. By creating an unassailable myth of the benefits of free trade, the neoliberal mantra of "no alternative to the market" has repressed any debate over the winners and losers in the new capitalist world order.

While global capitalism may be presented as the best of all possible worlds, in reality it is a ruthless, anarchic system that destroys everything in its relentless search for profits. In addition, it is inherently self-limiting both because of its wasteful and irrational use of natural, productive, and human resources and because world trade cannot continue to grow much faster than world income. The recent collapse of several Asian economies, combined with the sluggishness in the economies of Europe and Japan, underscores just how vulnerable the entire system is to its own internally generated limits. An obvious question that is never asked by Conservative and Liberal economists is: If all nations are to become rich by exporting to their competitors, who is importing and what is the source of their income? The fact is they have no answer because capitalism is incapable of sustaining balanced and sustainable growth for the benefit of the vast majority of people living under its domination.

Conservative and Liberal economists focus on the trade balance of particular countries, not on international firms, and therefore continue to fail to grasp the growing power of transnational corporations over individual nations. The World Bank estimates that about one-third of total world trade consists of transfers *within* the 350 largest multinational corporations. Intracompany trade, say between Ford plants in America and Mexico, often consists of sending parts or raw materials to one country and finished products back to the other. Such trade is also largely immune from import taxes and jobs are effectively outsourced to other countries. Nevertheless, free trade agreements such as NAFTA and the FTAA are designed to allow greater freedom for transnational capital to move across borders and thus take advantage of lower labor costs.

What about the supposed improvements in U.S. living standards due to the lowering of domestic trade barriers? While it is true that an infusion of foreign capital often entails the acquisition of state-of-the-art production facilities, rarely do the benefits trickle down to the average worker who will use the new machines and equipment. In fact, manufacturing plants in Mexico that employ the most advanced technologies have achieved quality and productivity standards that meet or exceed those in the United States. At this point, traditional economic theory would predict that real manufacturing wages would *have* to increase to U.S. levels following such a notable increase in Mexican labor productivity. Yet workers in Mexico earn much, much less on an hourly basis compared to American workers. Even allowing for generous assumptions about labor market reforms—including minimum wage, health, and safety standards—wages and working conditions remain much lower in Mexico than in the United States. In fact, while Mexico's manufacturing productivity rose by about 40 percent from 1980 to 1992, wages and benefits for manufacturing workers were only about two-thirds of their 1980 levels.

Neither increased job training nor a more efficient structure of production will guarantee a higher standard of living for American workers. This is because the rapid diffusion of technology and heightened competition in both labor and financial markets are swiftly destroying economic advantages that traditionally accrued to industrialized economies for relatively long periods of time. For example, computer programming and design were once thought to be the strict purview of highly trained "knowledge workers" living in the United States. Moreover, a range of high-tech support activities—especially data entry, coding, and computer support services—were also thought to be impervious to competition from workers in low-wage countries. But the widespread use of telecommunications satellites has enabled domestic corporations to employ Third World technical and professional workers at a fraction of the cost of their American counterparts. Today, a U.S. insurance company can hire a computer programmer in India and data entry clerks in Ireland—at one-half to one-third of American wages—to perform all data-processing tasks. Similarly, several high-technology companies such as Texas Instruments are employing mathematicians and other scientists in Russia to write computer software. Clearly, the relatively low value of the ruble and the rupee against the dollar make such arrangements highly profitable.

From a Radical perspective, the problem has been predictable. The internationalization of capital is only a further step in capitalism's irrational development. The strength of the American overseas economic operations of the 1950s and 1960s was the result of its power to exploit the so-called free world. This country's gains were others' losses. What Americans saw as a normal situation was an exceptional one. As the United States' capacity to exploit was successfully challenged by developing socialist countries and by increasing Third World independence and then by other capitalist economies, its premier position in world trade and finance has declined. As overseas growth ends, domestic contraction sets in. The specter of another worldwide capitalist depression looms larger. The crisis is, of course, a production crisis—too many goods and too few buyers. The newly industrialized nations of Southeast Asia have recently experienced such a crisis and have watched gains in living standards fizzle out. Even Japan, the once vaunted industrial powerhouse, faced a collapse of its financial system, despite an overabundance of savings and investment capital and nearly negligible interest rates. Economic growth in Japan has ranged from negligible to nonexistent for more than a decade.

What Is to Be Done?

The globalization of capitalism poses a vexing problem for mainstream economic theory. On one hand, the "triumph" of free markets over centrally planned socialist economies suggests that the private accumulation of capital is a fundamental precondition of political freedom. Nonetheless, it is also clear that placeless transnational corporations are undermining the economic sovereignty of capitalist democracies. Just as the classical English economist David Ricardo feared in 1817, global competition no longer allows "men of property to be satisfied with a low rate of profits in their own country." Even many Conservatives who extol the virtues of the capitalist work ethic (over sloth-promoting social welfare programs) harshly denounce free trade advocates and managed trade technocrats for their unpatriotic policies. Increasingly insecure about their futures, voters are courted by demagogic economic nationalists who want to close the borders to foreign capital and labor.

Is closing the borders to international trade the only viable solution? Not likely. Given the mobility of multinational corporations to move productive resources around the globe, actions by individual governments to control the movement of private capital are not expected to have much effect. Moreover, the growing role of international money managers and currency traders to rapidly mobilize and deploy huge amounts of financial capital is also undermining the power of central banks to control currency and monetary flows. Using sophisticated computer and communications technologies, these managers can instantaneously enter and exit stock and bond markets virtually anywhere in the world. The 1998 hedge fund crises are but one small example of the downside of bringing together technology and capital mobility for private gain.

The fundamental incompatibility between capital mobility and national sovereignty poses a profound, if not intractable, problem for world capitalism. The breakdown of international economic agreements, such as the Bretton Woods accords to control exchange rates, clearly suggests that the self-regulation of fundamentally irrational currency markets is not possible. Free-floating exchange rates can only result in short-term gains for currency traders and economic dislocation and crisis for the vast majority of people throughout the world. Thus it is incumbent on working people throughout the world not only to organize domestically, but also to reach out to their fellow workers outside their borders. Unions need to mobilize their political and economic resources with their counterparts all over the world to break the growing power of multinational financial capital. Unless international corporations are forced to equalize working conditions and wage-and-benefit standards for *all* workers, the relentless search for profits will compel them to drive down labor costs to levels existing in the poorest countries. Furthermore, international governmental organizations cannot be relied upon, or trusted, to act in the interests of workers; time and again organizations such as the WTO and IMF have shown themselves to be completely beholden to capitalists' interests, especially regarding the exercise of labor rights and environmental regulations. Without direct transnational solidarity between working people, standing together to challenge and overthrow the capitalist grip on the world economy, there is little hope. The new international economic order can only result in continued deterioration in the standard of living and overall quality of life for the vast majority of people living on the planet.

Part III

Conclusion

The Market Versus Planning and Controls

Which Strategy Works Better?

Whenever the legislature attempts to regulate the differences between the masters and their workmen, its counsellors are always the masters.

—Adam Smith, 1776

The world is not so governed from above that private and social interests coincide. It is not so managed here below that in practice they coincide. It is not a correct deduction from the Principles of Economics that enlightened self-interest always operates in the public interest.

—John Maynard Keynes, 1926

It used to seem to me that the drift of all Western countries was toward something like socialism. But now, when I reflect on what is happening . . . it is not so clear. There is a sense of return to the market, because the task of planning in a modern economy is so complex.

—Robert Heilbroner, 1986

Off-the-shelf utopias may be useful thought experiments, but they're of limited political use, except maybe as long-term inspiration. A future society has to emerge out of this one, on the basis of experimentation and struggle.

—Doug Henwood, 1997

The Problem

Throughout our examination of contemporary economic issues, there has been a consistent tension among the Conservative defense of a free and unregulated economy, the limited regulation objectives of the Liberals, and the general assault on free markets by Radicals. At issue has been the question of exactly how free or how planned the economy should be. In our closing debate, it is appropriate to deal with this question directly: Which strategy—the free market or some degree of planning and controls—is more likely to provide desirable outcomes?

Based on recent public opinion surveys, trends in American political rhetoric and practice, and events beyond the borders of the United States, an ordinary observer might quickly conclude that planning is in full retreat. Public support for the Keynesian social-engineering efforts of the 1960s and early 1970s withered by the late 1970s. Between 1980 and 1992, first with Ronald Reagan and then with George Bush, Americans elected presidents who, at least in terms of their public posture, were emphatically promarket. Democrat Bill Clinton entered office in 1992 sporting a sort of moderate Liberal posture, briefly turned leftward, and then, after his party lost both houses of Congress in 1994, moved toward a safer middle-ground position. He was reelected in 1996 after announcing that the era of big government was over. Meanwhile, within the domestic economy, "privatization" became an important new buzzword as extended discussions began to take place about spinning off certain longtime bastions of government power to the private sector. Schools, prison systems, and certain public welfare operations were in fact privatized in some areas of the country, and by 1997 there was serious talk of privatizing the Social Security system. With George W. Bush's election in 2000, the nation's political leadership took an obvious and clearly defined Conservative posture.

Beyond the nation's borders, however, the drift toward privatization and the introduction of market economic policies were much more striking, mostly because these shifts were taking place in economies long in the camp of the central planners. The collapse of the Soviet Union first opened Eastern Europe in 1989 to extensive experimentation with and implementation of a wide variety of market-directed economic policies. By 1990–91, in its reconstitution as Russia, the principal remnant of the former Soviet Union had hired a team of American free market advocates to advise the Russian authorities on the transition from a centrally planned communist state to a more democratically open and market-driven political economy.

However, the perilous decline in Russian living standards and life expectancy has undermined popular support for further privatization schemes. Meanwhile, China introduced *enterprise zones* and some limited experimentation with market economics in some of its southeastern provinces. However, the Chinese effort, promising as it is to free market advocates, remains suspect, still laboring under the cloud of that government's brutal reaction to the Beijing student uprising in the spring of 1989 and the considerable repression that persists throughout most of the nation.

Understandably, promarket advocates are quick to draw final conclusions on the basis of these trends. Yet what can we really conclude with certainty? Seven decades ago, in a world caught up in abject economic depression, the market system stood discredited in the eyes of many. However, market-based economics has obviously enjoyed a rebirth in recent years. The failure of the communist-bloc economies may say more about the effects of poor planning and the shortcomings of imposing ideology through the planning apparatus than about planning in general. After all, economic planning in various degrees remains alive and well in many nations, not the least of which are the highly successful cases of Sweden, France, and Germany. Nor can we ignore the fact that economic planning efforts have deep roots in the American past.

Someone unfamiliar with American history might conclude that current economic trends are a ringing and final referendum against any effort to construct even a modestly planned economy. Such a judgment would likely be premature. Popular political belief in the possibilities of national economic planning has frequently surfaced in the past and has been translated into policy. From Alexander Hamilton's *Report on Manufactures* to Henry Clay's American Plan to Woodrow Wilson's progressive New Freedom to Franklin Roosevelt's New Deal, the United States has undergone a number of periods in which varieties of faith in central planning were applied to the nation's economy. Nor were these experiments with planning mere artifacts of a distant political past.

As recently as the 1980–82 recession, even with a staunch defender of free market economics in the White House, another vision of central planning attracted considerable attention, this time with startlingly strong support in the business community. "Industrial policy," as it was known, promised to revitalize American industry through, among other things, the creation of a federal investment bank that would act as a lender of last resort to businesses, especially those rustbelt industries that were particularly hard pressed. Some industrial policy advocates urged that the United States develop its own version of Japan's then highly successful MITI (Ministry of International Trade and Industry). MITI had operated since shortly after World War II, directing Japanese industrial development and targeting winners and losers in Japan's export and domestic markets through its control over research and development funds, investment sources, and imports. However, industrial policy did have its critics in the United States, and it never developed to the point of proposing specific legislation. At any rate, its attractiveness diminished as the recession of the early 1980s lifted.

While the 1980s and 1990s will doubtless be remembered for the resurgence of market economic philosophy in the United States, some observers can be excused if they wondered aloud just how deep this redirection in American economic thinking really went. After all, the scare provided by the stock market crash of Black Monday, October 19, 1987, produced all manner of pleas from members of the business and financial communities for greater controls over securities trading. Similarly, the savings and loan crisis of 1988–89 triggered calls for greater regulation of American banking. And despite the expansive arguments on behalf of deregulation in general, surveys of public attitudes indicate no diminishing of the general population's support for environmental and consumer protection activities by government. In the fall of 2001, as smoke was still rising from the World Trade Center, the public clamored for "sky marshals" and federalized airport security while the airlines and segments of the tourist industry waited for federal assistance. Meanwhile, the 2001 bursting of the stock market bubble and increasing incidents of corporate fraud among such corporate giants as Enron and WorldCom pushed mindless devotion to market capitalism off center stage.

Given the cyclical nature of economic planning's popularity and its tendency to arise precisely as the general economy's performance sags, it is entirely possible that a national debate about industrial policy, full-employment planning, or perhaps even more radical and far-reaching planning efforts simply await the next significant slump in the economy.

Synopsis

For Conservatives, the adoption of national economic planning would mean the ending of capitalism as a social system and the imposition of an inefficient dictatorship in its place. Liberals, however, see planning as compatible with our mixed capitalist economy, since the essential elements of the system (private property and economic and political freedom) would actually be enhanced by the increased stability that planning would provide. To be sure, Liberals advocate only a limited system of planning. Radicals, meanwhile, see present planning proposals only as efforts to maintain the present inequalities and exploitativeness of the capitalist system. To them, planning is essential, but it must be done at the level of human needs, not those of the corporation.

Anticipating the Arguments

- What is the Conservatives' fundamental philosophical disagreement with centralized planning efforts?
- How do Liberals argue that planning and a basically capitalistic economic system are compatible?
- What do Radicals mean when they call for planning "for and by people"?

THE CONSERVATIVE ARGUMENT

At this stage in our discussion of contemporary economic problems, the Conservative response to the idea of national economic planning should be obvious—or perhaps it would be better to say *familiar.* National economic planning, in the sense that it means nonmarket, administrative decisions on output, pricing, employment, capital, and so on, is to be opposed as vigorously as possible. Planning is the final collectivist victory over freedom and individualism. When economic and political authorities, whether they be fascists or communists or even well-meaning Liberals, have the power to determine all important matters in the economy, there is little else left in life that is beyond their ability to control. The frightening scenarios in such books as *Brave New World* and *1984* are no longer merely science fiction.

The economic criticism of central planning is quickly summarized. First of all, it is profoundly inefficient in terms of theoretical economic principles. Second, empirical evidence on efforts at national economic planning (which is abundant) proves that such planning is ineffective.

National Planning: Theoretically Inefficient

As we know, under a market system prices are the signals for economic activity. The decision to produce a particular good can be calculated both in terms of the actual production costs of labor, capital, or resources and in terms of what that particular good costs compared to other goods. As long as the market designates the prices of the factors of production (labor, capital, and resources) and the prices of final goods, we have a rational basis for allocating resources to their best possible uses. As consumers or producers, we can make choices based on a steady and reliable measure of costs and benefits. This is not to say that prices will not fluctuate. Of course they will. They are supposed to fluctuate to reflect changes in demand and supply and thus changes in the cost structure or in consumer satisfaction.

Far from being anarchy, the market *is* a planning mechanism. The market works like a system and, as Adam Smith observed in an essay on astronomy written long before his *Wealth of Nations*, "a system is like a little machine." Like a machine, a market-planned economy has regulators that keep it in balance.

Administrative planning, on the other hand, has no natural internal or external checks on its effectiveness. In an administered economy, levels of output, employment, and the mix of goods are purely matters of political determination. It is not really important whether these goals are set by commissars, Harvard economists, or the duly elected representatives of the people; they are the result of human judgments. They reflect particular individual or collective biases. Not even a computer can tell what output and employment goals are correct unless it is programmed (by humans) to respond to certain criteria (selected by humans).

Defenders of planning may point out that high levels of growth and employment have been attained in certain planned economies. There is some truth to this, but the argument misses the point. Administrative planning in the Soviet Union during World War II and immediately afterward, and in developing nations more recently, was bound to have some success because of these nations' very primitive level of economic development. When you have nothing and plan something, you can hardly lose, especially if you have authoritarian control over the labor force. It is quite another matter, however, to maintain efficient administrative planning in an advanced, complex economy. This, of course, is exactly what the Russians, the East Europeans, and, to some extent, the Chinese discovered in the 1980s, as decades of inefficient planning brought economic growth to a standstill and discredited communism as an economic and political system.

Like market economies, most administered economies use prices to direct economic activity toward predetermined goals. But it should be remembered that these prices, like the goals themselves, are administratively determined. Prices, therefore, do not reflect costs as we speak of them but are merely a rationing technique used to direct labor, capital, output, and, ultimately, social behavior toward certain imposed objectives.

Space prohibits a more detailed theoretical attack on the output and pricing behavior of planned economies, but a brief survey of some of the problems encountered by such economies may demonstrate the essence of the Conservative critique.

National Planning: Ineffective in Practice

The Soviet Union was a striking example of what can happen when economic mechanisms are subordinated to clearly political objectives. Not unlike legislation American Liberals have sought to pass since the "glory days" of Roosevelt's New Deal, Soviet goals also included full employment, enforced price stability, and specific production targets for certain goods.

In the Soviet case, full employment meant a job for everyone. In an authoritarian collectivist society, this was not a great problem, but there is a big difference between putting people in jobs and having them perform productively. For instance, Soviet plant managers, given output goals by state planners (which were to be met *or else*), often feared a shortage of labor in the future and commonly hoarded workers. On other occasions, they had to hire labor as directed by state authorities, whether or not they needed it. In either case, the workers in question were underemployed. In terms of economic analysis, the result is obvious: inefficiency. Workers were hired without any view to their productivity. Wages were set by state planners, who had little or no knowledge of costs of production at a plant. Thus managers might reach their output targets, with workers *fully employed,* but the actual cost of goods (as reckoned by alternative uses of labor and capital) often were much higher than the planners could cover in setting a price. In real terms this meant that the whole society had to pay the actual costs by forgoing other goods. An inefficiently made tractor often "cost" many thousands of nonproduced consumer items.

The tendency to think only in output (quantitative) terms has qualitative effects too. Production rushed to meet a planner's goal may encourage defective and shoddy manufacture. Quick and flexible adaptation of production to meet changes in goals is very difficult. Planners lack the signals of prices based on supply and demand to tell them when and how to change the production mix. Plans become rigid, at both the plant and planning levels.

In the Soviet Union many of the worst features of central planning were eliminated over time. The introduction of linear programming, input-output analysis, and, finally, the computer did improve the accumulation and flow of information. The incredible lapses of mind that earlier had led to the production of motor vehicle engines and chassis but not the needed ball bearings for their wheels had generally disappeared by the 1980s. In fact, Soviet industry had achieved a measure of technological success in some cases (for example, space-related industries). However, as Gorbachev took over, the overall microeconomic decision-making process remained bogged down by the political administration of prices and wages and by mind-boggling distributional inadequacies. Even after years of sacrifice to build the industrial base of the society, ordinary Russians remained as they had always been—the balancing item in the central plan ledger. The errors of planners, even those with computers, were still to be paid for in relinquished consumer goods and in a scarcely improving standard of living. In the end, Gorbachev's timid efforts were his and the Soviet Union's undoing. Racked by strikes, internal economic crises and political disarray, and the secession of key states in the union, the USSR passed into history. Gorbachev was removed from power in December 1991, and in the fall of 1992, the Constitutional Court of Russia ruled that while communists could still enjoy local political rights and protections, the Communist Party, as a national political party, was illegal. Meanwhile, the party's financial assets and real property were placed under the control of the Russian Federation. The foremost model of the centrally planned, authoritarian state came to an end after a mere seventy-five years of existence.

Putting Planning Within an American Context

Critics will argue that the Soviet case is irrelevant to any planning situation affecting the United States. They will maintain, of course, that American *mixed capitalism*—a combination of a dependence on the market and relevant interventions to correct the market—is much different from a fully planned, authoritarian economic system. To Conservatives, though, the threat of planning is quite real. Talk of national economic planning goes back a long way in American history, and, as is evident in day-to-day government reaction to the issues discussed in this book, the tendency toward collectivist solutions to all economic problems, although diminishing a bit lately, remains strong. History shows that, once commenced, the march toward collectivism is hard to reverse. Today we may be talking merely of obtaining additional data for national planning or making full employment a law. Tomorrow the managed-economy objectives may be more personal to all of us— determining where we live, where we work, what we buy, and so on.

Conservatives are not anarchists. Indeed, they believe in planning, and today we have a high order of acceptable planning in the economy. This planning, however, is a function of *individual choices collectively expressed in the market.* As Milton Friedman has observed:

> Fundamentally, there are only two ways of coordinating the economic activities of millions. One is central direction involving the use of coercion—the technique of the army and of the modern totalitarian state. The other is voluntary cooperation of individuals—the technique of the market place. . . . Exchange can bring about coordination without coercion.*

The present in-between, never-never land of mixed American capitalism cannot continue long. *We must go either one way or the other in the future.*

The Dynamism of the Market

Critics of the market economy have always stressed that the fundamental weakness of a truly capitalist economic system is its recurring propensity toward varieties of instability. Such an idea is both overworked and misleading. As our earlier discussion should have pointed out, the failure of planned economic systems—such as the old Soviet Union— to meet individual needs can be vastly greater than the uncertainties a market order might create.

Yet, the critics do have a point. Market capitalism can be a disruptive system. Indeed, it should be. The driving force of a production-for-profit

---

*Milton Friedman, *Capitalism and Freedom* (Chicago: University of Chicago Press, 1962), 13.

market system is *change*—change in the goods that are produced, change in the way goods are produced and sold, and change from time to time in the distribution of the goods and the distribution of claims to goods produced. The great Austrian economist who for many years taught at Harvard University, Joseph Alois Schumpeter, called this process of capitalist uncertainty and change "creative destruction."

In the very processes of invention, innovation, and the resulting rise of new investment and production opportunities—always events encouraged in a market economic order—the society, said Schumpeter, would be swept by "gales of creative destruction." Perfectly serviceable factories and machines could be rendered obsolete instantly. Old capital investments could rapidly depreciate to scrap. Once-valued skilled labor could become redundant. Great redistributions of income and economic power could take place as new entrepreneurs with new ideas, driven by the desire to profit from their inventions and innovations, turned the old economic order upside down. But, Schumpeter maintained, the resulting destruction was worth the cost to everyone. Better goods, more efficiently produced, provided society with net positive gains even after the costs of destruction were subtracted.

Yet, as Schumpeter knew, there was always a variety of social groups who entrenched themselves against creative destruction. Labor unions, monopolistic business enterprises, bureaucracies of any kind, and their principal agent, government, all stand ready to protect the status quo by controlling, really strangling, change.

Those Liberal and Radical opponents of the market are not just advocates of a different view of economic progress and the benefits that thereby might be accorded. They are, in their hearts and minds, the enemies of progress itself.

THE LIBERAL ARGUMENT

By this point the Liberal propensity to approach contemporary economic problems in pragmatic and nondogmatic ways should be self-evident. Equally, it should be evident that both Conservatives and Radicals, despite their vastly different ideological agendas, share a peculiar tendency: to present economic behavior and economics itself as largely deterministic and mechanistic processes. That is, economic thinking and economic undertakings are viewed not as matters of human choice or as matters of cultural habit but as the unfolding of abstract and eternal verities that, quite simply, exist independently of human beings and of human history. The Radical argument has for the time being been shoved off into history's dustbin as a result of the failure of the Soviet Union. However, and regrettably for the discipline of economics, the Conservative vision has recently come to exercise considerable influence in mainstream American economic thought. It has also been gaining greater influence outside of the United States. Liberals cannot let this development go unchallenged and the debate over the comparative virtues of *the market* versus *employing planning and controls* is a good place to reveal the analytical and practical weakness of the Conservative argument.

The Narrow and Unrealistic Assumptions of Market-Logic Advocates

To see where Conservatives think they are going, it is necessary to understand the logic from which their argument proceeds. The argument, of course, was first set out by Adam Smith a bit over two hundred years ago and augmented and enriched a hundred years later by neoclassical economics. Together Smith and the neoclassical traditions are the foundations of modern Conservative emphasis upon market logic.

Market logic, first of all, presumes the existence of cultural and political stability as a given. Only amid this general external stability is it possible for a market to work according to a fairly consistent and predictable set of expectations. Second, market logic assumes the presence of *rational maximizing* behavior on the part of all individuals as a central element in the popular will of that society. Without social stability and without popular support for individual self-interest, the seeds of market logic cannot take root and give rise to appropriate practices of production-for-profit behavior. A third requirement specifies a *minimum government* condition to be present; in other words, a popular willingness never to tinker collectively with market outcomes. And, although the caveat hardly needs to be added, Conservatives believe the market, left essentially to its own dynamic, will be a competitive market. It should be remembered that all of these conditions are not viewed as mere accidental matters but as normal conditions that will naturally arise over time.

Right away, it becomes evident that a goodly portion of the world's population lives outside the conditions where a truly market-driven economic system could flourish. For instance, consider the problem of rational maximizing. The assertion that human beings are first and foremost acquisitive and self-interested individualists is impossible to prove and is easily disputed by real-world events. It goes without saying that much of the world is ruled by very different outlooks. The dominance of nationalistic, religious, and tribal orthodoxies that militate against individualistic and materialistic values poses an important practical problem in many nations for the development of a personal and social behavior that market-logic theorists describe as "human behavior" and as "natural." Much more troubling to market-logic adherents, however, is the fact that, even in social systems that have been receptive to individualist and materialist values and to the broad outlines of market logic, the tendency to tinker with and try to improve upon free market outcomes has been irresistible. While market-logic advocates rail against big government and its interference in the workings of the market, they offer no convincing explanation for the rise of this clearly *unnatural* tendency in the first place. After all the Conservative arguments against state interference in economic affairs have been reviewed, it still seems fairly obvious that big government with its planning and controls was not invented for the purpose of creating economic inefficiency and dependency.

Certainly in the United States, big government emerged initially as a corrective "political response" to problems viewed as inherent to free markets. It was from practical political experience, not an ignorance of economic logic, that Americans came to understand that a high order of personal freedom entailed much more than just having the right to be a rational maximizer and that individual economic freedom in no way ensured all individuals would enjoy fair and just outcomes in the marketplace.

The principal problem, then, that Conservatives have with regard to the accuracy of their market model and the relevance of its rational maximizer prescription is that none of the world's nations spells out citizens' rights and responsibilities in purely economic terms. The various freedoms and nonfreedoms that individuals have in virtually any society are derived from the prevailing political and social conventions deemed essential by that society to perpetuate and protect itself. Any particular society's taste for economic individualism and for free markets is necessarily constrained by these realities. In any case, the *political* requirements of a social order are set first and the acceptable range of economic behavior follows—a very different reality from the market-logic vision of things.

Putting the Role of the State in the Correct Perspective

Quite apart from the logical problems of Conservatives, there is the practical matter that history offers no convincing example of a successful free market economy. To be sure, there may have been some near misses. Perhaps England of the 1830s, the United States of the 1850s, possibly even Singapore a couple of decades ago demonstrated certain free market characteristics that were reminiscent of market-logic inspiration, but, on closer look, they were pretty pale copies, clearly not meeting the required standards.

With the possible exception of theological belief associated with religious faith, probably no set of formal arguments has endured so long in the absence of any convincing real-world evidence of their practicality and validity as those laid out by the classical advocates of market logic. Even formal scientific postulates in biology, astronomy, and physics have proven to be more adaptive to real-world constraints and the force of empirical evidence. Accordingly, for a very long time now, Conservative economic thinkers have had to spend much of their time explaining why their free market vision has not come to pass. Indeed, these explanations generally occupy more space in Conservative writings than the real body of Conservative analytical doctrine.

Variously over the years, labor unions, monopolistic business enterprise, socialists, communists, intellectuals, and many other groups have been singled out as part of the general "conspiracy" against free markets. And always the device these conspirators have employed to destroy or subvert true economic freedom has been the most malignant of human institutions: government. In any case, it is a heavy burden for Conservatives to bear, constantly having to explain why the "natural" conditions of a free economic order are forever undermined by "unnatural" conspiracies and events.

The Conservative assault on government, apart from its logical irrelevance, as we have earlier noted, rests on a revealing irony. It is true, of course, that Adam Smith intended his articulation of a market economy to free economic thinking (at least English economic thinking) from the hold long imposed by the mercantilist state. But Smith was no anarchist. He continued to assign to government, in his own version of state power, fairly considerable economic responsibilities. These powers Smith's followers ever sought to diminish. Yet, irony of ironies, the English classical economic tradition, the precursor of all market-logic efforts, only gained practical influence through its own, quite unnatural manipulation of government.

In England, as in other nations undergoing industrialization during the first half of the nineteenth century, it was the machinery of government—not the absence of such machinery—that was essential in rolling back the paternalism and protectionism of the feudal and mercantilist past. Repeal in 1846 of the Corn Laws protecting English agriculture, passage in 1832 of a new Poor Law that set aside the social protection of the unemployed in the name of a free labor market, and enactment of the Banking Act of 1844, which set Great Britain upon a gold standard, were efforts *by the state,* supported of course by the advocates of free markets, that paved the way for the temporary flourishing of laissez-faire economic conditions. As Karl Polanyi pointed out many years ago: "Laissez-faire itself was enforced by the state. . . . Laissez-faire was not a method to achieve a thing, it was the thing to be achieved."*

From the beginning, everywhere market capitalism surfaced in its varied forms, the state was the instrumentality through which it came into being. Capitalism was not obtained, as Conservative doctrine might lead one to believe, through evolutionary practice and the "natural" march of economic progress. Indeed, without the state's acting on behalf of a market capitalist agenda, there was no surety that capitalism—or at least capitalism as most Western nations have come to know it—would have emerged at all. And, when the experiments with a laissez-faire market system experienced difficulties from time to time, the state was to be used again and again in either its maintenance or its reform. By regulating away capitalism's more obnoxious social effects, and thereby at least maintaining the basic elements of production-for-profit, practical men of affairs, if hardly ever Conservative economic thinkers, recognized that saving half a loaf was better than no bread at all.

To be sure, many of the market-driven economic tools of Conservative economic theory have been and continue to be useful analytic devices. Liberal economic analysis, as it is known and taught in the United States, is built, after all, on the foundation of classical economics. But the larger vision of Conservatives is another matter. Their faith in the efficient and fair functioning of an economy free of all planning and controls is blind to the flaws of its own logic and overlooks the evidence of history. It is a hopelessly mechanical argument in which iron-clad

---

*Karl Polanyi, *The Great Transformation* (New York: Rinehart, 1944), 250.

economic "laws" can be used to justify great varieties of inequity and unnecessary pain. Capitalism as a system may be able to function and thrive, but only with periodic adjustment and repair.

The Objectives of Liberal Interventionism

A quick review of the Liberal arguments in each of the preceding economic issues provides a range of the types of tinkering Liberals are content to support. The Liberal view is certainly not the collectivist vision Conservatives assign to it.

Contrary to the Conservative outlook, planning is not necessarily communism, nor is it authoritarianism of any special breed. Planning is essential to maintaining the American democratic capitalist tradition. To the Liberal, of course, "democratic" is much more important than "capitalist" in a generic sense. The economic experiences of the United States and all other basically capitalist countries indicate quite clearly that only planning can save the private-property, production-for-profit system from self-destruction.

Although he has not always been in the mainstream of Liberal opinion, John Kenneth Galbraith's observations of over three decades ago fairly represent the Liberal position of today. After weighing the growing problems of American industrial society, Galbraith concluded:

> It is through the state that the society must assert the superior claim of aesthetic over economic goals and particularly of environment over cost. It is to the state we must look for freedom of individual choice as to toil. . . . If the state is to serve these ends, the scientific and educational estate and larger intellectual community must be aware of their power and their opportunity and they must use them. There is no one else.*

THE RADICAL ARGUMENT

Despite the current Conservative celebration of a renaissance of free market thought and practice, capitalism has for a considerable period of time moved inexorably toward greater central control. Although there is much debate on how close we really are to a formally planned and con-

---

*John K. Galbraith, *The New Industrial State* (Boston: Houghton Mifflin, 1967), 335.

trolled economy, Radicals would generally agree that it is the next great leap in capitalist development. From laissez-faire to monopoly capitalism to state-corporate regulation to formal planning, capitalism runs its course in its effort to secure profit and protect itself. The obvious irony, of course, is that planned capitalism is a contradiction in terms. As the basic economics textbooks tell us, capitalism emerged as a philosophy espousing, in theory at least, total economic and personal freedom. Alas, in the practical world, it ends as a statement on behalf of authoritarianism.

From the Radical perspective, it is necessary to get beyond the thoughtless celebration of market economics that presently pervades popular opinion and political rhetoric in the United States. Quite simply, this resuscitation of capitalist ideology has served to obscure the capitalist reality we in fact live in and to mystify for many the actual workings of modern capitalism. Yet the symbiotic relationship between capitalist enterprise and the modern capitalist state persists just below the surface of everyday economic life if only we care to dig beneath the veneer of Conservative ideology.

Capitalism Needs Planning

Ideologies, even after they have proved worthless, die hard, often convulsively. It remains to be seen how the outmoded rhetoric of laissez-faire or even the more sophisticated mixed-economy philosophies will pass into history. They are deeply rooted in the individual practice and thought of American citizens, and their public defenders are still loud and shrill. Nevertheless, as our discussions of other contemporary issues should indicate, the use of government controls and planning in the economy is apparent everywhere.

This process is not really very new. It originated in the late nineteenth-century response to the growing crises of American capitalism. Troubled by periodic panics or recessions (in 1873, 1884, 1893, and 1907), chronic excess capacity and overproduction, and anarchic market conditions, and threatened by increasingly radicalized labor strife, American capitalism depended more and more on state intervention. We have elaborated on these interventions in our discussions of stabilization policy, government deficits, unemployment, and international trade. As the state became a partner in supporting business, American corporations enlarged their monopoly powers through concentration and control.

This growth of state-corporate integration has been euphemistically termed the "mixed economy" in economics texts. Uninformed Conservatives have attacked this integration as the domination of business by the state, without even stopping to ask just whose interests the state has represented. They fail to see that, quite as Marx specified, "the State is the form in which the individuals of the ruling class assert their common interests."

Capitalist production has proved to be extraordinarily rational in a microeconomic sense. The organization of production, labor, and capital for any particular firm is governed by economic rules of behavior (we call it the price system) that, for an individual entrepreneur, give key signals on how best to attain profit objectives. Yet, in totality, the capitalist system is irrational. Though the actions of any given firm are rationally planned or calculated with profit in mind, the actions of all firms taken together produce macroeconomic and social disorder. There is a lack of coordination and integration, even among monopolistic capitalists, in dealing with different industries and different sectors of the economy. Rational control of the whole labor force, of total output, and of investment alternatives is lacking.

The boom-bust rhythm of the business cycle, although recently muted when compared to the past, is still evident—but with a difference. Today's highly integrated and automated production is extremely vulnerable to even the slightest variations in sales, profits, and output. In the past, when industry was predominantly labor-intensive, a business downturn amounted mainly to sending the workers home with empty pay envelopes and waiting until things got better. Today, with greater capital usage and production on an international scale, nonproduction presents a firm with greater losses. These, in turn, adversely affect financial markets and the international structure of business.

Moreover, modern capitalism has so penetrated the world that it is limited in its ability to acquire new markets, so essential to its survival. At the same time, as we have noted repeatedly before, capitalist production can be carried on at higher output levels using less labor power. As a result, the crowning irrationality of the system is that it can produce more and more, but labor becomes increasingly redundant and markets harder to find.

The chronic tendency toward unemployment and excess capacity, the steady threat of inflation, and the worsening balance-of-trade situation leave few options for American capitalism. As the Liberal John Kenneth

Galbraith has argued for years, the next step in capitalist development is to transcend the market and modern Keynesian efforts to correct it and to move straight toward direct economic planning and controls. Only through such efforts can capitalist irrationality be controlled. Planning presents possibilities for reorganizing the capitalist processes of production and accumulation and at the same time can legitimize or bring order to labor markets.

Planning for Profits, Not People

One of the great self-deceptions of Conservative economic thought is the doctrinaire view that planning is inimical to market-based economic behavior. It is wrongheaded as a logical matter and a positively silly notion as a matter of real-world practice. Capitalists, whether we are talking of giant corporations or small mom-and-pop operations, do not earn their profits accidentally. In any case, it would be absurd to suggest that Microsoft, General Motors, and Citicorp do not have a plan for their business operations, that at the end of the year of producing and selling goods and services willy-nilly they are randomly surprised or dismayed when they tally their sales and expenses.

No one in their right mind would seriously argue that planning is not an essential element of every business enterprise's operations. Planning within the modern enterprise is, of course, much more important than it was at the dawn of the capitalist era when Adam Smith and his colleagues were working out the "rules" of a market economy. This does not reflect so much a philosophical change in capitalists' approach to the everyday matter of obtaining profit as it does the vastly increased complexity of the goods they make and the techniques necessary to manufacture and sell these goods.

However, if planning is important as an everyday operational function within a business, why are planning efforts between and among businesses and planning utilizing government not seen as natural progressions for capitalism as a system? Obviously, the Conservative assault upon planning is a spurious argument not taken seriously by real-world practitioners of production for profit.

In fact, business enterprisers—especially large business enterprisers— see real gains and opportunities to be obtained from planning. During the late 1970s and into the 1980s, as the American economy sagged through a particularly unimpressive period of slow growth, high unemployment, and lowered profits, many in the business community flirted publicly with the idea of enlarging the federal government's role as a central planner. Many spoke warmly on behalf of an *industrial policy* that embraced a joint government-business coordination of investment, labor, and trade policies to deal with the then preoccupying concern about the *deindustrialization* of America. To be sure, this enthusiasm for planning has flagged a bit over the past two decades as the American economy's performance and prospects brightened. But when the boom turns to bust, as it surely will and as it always has, it is reasonable to expect that capitalists will rediscover industrial policy.

Regardless of the simplistic Conservative notion that all centralized efforts at economic planning and control are threats to a production-for-profit system, Radicals understand the real issues in any discussion of planning to be very different matters. The crucial question that any inquiry into economic planning should raise is: planning by whom and for what objective? Planning of an industrial policy variety still operates within the capitalist firmament. It amounts to planning by capitalists, or their agents, for the purpose of maintaining profits for business enterprises and profit-making as a social objective. The name of the game in capitalism is still profits, and, contrary to Liberal apologists, the name does not change when essentially capitalist systems adopt centralist planning techniques.

As long as business profitability is the guiding force of planning efforts, Americans will never be able to transcend the limitations of the social order under which they live. Quite literally, all human experience will remain subservient to and positively limited by the eternal quest for *the bottom line*. Radicals have a different prescription for the economic order: Planning should first and foremost be about meeting the needs of real living and breathing people.

The Radical Alternative: Planning for and by People

Although Radicals may be divided on the means by which social planning is to be achieved, there is greater agreement on *how* such planning should proceed once it is established. Most American Radicals would reject out of hand the varieties of social planning demonstrated by such socialist nations as the Soviet Union or China. These efforts at state planning simply lost sight of the major objective of any rational and humane planning: *people.* In these cases, plans were developed and imposed from above by central planning or political authorities whose decisions had no more to do with workers' and consumers' needs than decisions currently being made by Exxon or IBM officials.

The first and unifying rule for Radicals with regard to planning is that the planning process must begin with popular participation and must be conceived to deal with people's problems.

The complexity of modern economies and the immensity of providing people with the opportunities to plan such economies, of course, seem so formidable as to make most citizens believe that popular planning is simply impossible. Radicals reject such a view out of hand. To do anything else would be to submit to the tyranny that is the capitalist mode of production. There are, of course, many levels of planning, from decisions pertaining to a particular plant or factory to broad national output targets. Obviously, the more distant the level of planning, the more difficult individual participation becomes. Nevertheless, society now has the appropriate means of production, such as computer and information processing technologies, to make widespread planned coordination between producers and consumers a reality. Innovations such as bar code technologies and integrated communication and computer networks can facilitate a speed and depth of coordination and allocation that is far superior to anarchic capitalist markets. Recognizing that the Soviet and Chinese communist cases are examples of what can happen when planning lacks the requisite information processing and coordination capabilities and becomes too abstracted from popular input, the object is always to keep as much of the decision making at the lower levels as possible and, when that is no longer a reasonable alternative, to devise the broader elements of the plan through as democratic a means as possible.

Workers or their directly elected representatives must be the basis for local output, pricing, and workplace decisions. Such decisions, of course, must be made with an eye to the general welfare. No worker or group of workers has the right to earnings obtained by sacrificing consumers or some other group of workers. That would merely be capitalism reappearing in the disguise of socialism, and it would lead to the same kind of exploitative conditions we now live under. Thus it is obvious that workers must be joined by consumers in the local or lower-level planning activities. Organizing broad popular participation in the planning process will not be easy, nor is there absolute certainty that a democratically devised plan will not be guilty of error and even failure. It is comparatively easy for Conservatives and Liberals to paint a picture of chaotic planning meetings as various representatives of workers, managers, and consumers determine key economic objectives. However, they miss two very important points. First, the failures of such planning efforts can be little worse than the current private planning "successes." Second, even at its worst, planning based on workers' and consumers' participation *is* democratic planning and *is* consistent with the professed ideals of a democratic society.

Regardless of the precise methods ultimately devised to facilitate participatory planning—and trial and error will certainly play a role in selecting planning goals—the Radical holds to a basic belief that the people must be the architects of their own society. The basic economic decisions of *what* is produced, *how,* and *for whom* must not be entrusted to an elite, whether they be capitalists, political commissars, or excommissars turned capitalist.

The late Radical economic and social historian William Appleman Williams put it this way:

> Hence the issue is not whether to decentralize the economy and politics of the country, but rather how to do so. . . . This literal reconstructing and rebuilding of American society offers the only physical and intellectual challenge capable of absorbing and giving focus to the physical and intellectual resources of the country during the next generation. . . .
>
> Throughout such a process, moreover, the participants will be educating themselves . . . for their membership in the truly human community they will be creating. In the end they will have built a physical America which will be beautiful instead of ugly, and which will facilitate human relationships instead of dividing men into separate functional elements. They will have evolved a political system which is democratic in form and social in content. And they will be prepared . . . to function as men and women who can define their own identity, and their relationships with each other, outside the confining limits of property and the bruising and destructive dynamics of the competitive marketplace. They will be ready to explore the frontier of their own humanity.*

---

*William A. Williams, *The Great Evasion* (Chicago: Quadrangle Books, 1964), 175–76.

Final Thoughts and Suggested Readings

Having reached the end of this volume of debates on contemporary economic issues, it is probable that the reader expects (perhaps even hopes for) the authors to make their pitches—to say straight out which of the representative paradigms is correct and which is not, perhaps each one to unveil his own grand program. Indeed, the opportunity is tempting. For an economist, it is practically a reflex to try to get in the last word, especially one's own last word. However, after much thought, we decided that such conclusions would spoil the entire effort. This book was undertaken to present the differing ideological alternatives as objectively as space and writing talents allowed so that the reader would be free to make personal choices on matters of economic policy.

We can hear some readers complaining: "Cop-out! You're avoiding presenting your own preferences and your own conclusions. You've taken the easy way out of the swamp." Not so. Delivering our own final polemics would in truth be ever so easy. But the book has been about questions and choices. The reader, then, shall be left in the uncomfortable position of making a choice among the paradigms and policy questions surveyed here. And that is the way it should be.

This perspective, however, must not be misunderstood. The authors have not intended to produce a relativistic conclusion in which any choice will do and one choice is as good as any other. The point is for the reader to make a *good* choice, and some policy choices *are* better than others. However, only a reasoned analysis of the facts and a critical study of the truths of this world will permit any of us to make wise choices.

The British economist Joan Robinson has said it best:

> Social life will always present mankind with a choice of evils. No metaphysical solution that can ever be formulated will seem satisfactory for long. The solutions offered by economists were no less delusory than those of the theologians that they displaced.
>
> All the same we must not abandon the hope that economics can make an advance towards science, or the faith that enlightenment is not useless. It is necessary to clear the decaying remnants of obsolete metaphysics out of the way before we can go forward.
>
> The first essential for economists, arguing amongst themselves, is to "very seriously," as Professor Popper says that natural scientists do, "try to avoid talking at cross purposes."*

Before we can "avoid talking at cross purposes" on economic matters, we must understand our fundamental differences in opinion and interpretation. We hope this book has identified some of these important differences for the reader.

In undertaking this task, the authors were sorely tested. While trying to submerge our personal biases, we also had to master the biases of others. Perhaps we have not entirely succeeded on either count. Only the reader can judge. Nevertheless, such an endeavor has been extremely educational.

For readers who desire to dig deeper into economic ideologies and their application to contemporary issues, the following bibliography offers some landmark readings in the respective Conservative, Liberal, and Radical schools of economic thought.

Conservative

Banfield, Edward C. *The Unheavenly City.* Boston: Little, Brown, 1970.

Buckley, William. *Up from Liberalism.* New York: Honor Books, 1959.

Friedman, Milton. *Capitalism and Freedom.* Chicago: University of Chicago Press, 1962.

————. *Free to Choose.* New York: Harcourt Brace Jovanovich, 1980.

Gilder, George. *Wealth and Power.* New York: Basic Books, 1981.

Hazlitt, Henry. *The Failure of the "New Economics": An Analysis of the Keynesian Fallacies.* New York: Van Nostrand, 1959.

Kirk, Russell. *The Conservative Mind.* Chicago: Regnery, 1954.

---

*Joan Robinson, *Economic Philosophy* (Garden City, NY: Anchor Books, 1964), 147–48.

Klamer, Arjo. *Conversations with Economists*. Totowa, NJ: Rowman and Allanhold, 1983.

Knight, Frank. *Freedom and Reform*. New York: Harper and Row, 1947.

Malabre, Alfred E., Jr. *Living Beyond Our Means*. New York: Vintage Books, 1987.

Marshall, Alfred. *Principles of Economics*. New York: Macmillan, 1890.

Rand, Ayn. *Capitalism: The Unknown Ideal*. New York: New American Library Signet Books, 1967.

Schumpeter, Joseph. *Capitalism, Socialism, and Democracy*. New York: Harper Brothers, 1942.

Simon, William E. *A Time for Action*. New York: Berkley, 1980.

Simons, Henry C. *A Positive Program for Laissez-Faire*. Chicago: University of Chicago Press, 1934.

Smith, Adam. *An Inquiry into the Nature and Causes of the Wealth of Nations*, 1776.

Stein, Herbert. *Presidential Economics: The Making of Economic Policy from Roosevelt to Reagan and Beyond*. New York: Simon and Schuster, 1985.

Von Hayek, Friedrich. *The Road to Serfdom*. Chicago: University of Chicago Press, 1944.

Von Mises, Ludwig. *Socialism: An Economic and Sociological Analysis*. New Haven: Yale University Press, 1959.

Liberal

Berle, Adolf A. *The Twentieth-Century Capitalist Revolution*. New York: Harcourt Brace Jovanovich, 1954.

Clark, John M. *Alternative to Serfdom*. New York: Random House/Vintage Books, 1960.

———. *Social Control of Business*. New York: McGraw-Hill, 1939.

Friedman, Benjamin. *Day of Reckoning*. New York: Random House, 1988.

Galbraith, John Kenneth. *The New Industrial State*. Boston: Houghton Mifflin, 1967.

———. *The Affluent Society*. Boston: Houghton Mifflin, 1971.

———. *Economics and the Public Purpose*. Boston: Houghton Mifflin, 1973.

———. *Economics in Perspective*. Boston: Houghton Mifflin, 1987.

Hansen, Alvin. *The American Economy*. New York: McGraw-Hill, 1957.

Heilbroner, Robert. "The Future of Capitalism" in *The Limits of American Capitalism*. New York: Harper and Row, 1966.

———. *The Nature and Logic of Capitalism*. New York: Norton, 1985.

Heller, Walter W. *The Economy: Old Myths and New Realities*. New York: Norton, 1976.

Keynes, John M. *The General Theory of Employment, Interest, and Money*. New York: Harcourt Brace Jovanovich, 1936.

Lekachman, Robert. *The Age of Keynes*. New York: Random House, 1966.

Okun, Arthur M. *The Political Economy of Prosperity*. New York: Norton, 1970.

Reagan, Michael D. *The Managed Economy*. New York: Oxford University Press, 1963.

Reich, Robert B. *Tales of a New America*. New York: Times Books, 1987.

Shonfield, Andres. *Modern Capitalism: The Changing Balance of Public and Private Power*. New York: Oxford University Press, 1965.

Thurow, Lester C. *Dangerous Currents*. New York: Basic Books, 1980.

———. *The Zero-Sum Solution*. New York: Simon and Schuster, 1985.

Radical

Baran, Paul. *The Political Economy of Growth.* New York: Monthly Review Press, 1957.

Baran, Paul, and Paul M. Sweezy. *Monopoly Capital.* New York: Monthly Review Press, 1966.

Botwinick, Howard. *Persistent Inequalities.* Princeton, NJ: Princeton University Press, 1993.

Bowles, Samuel, and Herbert Gintis. *Property, Community, and the Contradictions of Modern Social Thought.* New York: Basic Books, 1986.

Bowles, Samuel, and Richard Edwards. *Understanding Capitalism.* New York: Harper and Row, 1985.

Brouwer, Steve. *Sharing the Pie: A Citizen's Guide to Wealth and Power in America.* New York: Henry Holt and Company, 1998.

Domhoff, William. *Who Rules America?* Englewood Cliffs, NJ: Prentice-Hall, 1967.

Dowd, Douglas. *The Twisted Dream.* Cambridge, MA: Winthrop, 1974.

Duboff, Richard. *Accumulation and Capital.* Armonk, NY: M.E. Sharpe, 1990.

Franklin, Raymond S. *American Captialism: Two Visions.* New York: Random House, 1977.

Gordon, David M. *Fat and Mean.* New York: The Free Press, 1996.

Henwood, Doug. *Wall Street.* London: Verso, 1997.

Kolko, Gabriel. *Wealth and Power in America.* New York: Praeger, 1962.

Magdoff, Harry. *The Age of Imperialism.* New York: Monthly Review Press, 1967.

Mandel, Ernest. *Marxist Economic Theory.* New York: Monthly Review Press, 1967.

Marx, Karl. *Capital.* 1867.

O'Connor, James. *The Fiscal Crisis of the State.* New York: St. Martin's Press, 1973.

Robinson, Joan. *An Essay on Marxian Economics.* London: Macmillan, 1942.

Shaikh, Anwar M., and E. Ahmet Tonak. *Measuring the Wealth of Nations.* Cambridge: Cambridge University Press, 1994.

Sherman, Howard. *Radical Political Economy.* New York: Basic Books, 1972.

———. *Stagflation: A Radical Theory of Unemployment and Inflation.* New York: Harper and Row, 1976.

Strachey, John. *The Nature of Capitalist Crisis.* New York: Covici, Friede, 1933.

———. *The Theory and Practice of Socialism.* New York: Random House, 1936.

Sweezy, Paul. *The Theory of Capitalist Development.* New York: Monthly Review Press, 1942.

Williams, William A. *The Great Evasion.* Chicago: Quadrangle Books, 1964.

Index

A

Aggregate demand–aggregate supply
model, 63

B

Barro, Robert, 132
Benn, Tony, 23
Black Tuesday
stock market collapse of 1929, 36
Bluestone, Barry, et al., *Corporate
Flight: The Causes and
Consequences of Economic
Dislocation*, 119
Bretton Woods system, 190
Bush, George W., 35, 87
Business cycles. *See* Macroeconomic
stability

C

Classical economics
decline of and reversal, 39–42
Clay, Henry, 177
Clinton, William, 35
Cohen, Wilbur, 155
Comprehensive Employment and
Training Act (CETA) of 1973, 125
Consumer price index (CPI)
historical record, 136
Cyclical budget deficit, 99

D

Debt
public and private growth, 108
Direct investment abroad, 205

E

Economic growth, 60
Conservative view, 68
regulatory burdens and
disincentives, 70
Conservative critique of Johnson's
Great Society, 69
Conservative program for stabilization
and growth, 70–72
historical record, 62–64
Liberal view, 73
Radical view, 80
Economics a science, 6
Economics texts, 7
Employment Act of 1946, 49–50, 61

F

Federal budget
balancing, 87
budget deficit, 88, 90
Bush deficits, 97, 103
Conservative view, 93
deficits as source of inflation and
unemployment, 93
cyclical budget deficit, 99
deficit
crowding out effect, 96
deficits and trade balances, 96
introduction to budget philosophies
annually balanced budget, 88
cyclically balanced budget, 88
functional finance, 88
Liberal refutation of crowding-out
effect, 99
Liberal view, 97
debt in perspective, 98

Federal budget *(continued)*
  Radical view, 103
    misplaced focus on federal deficits,
      108
    Reagan deficits, 89
    relationship of deficits to debt, 88–89
    structural budget deficit, 99
    war against Afghanistan and Iraq, 92
    war on terrorism, 103
Federal debt, 88
  monetizing the debt, 94
  sources, 98
Federal debt as share GDP, 89
Flexible exchange rates, 189
Ford, Henry, II, 20
Friedman, Milton, 12, 13, 60, 132, 147,
  155, 188, 221

G

Galbraith, John Kenneth, 19, 20, 227, 229
General Agreement on Tariffs and Trade
  (GATT), 201
German hyperinflation, 133
Gilder, George, 60
Government spending
  percent of GDP, 105
Gramm-Rudman-Hollings Act of 1985, 91
Great Depression, 36
  bank failures, 42

H

Hamilton, Alexander
  Report on Manufactures, 215
Hansen, Alvin, 18, 19
Heilbroner, Robert, 20, 213
Henwood, Doug, 87, 213
Humphrey Hawkins Full Employment and
  Balanced Growth Act of 1978, 110

I

Ideologies, 8
Inflation, 132
  Conservative view, 138

Inflation
  Conservative view *(continued)*
    need to control inflation, 142
  defined, 133
  Liberal view, 144
    managing inflation, 148
    money supply, 147–48
    random shocks and structural
      change, 145
    Taylor Rule, 148
  price controls, 145
  Radical view, 148
    class interests, 152
    false trade-off of inflation versus
      unemployment, 150
    inherent instability of capitalism, 152
    Radical agenda for equity and price
      stability, 153
Interest on federal debt as share of GDP,
  89
International
  basics of international economics, 183
International economics, 179
  Conservative view, 186
    arguments against protectionism,
      186
    international crisis as failure of
      domestic policies, 193
    necessity of floating exchange rates,
      189
    necessity of free trade, 186
    trend toward freer trade, 194
  events leading to a change in U.S.
      international position, 181–83
  Generalized System of Preferences
      (GSP), 200
  Liberal view, 195
    case for modified protectionism,
      198
    need for rules and enforcement, 201
    trade crisis of the 1980s, 195
  Radical view, 204
    cheap raw materials and labor, 204
    collapse of the empire, 206
    exhaustion of domestic markets,
      204

International economics
  Radical view *(continued)*
    global competition and the race to
      the bottom, 207
    international class unification to
      offset power of transnational
      corporations, 210
    power of transnational corporations,
      207
    profit motive for international trade,
      203
    rise of the American empire, 204
  suspension of gold conversion, 191
  tariffs
    historical record, 199

J

Johnson, Lyndon, 16, 21

K

Karl Polanyi
  The Great Transformation, 226
Kelly, James, 145
Kerry, John, 109
Keynes, John Maynard, 3, 14, 17, 37, 60,
  87, 132, 144–45, 179, 213
  caution about deflation, 125
  General Theory of Employment,
    Interest, and Money, 37, 145
  New Economics, 37
Keynesian economics
  World War II tests spending policies, 73

L

Lenin, V.I., 179
Liberal paradigm, 15

M

Macroeconomic stability, 35
  Conservative critique of Keynesians,
    111
  Conservative view, 39

Macroeconomic stability *(continued)*
  Liberal view, 46
    collapse of the Classical orthodoxy,
      46–48
    victory of the New Economics, 49
  Radical view, 52
Mankiw, N. Gregory, 109
Market versus planning
  collapse of the Soviet Union, 214
  Conservative view, 217
    national planning ineffective in
      practice, 219
    national planning inefficient in
      theory, 217
  Liberal view, 222
    objectives of Liberal intervention, 227
    role of the state, 225
    unrealistic assumptions of market
      advocates, 223
  Radical view, 227
    capitalism needs planning, 228
    planning as a Radical alternative, 231
    planning for profits, not people, 230
Marx, Karl, 6, 25–30, 35, 109, 132
Marxist
  critique, 24–28
McConnell, Campbell R., 181
Ministry of International Trade and
  Industry (MITI), 216
Monetarism, 139
Mundell, Robert, 193

N

National Recovery Administration, 18
New Deal, 18
Non-accelerating inflation rate of
  unemployment (NAIRU), 114
North American Free Trade Agreement
  (NAFTA), 181

P

Phelps, Edmund, 126
Pine, Patricia P., 155
Polanyi, Karl, 222

Productivity
  historical record, 63, 65
  living standards and, 65
Productivity slowdown, 65–66
Progressive Era, 17

R

Radical paradigm, 22–30
Random shocks and structural changes,
  145
Rational expectations, 95
Reagan, Ronald, 14
Reaganomics, 15
Ricardo, David, 6, 179, 209
Robinson, Joan, 236
Roosevelt, Franklin, 35, 155
Rule of 72, 63, 65

S

Say, Jean Baptiste, 40
  Say's Law, 40, 47
Schumpeter, Joseph, 222
September 11, 2001
  in context of U.S. international
    position, 183
  economic impact, 38
  impact on federal budget, 92
  Federal Reserve policy, 149, 152
Simons, Henry C., 13
Smith, Adam, 6, 10–12, 87, 213
Smoot-Hawley Tariff, 43, 199
Social Security, 155
  "beaver solution," 157
  Conservative view, 160
    Conservative solutions, 165
    financing myths, 161
    undesired effects, 162
    tax rates, 163
  financing problem, 158–59
    solutions, 159
  Liberal view, 167
    dependency ratios, costs, and
      economic growth, 169–71
    system is affordable, 171

Social Security (*continued*)
  Old-Age, Survivors, and Disability
    Insurance (OASDI), 156, 158
  population problem, Thomas Malthus,
    156
  Radical view, 173
    budgeting and "legitimation
      schemes," 174
    rowing fiscal crisis, 175–77
Soros, George, 180
Special drawing rights (SDRs), 192
Stagflation, 42
Stock market collapse, 36
Strange, Marty, 35
Supply-side economics, 51, 62

T

Tariffs, 199
Taylor, John, 148
Terrorist attacks. *See* September 11,
  2001
Treaty of Maastricht, 181

U

Unemployment, 109
  Conservative view, 113
    antidiscrimination laws and failed
      employment policies, 116
    efforts to offset structural
      unemployment, 116
    failed employment policies, 114
    failed employment policies caused
      by support of labor unions,
      114
    minimum wage, 115
    natural rate of unemployment,
      113–14
    nonaccelerating rate of
      unemployment (NAIRU), 114
    unemployment insurance and Social
      Security, 115
    unemployment problem overstated,
      117

Unemployment *(continued)*
  Liberal program, 123
    public service jobs, 125
    wage subsidies, 126
    youth programs, 124
  Liberal view, 118
    examples of structural shifts, 120
    high cost of joblessness, 119
    historical overview of structural
      unemployment, 119
    of NAIRU, 118
  Radical view, 126
    capitalism as usual, 126
    capitalism benefits from
      unemployment, 128

Unemployment
  Radical view *(continued)*
    understating the problem, 129

W

Wealth of Nations. See Smith, Adam
Williams, William A., 233
Workforce Investment Act of 1998, 124
World Trade Organization (WTO), 187

Z

Zoellick, Robert, 180

About the Authors

Robert B. Carson is professor emeritus with the Division of Economics and Business at the State University of New York College at Oneonta. He pioneered the unique approach of teaching economics by addressing economic issues from the Conservative, Liberal, and Radical positions with the first edition of *Economic Issues Today* in 1978. He has authored twelve books on economics, including *What Economists Know* (1990), which has been reprinted abroad in Spanish, Portuguese, Russian, and Arabic editions. Dr. Carson is an expert on the public regulation of American railroads.

Wade L. Thomas is professor of economics and assistant dean of the Division of Economics and Business at the State University of New York College at Oneonta. Dr. Thomas served two terms as president of the New York State Economics Association, and serves as the organization's Web coordinator, and received the association's Distinguished Fellow Award in 2004. In addition to publishing journal articles on the economics of franchising, health care, and antitrust, he coauthored *The American Economy: Contemporary Problems and Analysis* (1993) with Robert B. Carson.

Jason Hecht is associate professor of finance in the School of Administration and Business at Ramapo College of New Jersey. He has published in both academic and business publications including the *Journal of Economics and Business* and the *Cambridge Journal of Economics*. Dr. Hecht previously worked as an economist in the property-liability insurance industry for many years and continues to consult for this industry.